Dimensions. Journal of Architectural Knowledge
01/2021

Research Perspectives in Architecture

Issue Editors
Katharina Voigt, Uta Graff, Ferdinand Ludwig

Advisory Board
Isabelle Doucet, Uta Graff, Susanne Hauser,
Klaske Havik, Jonathan Michael Hill, Wilfried Kühn,
Ferdinand Ludwig, Meike Schalk, Katharina Voigt

Editorial Context
BauHow5 and associated institutions
Bartlett University College London, Great Britain
Chalmers University Gothenburg, Sweden
Delft University of Technology, Netherlands
Swiss Federal Institute of Technology Zurich, Switzerland
Royal Technical University of Stockholm, Sweden
University of the Arts Berlin, Germany
Technical University of Vienna, Austria
Technical University of Munich, Germany

[transcript]

Dimensions. Journal of Architectural Knowledge
is initiated and founded by Uta Graff, Ferdinand Ludwig and Katharina Voigt.
Initial funding for the journal is provided by the Technical University of Munich.

Coordination and organization by Uta Graff, Ferdinand Ludwig and Katharina Voigt.
Contact: dimensions@bauhow5.eu

This journal is published bianually (in spring and autumn). The printed editions are available for annual subscription directly from the publisher. The retail price incl. shipment within Germany is 75,00 € and for international purchases 85,00 €. The electronic version is available free of charge (Open Access). All information regarding notes for contributors, subscriptions, Open Access, back volume and orders is available online at https://www.transcript-publishing.com/dak

Bibliographic information published by the Deutsche Nationalbibliothek
The Deutsche Nationalbibliothek lists this publication in the Deutsche Nationalbibliografie; detailed bibliographic data are available in the Internet at http://dnb.de

This work is licensed under the Creative Commons Attribution 4.0 (BY) license, which means that the text may be be remixed, transformed and built upon and be copied and redistributed in any medium or format even commercially, provided credit is given to the author. For details go to http://creativecommons.org/licenses/by/4.0/
Creative Commons license terms for re-use do not apply to any content (such as graphs, figures, photos, excerpts, etc.) not original to the Open Access publication and further permission may be required from the rights holder. The obligation to research and clear permission lies solely with the party re-using the material.

First published 2021 by transcript Verlag, Bielefeld
© **Katharina Voigt, Uta Graff, Ferdinand Ludwig (eds.)**

Cover layout: Uta Graff, Technical University of Munich
Copy-editing: Madison Erdall and Katharina Voigt, Technical University of Munich
Editorial Consulting: Ria Stein, Berlin
Proofreading: Lisa Goodrum, London
Typeset: Katharina Voigt
Printed by Majuskel Medienproduktion GmbH, Wetzlar
ISSN 2747-5085
eISSN 2747-5093
Print-ISBN 978-3-8376-5809-5
PDF-ISBN 978-3-8394-5809-9

Printed on permanent acid-free text paper.

Contents

INTRODUCTION

Editorial
Katharina Voigt, Uta Graff, Ferdinand Ludwig 7

Research Perspectives in Architecture
Uta Graff 11

METHODOLOGIES AND PERSPECTIVES OF RESEARCH IN ARCHITECTURE

I. DESIGN PROCESS / DESIGN-BASED RESEARCH

Collage-Based Research and Design
Sarah Wehmeyer 25

Embodied Knowledge, Tool, and Sketch:
Intuitive Production of Knowledge in Architectural Design
Nandini Oehlmann 37

Data-Driven Research on Ecological Prototypes for Green Architecture: Enabling Urban Intensification and Restoration through Agricultural Hybrids
Defne Sunguroğlu Hensel 47

Reflexions on the Plurality of Methods in Architecture
Oya Atalay Franck 55

II. REFLEXIVE RESEARCH

Reflexive, Reflexivity, and the Concept of Reflexive Design
Margitta Buchert 67

Architecture Schools and Their Relationship with Research: It's Complicated
Jan Silberberger 77

Thinking the Transformative
Steffen Bösenberg 85

III. QUALITATIVE RESEARCH

Research through Design under Systematic Quality Criteria: Methodology and Teaching Research
Sören Schöbel, Julian Schäfer, Georg Hausladen 99

Architects as Public Intellectuals: How Far Beyond Can We Go?
Hannah Knoop 111

Playing Seriously: An Introduction to Corporeal Architecture, Neuroscience, and Performance Art
Maria da Piedade Ferreira 119

IV. PERCEPTION-BASED RESEARCH

These Are Only Hints and Guesses
Francesca Torzo 133

Corporeality of Architecture Experience
Katharina Voigt 139

Researching Non-Conscious Dimensions of Architectural Experience
Marcus Weisen 149

V. ARCHIVAL RESEARCH

What the Files Reveal: Making Everyday Architecture Talk
Benedikt Boucsein 163

Architectural Drawings:
Teaching and Understanding a Visual Discipline
Peter Schmid 173

Archives, Bureaucracies, Architecture:
Now You See Me, Now You Don't
Anna-Maria Meister 181

VI. INTERDISCIPLINARY RESEARCH

Research / Design and Academia
Susanne Hauser 191

What is Architectural Psychology?
Alexandra Abel 201

On the Entanglement between Sociology
and Architecture in Spatial Research
Séverine Marguin 209

RESUMEE

Reflection
Ferdinand Ludwig and Katharina Voigt 223

CONTRIBUTORS

Biographies 237

Editorial

Katharina Voigt, Uta Graff, Ferdinand Ludwig

Within the manifold landscape of academic journals, *Dimensions. Journal of Architectural Knowledge* underlines the plurality of methodological approaches and working methods in the field of architecture – scientific and practical, theoretical and applied. By emphasizing the commonalities of methodologies and approaches, it unites different lines of enquiry under the overarching theme of their respective methodology, aiming to foster the reciprocal conditionality of thinking and making in the discipline of architecture. Superordinate topics and research questions are addressed by architectural, theoretical, and trans-disciplinary means, equally contributing to knowledge-creation in architecture. It is the goal of this journal to unravel the anthology of methods and ways of knowing genuine to the discipline. This journal provides a platform for researchers who work with established scientific methods as well as for practitioners that use applied forms of investigation, specifically focusing on the framework of methodologies true to the discipline.

Research Perspectives in Architecture, the inaugural issue, marks the prelude of a journal, presenting the spectrum of methodological focal areas, which will be examined with greater depth in the following editions. It opens the field of investigation within the discipline of architecture, exploring how different perspectives and applied methodologies encourage varying research questions, findings, and ways of knowledge creation. This issue investigates the following lead question: Which methodological approaches are used in research on architecture, landscape architecture, and urban design? Accentuating the methodological framework of research, the journal focuses on genuine methodologies applied in scientific architectural research and particularly on those derived from architectural practice and design. Furthermore, it investigates how established scientific methods from other fields can be adapted for architectural research. The methodologies and

---

Corresponding authors: Katharina Voigt; Uta Graff; Ferdinand Ludwig (Technical University of Munich, Germany); katharina.voigt@tum.de; http://orcid.org/0000-0002-2547-8292; uta.graff@tum.de; http://orcid.org/0000-0002-9185-7514; ferdinand.ludwig@tum.de; https://orcid.org/0000-0001-5877-5675.
Open Access. © 2021 Katharina Voigt; Uta Graff, Ferdinand Ludwig published by transcript Verlag.
This work is licensed under the Creative Commons Attribution 4.0 (BY) license.

approaches emphasized in this issue form the basis for further development of a methodological spectrum in the discipline of architecture. The overarching aim of this journal is to exploit the methodological plurality in scientific research in architecture, in order to highlight the variety of possible methodological attempts and relate to the originality of genuine architectural methods of knowledge creation – be it conceptual, practical, or scientific.

Introduction

According to the mission statement of the Technical University of Munich, Department of Architecture, »Architectural design (German: »Entwerfen«) is the core of the department and the exploration of complex aesthetic and spatial solutions its primary objective. […] The academic discipline of architecture involves skills from different backgrounds including engineering, humanities, and social sciences, each of which flows into architectural teaching and research at all levels.«[1] Scientific research in our department has so far focused on the areas of »Integrated Building Technologies«, »Cultural Heritage, History and Criticism«, and »Urban and Landscape Transformation«, namely in three out of four focus areas. In the field of Architectural Design, the number of research projects and PhD candidates are only gradually increasing although this field is referred to as »the core practice, which serves as a common basis for all teaching and research activities.«[2] The research at the core of our discipline is still fraught with many uncertainties, and the necessary methods cannot be adopted from other disciplines.

The initiation of this journal is driven by the intention to investigate this key question: How can we strengthen research in the core area of architecture?

As an impetus toward answering this question, we submit the following five methods of architectural research for discussion: Design-based research and the process of architectural design, reflexive design and research, qualitative research, experience-based methodologies, and archival forms of research. Various overlaps between these different methodical approaches

---

1 https://www.ar.tum.de/fakultaet/wir-ueber-uns/mission, accessed May 28, 2019.
2 ibid.

exist. Their specific characteristics, their adequateness for relating research questions, and their potentials and challenges will be described on a superordinate level in the introduction of the respective chapter. Furthermore, they will be superimposed and proven by exemplary research approaches displayed in the individual contributions. It is the journal's goal to discuss relevant positions in the context of specific research questions and against the background of their methodological approaches and their respective potential for the discourse in architecture.

With the initiation of the international conference »*Research Perspectives in Architecture*« which was funded by the German Research Foundation (DFG), project number 428316702, and took place at the Technical University of Munich in July 2019, as well as with the initiative of this journal, our aim is to trace architectural ways of knowing. Displaying the diversity of methods in architecture, the first day of the two-day conference focused on different methodologies and research approaches. The methodological spectrum was presented in brief lectures on methods of current research and doctoral projects. The second day broadened the methodological discourse and provided an exemplary insight into methodologically independent research programs in architecture. We were hitherto not interested in completeness, but rather in stimulating discussion, and we conceived of the conference as a first step toward consensus and clarity in the range of research methods in architecture.

In order to contextualize recent research in the discipline of architecture within the greater realm of the history of architectural knowledge creation, we are eager to raise three questions, directed to the past, present, and future state of the discipline:

- Where do we come from?
- Where are we now?
- Where are we going?

Research on a superordinate level on overarching questions has been introduced rather recently to the field, representing a scientific and academic transition within the discipline.

Research Perspectives in Architecture
Uta Graff

»Working in philosophy – like work in architecture in many respects – is really more a working on oneself. One's own interpretation. On one's way of seeing things. (And what one expects of them.)«

Ludwig Wittgenstein: 1931, 472.

Research Perspectives in Architecture

Uta Graff

Keywords: Architecture; Architectural Design; Design Process; Reseach through Design; Reseach on Architectural Design; Design as Research Methodology; Intuition and Understanding.

Research in Architecture

Research in architecture is explicitly concerned with an examination of the various inherent potentials of architecture, its principles and rules, practices and processes, techniques and tools and, correspondingly, with the ways of thinking and methods constitutive for the design.

At the beginning of the 21st century, developments in higher education policy led to increasing recognition of research as a scientific achievement and thus to the opportunity to cast an exploratory glance into creative disciplines such as architecture, where, until then, research had almost exclusively taken place in the technical and theoretical fields, instead of the actual core domain of the discipline. This notion has since been increasingly analyzed, with the gaze often being directed from outside the process and its tools, but sometimes also from within the discipline itself. The view from outside often remains an approximation to the core domain of the discipline. The view from within the discipline, on the other hand, is increasingly directed toward the design process and the knowledge implicit in it. This research approach is able to fathom the core and thus convey the knowledge gained.

Following the UNESCO definition, research is »any creative systematic activity undertaken in order to increase the stock of knowledge, including knowledge of man, culture, and society, and the use of this knowledge to devise new applications.«[1] Making this knowledge accessible is necessarily and indispensably linked to this.

The main domain of architecture offers very different approaches and possibilities for research. This raises the question of how research areas in

---

1 http://stats.oecd.org/glossary/detail.asp?ID=2312, accessed October 10, 2020.

Corresponding author: Uta Graff (Technical University of Munich, Germany); uta.graff@tum.de; http://orcid.org/0000-0002-9185-7514
Open Access. © 2021 Uta Graff, published by transcript Verlag.
This work is licensed under the Creative Commons Attribution 4.0 (BY) license.

the core discipline of architecture can be differentiated. In order to propose an approach to this, I will first of all focus on design as the key competence of the discipline of architecture. In doing so, I will provide an insight into this creative activity, which operates with both facts and assumptions and, as an object of research, demands a variety of perspectives.

Architectural Design as Core Competency

Design is the core competence of the discipline of architecture. Designing, as an overarching, integrative process, means gaining an idea of what one is projecting and to sharpen and substantiate this idea. Concretization in this context means not so much the structural realization of an architectural project, but rather the clarification and specification of ideas during the design and planning process.

During the design process, the architectural concept is clarified and its language becomes more tangible, with all its contextual and typological, its spatial and material, its structural, constructive, and technical characteristics. In other words: Conceived architecture becomes real architecture, a specific place where life takes place. After all, architecture doesn't mean anything, »it reaches beyond sign and symbols«[2]. It contains the spaces in which we live.[3] This clearly shows the complexity of architectural thinking, which is subject to a wide range of requirements and in whose concretization numerous specialist disciplines are involved.

An essential aspect of architectural design is the development of concepts, which, as an idea or set of principles, underlies the process and thus the work that is created. Abstract thinking and practical work are essential skills for the design work of the creating architect. This creative process of architectural conception and concretization is about sharpening the concept in thought and concretizing it with spatial architectural means. This process is target-oriented, but not linear. The constant reconciliation, weighing up, and examining of all requirements and concerns obliges to precise questioning

---

2 German original: »Sie liegt jenseits der Zeichen und Symbole.« Zumthor 1992: 42. Translation: Uta Graff.

3 »Architecture has its own realm. It has a special physical relationship with life. I do not think of it primarily as either a message or a symbol, but as an envelope and background for life which goes on in and around it, a sensitive container for the rhythm of footsteps on the floor, for the concentration of work, for the silence of sleep.« Zumthor 2006: 12.

and thinking, which is always critical of itself and does not tolerate coincidences and mere forms which, at best, seem fashionable.

The cultural scientist Susanne Hauser understands design as a cultural technique and expects architectural designs to »bring something new into the world« (Hauser 2011: 365. Translation: Uta Graff).

»Designs are not necessary where all questions are answered and all problems solved. The more questions are open, the more clearly design emerges as a problem-solving activity. It then becomes evident that designs do not deal with completely defined processes, but with not knowing, uncertainty, and unpredictability. Indeed, designs point to a future that in many respects can only be imagined. Although they inevitably take their starting point from current conditions [...], they define conditions and goals of interest to the present. But they are oriented toward and beyond future [...] uses and purposes« (ibid.).[4]

According to Hauser, the special interest in the methods of design lies »in this special relationship to accepted and rejected possibilities of future developments and in the fascination that emanates from the option of their determination and determinability« (ibid.: 3). The interest in the process itself, the tools used, and the methods pursued in this processual procedure are not surprising, as its exploration makes it possible to understand creative processes. So the question arises, among others, which criteria design is based on? Which rules underlie certain decisions? Which conscious or subconscious aspects constitute important milestones in the process? In the phase of the design process, numerous possibilities are open, which are continuously collected, explored, and evaluated, rejected and excluded, respectively integrated, transformed, and substantiated. Understood as a cultural technique, »architectural design is understood as a heterogeneous aesthetic,

---

4 German original: »Entwürfe sind nicht erforderlich, wo alle Fragen beantwortet und alle Probleme gelöst sind. Je mehr Fragen offen sind, umso deutlicher tritt das Entwerfen als eine problemlösende Aktivität hervor. Es wird dann erkennbar, dass Entwürfe nicht mit vollständig definierten Prozessen umgehen, sondern mit Nicht-Wissen, Ungewissheit und Unvorhersehbarkeit. Denn Entwürfe weisen in eine Zukunft voraus, die in vielen Hinsichten nur imaginiert werden kann. Sie nehmen zwar ihren Ausgang unweigerlich von aktuellen Gegebenheiten [...], sie definieren gegenwärtig interessierende Bedingungen und Ziele. Doch richten sie sich aus auf künftige [...] Nutzungen und darüber hinausgehende Zwecke.« Hauser 2011: 365. Translation: Uta Graff

symbolic, and technical practice for the conception of imaginary worlds in which cultural and social projections are articulated. In this respect, design can be understood as a basic cultural technique for shaping the future« (Gethmann/Hauser 2009: 11. Translation: Uta Graff).

For this process, two basic requirements are necessary in addition to all specialist knowledge: intuition and understanding. Indeed, the power of a good design lies in the authors themselves, in their »ability to perceive the world with both emotion and reason« (Zumthor 2006: 65). The perception, recognition, and interpretation of the characteristics and potential of a place and a task are determined by both intuition and reason. Observation and evaluation are carried out in accordance not only with subjectively perceivable criteria but also with objectively ascertainable ones. In this sense, the design work always has to deal equally with specialist knowledge as well as »personal biographical experiences of architecture« (ibid.: 65).

Intuition is closely related to an inner validity of circumstances based on experience. It is often the basis for making the right decision without understanding the underlying relationships. The mind, on the other hand, fathoms the connections and has a capacity for language, mediation, and criticism. Accordingly, empathy and the ability to judge are prerequisites for conception and design.

In the case of a successful design, it is not clear whether the starting point was the sensual-intuitive or the intellectual-mental perception of the concrete location and task. Based on the assumption that a mixture of both is inherent in a good design, it is necessary to synchronize thinking and acting as a consequence of knowledge and intuition in the process. The exploratory screening, the fathoming, understanding, and making available of knowledge about the methods, techniques, and tools of the process has to do with these criteria.

> »For an investigation of design, this is a challenge, because there is the possibility that in these processes a knowledge develops which can only be made accessible through executions and only in the passage through these practices« (Hauser 2011: 372).

Research Fields in the Context of Architectural Design

Architectural design is linked to different dimensions of architectural knowledge and to complex cognitive processes. A differentiated view on the methods of design reveals their multi-dimensionality and allows for their overarching reflection. It should be anticipated that among the possible different research approaches, a clear distinction must be made between knowledge in design or knowledge from the design process and scientific knowledge in architecture. This discrepancy constantly emerges as a result of different expectations of research in the various fields of architecture and is constantly being discussed anew divergently.

With the focus on the core discipline of architecture, three areas that are fundamentally different from each other in terms of methodology can be distinguished:

1. Research through Design
2. Research on Architectural Design
3. Design as Research Methodology

In each case, this involves a differentiated approach and a genesis of knowledge in the context of architectural design in different ways.

Research through Design. Research through design is a practice-based research approach. Research using the method of design plays a central role in this. Since design processes are an integral part of this research, the reflection of creative processes as well as the analysis of tools and techniques immanent to design form a focus area of Research through Design. In this context, designing as an independent method offers a possible mediation between seemingly incompatible areas of knowledge.

Research on Architectural Design. In research on architectural design, the focus is on the analysis of the design process. The main aim of Research on Architectural Design is to work out the interactions between anticipation and experience in conception and perception and, in particular, to visualize the characteristics and potentials inherent in the process and to make this knowledge accessible.

Design as Research Methodology. Design as research methodology entails the elaboration of working methods of research through the design. This research approach extends beyond the knowledge inherent in design and focuses on both the process and the original methods of architectural design. It is concerned with the genuine design methodology of architecture as an immanent knowledge to be made explicit, as well as the equal consideration of relevant tools and techniques, processes, and results of design.

In all sections, criteria must be specified which can be used in the future to record and name the quality of architectural designs. Moreover, criteria must be developed which can be used to record, describe, and evaluate the quality of research results in one of the designated areas.

Integrative Interdisciplinary Approach. There is no question that research in the core area of architecture is based on an interdisciplinary approach and is accompanied by the corresponding research methods. After all, architecture is not only inherently a multi-disciplinary field, but has always been an interdisciplinary science. The discipline of architecture and its core competence of design is immanent in today's specialist cultures, which are the product of a frequently dissected knowledge landscape and have to be learned again with great difficulty. It is the self-evident coordination of factual knowledge on the one hand with heuristic assumptions on the other, which, as necessary foundations, determine the process and the emergence of the successive solution phases. It is the handling of disparate methods and terminologies, the mutual exchange between theory and practice, and the combination of a scientific analysis based on reason with an artistically intended speculative conception that formulate the core of the architectural work. The integration of scientific, design, and technical aspects in a convincing holistic work is the achievement of a thinking and acting architect.

Accordingly, research in the core discipline of architecture entails a spectrum of possible views and opens up research perspectives of architecture while enabling a change of perspective. Interdisciplinary work and its inherent transfer of methods broadens the view and is beneficial and purposeful when it comes to the genesis of knowledge in creative disciplines, such as architecture, that operate with diverse cultural techniques. The three areas of research highlighted – research through design, research on architectural design, and design as research methodology – explore the object of research of creative processes and their techniques in methodologically different ways.

Exploring the core of architecture entails grasping its process, techniques, and methods and understanding them as cultural achievements, as well as fostering the highest goal in the discipline of architecture, the creation of space in all its dimensions and by any means.

References

Gethmann, Daniel/Hauser, Susanne (2009): *Kulturtechnik Entwerfen. Praktiken, Konzepte und Medien in Architektur und Design Research*, Bielefeld: transcript Verlag.

Hauser, Susanne (2013): »Verfahren des Überschreitens, Entwerfen als Kulturtechnik«, in: Sabine Ammon/Eva Maria Froschauer (eds.), *Wissenschaft Entwerfen: Vom forschenden Entwerfen zur Entwurfsforschung der Architektur*, Paderborn: Wilhelm Fink Verlag.

Wittgenstein, Ludwig [1931]. *Bemerkungen über die Farben. Über Gewißheit. Zettel. Vermischte Bemerkungen.* – English translation: Georg Henrik von Wright (ed.): Culture and Value, London: Wiley-Blackwell Publishers, 1998.

Zumthor, Peter (1992): *Eine Anschauung der Dinge. Über die Sprache der Architektur*, Haldenstein.

Zumthor, Peter [1998]: *Architektur denken.* – English translation: *Thinking Architecture*, 2nd expanded edition, transl. by Maureen Oberli-Turner, Basel: Birkhäuser, 2006.

Design Process / Design-Based Research

Katharina Voigt

This chapter elaborates on different ways of architectural knowing and the constitution of knowledge by architectural means. The chapter equally takes into account the design process – as one of the key elements of the discipline – and design-based research attempts in the field of architecture. It seeks to reach beyond the ambiguity of the knowledge of architectural design and the conception of design as a process of knowledge creation. In this regard, the chapter aims to overcome the discrepancy between the inherent knowledge of architectural design and an implicated meta-level of design research. While the creation and production of knowledge has always been an inherent part of architectural design, the reflection of its methodological procedures, the specification of methodologies, and their significant application to referable questions constitute a contemporary thread in the field.

The particularity of design methods has only very recently become an explicit element of the discourse, alongside the growing debate on the scientific potentials and challenges facing the discipline. Throughout the discipline of architecture, the notion of methodological endeavors has foremost been directed at the challenges of the design task, aiming to find the most suitable procedures to solve the overarching challenges of the project. So far, superordinate topics from the disciplinary realm of architecture have merely been addressed by the transposition of methodologies established in other disciplines and fields of research.

The unraveling of an underlying methodological fabric of the design process holds the potential to increase awareness for genuine architectural knowledge and exploits its inherent working methods and acquaintance of comprehension – an aim which design-based research contributes to fruitfully. The design process itself resembles a cogntive structure of thoughts, ideas, and choices, dependent on the interrelating, consecutive development and draft of concretization; reconsideration, revision, specification, decision, and choice-making are essential to the processes of architectural design and conception. By tracing this stream of consciousness through the established methodologies and by addressing the tools and agencies involved in emphasizing specific architectural knowledge through architectural means, it becomes apparent that a greater awareness of the different dimensions of the design process fosters the integration of specific architectural ways of working in architectural research. Only very recently, a shift of perspective has occurred in the field of fundamental and superordinate architectural research, as genuine methodologies from the discipline of architecture are being applied to this research. The more we reflect on this notion, the more we can benefit from such methodological knowledge.

Design-based research provides an attempt to explore, define, access, and integrate genuine architectural methodologies and procedures in architectural research. The reconsideration of original architectural methodologies and the investigation into explored working methods enable researchers to use their established tools and ways of working, their means of analysis, comparison, and evaluation, as well as their tools for the creation as well as the production and invention of profound – either scientific or applied – ideas and significant positions in the discourse. An analysis of established methodologies strives to discover inherent architectural tools for research, from which a discipline-specific methodological spectrum and ontology of architecture ensues. The broad variety of tools and media applied in the design process bears the potential to contribute as equally fruitful catalysts to the research process. In design research, the tools and results of the creation process – like sketches and drawings, different types of models, and all others – are treated as experimental findings, made explicit, critically examined and developed, and, if needed, are subject to further revision. The design itself and its corresponding creational processes appear as tools – as well as subjects – of research.

The four following contributions address different aspects of the broad field of potential adaptations from architectural design to research in architecture. They highlight the investigation of specific tools and techniques of the design process, emphasize the transfer, applicability, and adaptation of preconceived knowledge to specific design and research tasks. They also reflect the potential of genuine methodologies, inherent to the discipline, and their capacity to be just as productive in applied design and scientific research.

Collage-Based Research and Design

Sarah Wehmeyer

Editorial Summay: In her contribution »Collage-Based Research and Design«, Sarah Wehmeyer addresses the distinct differentiation between design-based and design-related forms of investigation in architecture. Hereby, she fosters reflexive design and research processes and practices as sources of »design-specific knowledge«. In this regard, she highlights applied artistic and superordinate theoretical aspects as well as discusses practical skills and scientific capacities inherent to the medium of collage as an architecture-specific tool for design and research. This contribution can be read as a precise and distinct examination of the collage as an artifact, media of design, knowledge creation, and communication, and as an alternative – artistic-reflexive – methodological approach to research in architecture. [Katharina Voigt]

Keywords: Collage; Artistic Concepts and Reflection; Reflexive Design; Reflexive Research Practice; Design-Specific Knowledge; Media of Knowledge; Image as Knowledge Component.

Architectural Ways of Researching?

Due to a new self-understanding in the context of the academic landscape, architects are increasingly showing an interest in not only defining design as a generative and integrative field of research, but also in seeking their own »architectural« ways of researching. Discourses of both design-based and design-related research play a central role in this context. From varying perspectives, they discuss new notions of traditional research definitions that are rooted in the methodological framework of the humanities and other theoretical research attempts. Further, they contemplate their methodological expansion and connection to the wider spectrum of processes, practices, and instruments offered by the core competence of architecture: the design. While some positions hereby focus on the design (process) itself as the main methodological basis (Fraser 2013; Weidinger 2013), other formats, such as the Reflexive Design, highlight possible crossovers and interactions of design and research as generative epistemological processes (Buchert 2014; Buchert 2016; Buchert 2018).

Corresponding author: Sarah Wehmeyer (Leibniz University Hannover, Germany); s.wehmeyer@igt-arch.uni-hannover.de; https://orcid.org/0000-0002-8095-4418
Open Access. © 2021 Sarah Wehmeyer, published by transcript Verlag.
This work is licensed under the Creative Commons Attribution 4.0 (BY) license.

Research-Oriented Design

Such a coevolutive approach as a specific form of architectural research is promoted by the concept of research-oriented design [forschendes Entwerfen]. The term, which may initially appear paradoxical, describes an intended procedure that connects the search for compositional order – the design – with the search for design-specific knowledge – the research (Buchert 2011: 77–78). It is assumed that the architect not only aims to realize a built space or object, but also to raise specific questions and investigate them during the design process and beyond. These questions may be individually design- or project-related and may concentrate on collective social, economic, or other topics of discussion, as well as address overarching aspects of design.

Correlative + Reflexive. Research-oriented design does not seek to scientificize or rationalize the design process, as was attempted in the 1960s with the Design Methods movement (Schrijver 2014: 61–63). Rather, the intention is to emphasize the potential of the complex ordered design process as an iterative development, in which, as Donald Schön describes it, phases of analytical, reflective, and synthetic activities are mutually connected and repeated (Schön 1991: 94–95, 280). A further key characteristic concerns Michael Polanyi's concept of tacit knowledge: this never completely tangible network of images, analogies, and syntheses, which precedes, supports, and exceeds the design process (Buchert 2011: 79–83; Polanyi 1966). It manifests itself in the interaction between different design practices and instruments, in (un)built products as well as in individual archives. As designers in creative phases primarily concentrate on the desired outcome, the generative potential of this specific knowledge plays an accompanying, yet unnoticed role (Schön 1991: 282). Research-orientated design strives for conscious reflexive phases of alienation, review, consolidation, and abstraction that focus on the designed object as well as on the architect and their actions to gain access to individual design-related insights (Ammon/Froschauer 2013: 16; Buchert 2014: 33, 47). In this manner, the twofold motivated search should not be understood as research linked to a singular design project. Instead, in its reflexive capacity, it describes a project-overlapping research ambition, which includes both the (further) development of different project conceptions as well as the concretization of individual basic conceptions.

Instruments. Which instruments and practices support and catalyze the research-orientated design as a medial and/or methodological constant? How is design-specific knowledge captured in material and visual objects and how do these research results become accessible and applicable to others? While the tools of the architect and their influence on the design process have already been addressed in various publications (e.g. Gänshirt 2021), the investigation of their formative role at the interface of design and research processes as well as their knowledge transfer qualities remains in its infancy. Robin Evans for instance tried to decipher the correlations between architects, drawing projections, collective spatial ideals, and the perception of the built object, both linguistically and with his own graphic illustrations (Evans 2011: 192). Subsequent positions have since emerged, exploring the qualities of architectural drawing beyond its function of constructive support and means of representation (Kienbaum 2016). Similarly, the notion of the model as a tool for the production of ideas with research qualities (Oechslin 2011; Ursprung 2013) as well as architectural photography receive increasing focus in scientific observation (Schrijver 2014: 63–65). In the quest for hitherto unknown research-orientated design instruments, both our own everyday design practices as well as the work of individual architects, since modernity to the present day, can serve as exciting sources. Against this background, this dissertation (re-)discovers the collage as a basis for architectural action and thought. The aim is to identify the practical skills and scientific capacities that the collage generates as an architecture-specific design and research tool.

Re-Think Collage!

Collages are currently experiencing a comeback as an alternative form of architectural visualization in addition to established forms of architecture representations such as maps, plans, and renderings. Spatial atmospheres are increasingly created through digitally or analogously generated layering of different, abstract colors or material surfaces and fragments of pictures. Beyond the visual succinctness of these images, special attention must be paid to certain contemporary architects, such as OFFICE and Dogma from Brussels or the Mexican Tatiana Bilbao; such architects demonstrate – in their individual interaction with collage – an intensified artistic and research-orientated access to the design process. The ongoing dissertation ties in with this point and focuses on the potential that collage and collaging offer for conceptualizing and researching on architecture and urban space, as well as for reflecting on individual design competences, ideals and values and develop them further. Moreover, the question arises whether and how the collage – as a reflexive approach to creative processes – implicitly or explicitly supports the genesis of design-specific knowledge. Situated in a phenomenological hermeneutic research tradition, the dissertation is structured in different methodical steps. The main part is conceived as a case study analysis of the already mentioned architectural firms. Through scientific investigation and supplementary interviews, it will be explored when and with which perspective they use the digitally or analogously composed collage as a form of visualization, design instrument, or research medium. Furthermore, the aim is to address the collage not only as an object of research, but also to prove it as a practice itself. The test field consists of a collage-based design and research study in conjunction with the doctoral thesis; it creates the space to rethink and examine the methods and objectives of the architects and to expand the research findings regarding the authors' own work as architects and theorists.

The theoretical and practical exploration of the collage is tied to the discourses on research-orientated design as a specific facet of reflexive design. As a scientific classification of the collage as a knowledge-generating and -mediating instrument is missing in this research context, the scope of possibilities and potentials will be discussed within the framework of the dissertation and in excerpts in this article.

Collage-Based Research and Design

A collage is not a simple illustration of the present or future world. Rather, it creates its own pictorial reality with simultaneous layers of different meanings and realisms, evoked by the layered coexistence of image fragments from different contexts. This recycling of fragments and statements as well as the provoked openness of interpretation is often combined with a critical intention that addressed issues of society, design, and perception (Schneede 2001: 77). The specific dialectic of the collage has been interpreted in many ways in the fine arts since the first papier collé (Jürgens-Kirchhoff 1984: 42) and has just as often been a graphic and conceptual reference for architects (MoMA 2014; Shields 2013).

Retrospective. The fact that some of these characteristics even enabled individual architects to gain new insights into spatial forms of expression, as well as into their own design practices and values, was conveyed in several architecture theory publications. Neil Levine and Martino Stierli show, for example, that the collage-specific interplay of flatness and depth has been a fundamental practice for Mies to understand, develop, and communicate his specific spatial principles, such as the staging of material surface as space-defining walls (Levine 1998; Stierli 2011: 409–410). Based on the creative actions of Superstudio and Archizoom, Marie Stauffer has demonstrated how the collage is used as a tool alternative to language in its interface between reality and vision. Firstly to deal more independently with design and social issues, and secondly to provoke public discourse by publishing the ideas gathered as a common visual shock therapy: the negative utopia of total urbanization and consumption as manifested in the Continuous Monument or the No-Stop City (Stauffer 2007: 10–19).

Contemporary Applications. »A Grammar for the City« (2005) developed together by OFFICE and Dogma (see fig. on next page) is one interesting example for a current collage-based research and design project. The design for a new South Korean capital[1] is both a competition entry as well as a component of a wider context of projects and collages (re)searching design strategies that serve as architectural solutions to uncontrolled urbanization and loss of public space. The architects consciously refer to already available design-related knowledge – the rational positions of the 1960s – and apply it with the prospect of further developing their own design-specific insights. The intention is the continuous improvement of their individual typologies »building-as-wall« und »square-as-room« as possible answers to their own ideals (Aureli/Tattara 2017: 61; Borasi 2017: 11–13; Wehmeyer 2018). Thus, in the project series, including »Stop City« and »Lokomotiva 3« by Dogma or »Tower and Square« by OFFICE (see fig. on next page), accompanying research activities can be identified in which the studies of urban vocabulary and the design of urban architecture and spaces become one.

---

1 In 2005, a competition was held to develop a new multi-functional administrative city in South Korea, in response to the enormous dominance exerted by the metropolitan area of Seoul and in an attempt to foster decentralization.

Urban walls and rooms
A grammar for the city (2005)
OFFICE + DOGMA

Towers + squares (2004)
OFFICE 09

To convey the gained insights not only linguistically, but also graphically, OFFICE and Dogma utilize the collage to display a visually striking image. The white surface is chosen to symbolize and accentuate the role of architecture as a structuring »wall« that acts in the background, while the monochrome or color-intensive photographic images present the square interspaces as generous »rooms« open to urban unfolding (Aureli/Tattara 2017: 61). The different atmospheres evoked by this monumental and yet restrained design grammar would have been difficult to describe in words but become visually explicit through collage. However, the question still remains of how these aspects of design-related knowledge may be generated in interaction with collage. When juxtaposing intentions and pictorial rhetoric of the contemporary and the earlier collages, several inspiring observations can be made.

Cognitive Performances

Visual Training. A distinct feature of these contemporary collages is the carefully composed dialogue of two components: Abstract white surfaces in combination with photographic backgrounds create the specific interplay between planarity and depth that Mies already successfully used to train his perception. OFFICE and Dogma also appear to activate the process of composing the image space as a practice for honing their own design-related competences. The interplay between two-dimensional surfaces and three-dimensional space acts, in this context, as a method of training their perception of urban scenes as spaces and walls.

Critical Image. Correspondingly, it appears that contemporary architects, similar to Superstudio and Archizoom, use collages in their original artistic intention as critical mirror images of reality. The floating state between abstraction and realism initiates a new, more exaggerated and dramatic perspective of the omnipresent and familiar theme of urbanization. The recipient is left in uncertainty as to whether the vertical densification and absolute definition of the city's basic form via walls and towers represents an already existing or a future state of habitat. It also remains unclear whether the white surfaces display serious or ironic typological solutions. In this regard, the collage reveals its fundamental quality as an artistic artefact by leading the recipient to new insights and knowledge through confrontation, critical self-reflection and association. It calls for thinking beyond the written and visual manifests, beyond the here and now, and rather for relating one's own stance and action to the environment and fellow human beings, with regard to the past, present, and future. In this way, the collage – as well as an architecture – mediates between the world and mankind, it points out aspects that cannot be described methodically or conceptually (Buchert 2011: 44–47). To create this mediation, the collage requires that complex contents are abstracted into striking but also mind-opening visual statements. As Evans already recognized in relation to projections (cf. Evans 1995), the collage provokes the genesis of new findings through focusing, abstracting, and transferring ideas to paper, more in the process of making than explicitly intended.

Reflexive Components. Keeping the collage in mind as a »practice«, further possibilities for the genesis of design-related insights emerge with regard to Donald Schön. The urbanist and sociologist questions how practitioners examine themselves in action without being paralyzed by the complexity of information, dependencies, and background knowledge that are usually handled implicitly. Observing the architect, Schön detects the everyday practice of sketching as intuitive yet unrecognized conscious access to reflection and, in this sense, as a targeted way of grasping aspects of silent knowledge. Schön describes how hand drawing slows down the process of designing and at the same time constructs a parallel, »virtual world« on paper, in which the architect finds the time to reframe, vary, or experiment with their ideas (Schön 1991: 277–279). Viewing the process of collaging, one could interpret the different steps – from selecting and cutting out to layering and relating – as similar generative moments of deceleration. Aware of this capacity, architects could intentionally use the practice as a reflexive tool to establish personal think tanks in uncertain or stagnating situations of designing or researching and to restructure thoughts and receive new creative input. The persistent but varying creation of collages, as can be observed in the case studies, is understood here as a first indication that Dogma and OFFICE may have intuitively appropriated this potential. Furthermore, it may imply that the architects use collages to document and archive their designs, as well as their design-related knowledge. Due to their high level of abstraction, collages can therefore be read as individual image studies and visual knowledge archives, which allow the architects – during the process and afterward – to distance themselves from their work in order to examine, compare, and rethink ideas and syntheses. It seems as if the collage is now also consciously integrated as an »object« into the design and research processes in order to enable its reflexive qualities of supporting the self-critical development of stances and values. As collages are constantly published in exhibitions and publications, they can also be understood as a collectively accessible knowledge pool that we can refer to.

The Difficult Whole

Collage and Research. The knowledge-generating and -communicating potentials of the collage identified so far appear to simultaneously reveal their limits. Even if the collage is based on rational actions, it reflects a subjective point of view and allows only limited direct inference of the theories behind the picture or of a clear documentation of findings. It »encodes« the researcher's message in a certain visual way, so that complementary, descriptive methods are required. Moreover, it seems beneficial to have some prior knowledge of the ideal dimensions of collages in order to be able to interpret and use them as a critical instrument of analysis and representation. However, it is precisely its characteristic as a complex entity that makes the collage so interesting for research in architecture, offering an architecture-specific access to investigate research questions and create research findings. In their complementary interaction of objective and subjective factors, in their reflexive and artistic dimension and finally in their associative effect, collages embody fundamental qualities of designing and receiving architecture.

Design and Research. In the quest for discipline-specific ways of researching, the activation or adoption of design practices as research practices can forge new perspectives. Yet the limits and risks of such approaches should always be integrated into the discourse. Simply equating design and research could lead to a loss of relevance for theory, often critically perceived in practice anyway. The compulsive attempt to embed design in research, in turn, could overwhelm especially young scholars in their PhD projects. This raises the question of whether a »classical« dissertation that includes research inquiries into the phenomenological, i.e. also about the interaction of subject and object, is not already architecture-specific research. However, alternative research approaches, exemplified by the collage, clarify the enriching potential for reflection and communication that the interplay of theoretical and practice-based practices as well as verbal and visual patterns offers for (architectural) research.

References

Ammon, Sabine/Froschauer, Eva Maria, eds. (2013): *Wissenschaft Entwerfen: Vom forschenden Entwerfen zur Entwurfsforschung der Architektur*, Paderborn: Wilhelm Fink Verlag.

Aureli, Pier Vittorio Aureli/Tattara, Martino (2017): »Is this a city?«, in: Kersten Geers, David van Severen (eds.), *OFFICE Kersten Geers David van Severen, Volume 1* (exhibition catalogue, BOZAR Centre for Fine Arts Brussels, 2016), Cologne: Verlag der Buchhandlung Walther König, 61.

Borasi, Giovanna (2017): »Hunting for the Present in the Past«, in: Kersten Geers/David van Severen (eds.), *OFFICE Kersten Geers David van Severen, Volume 1*, (exhibition catalogue, BOZAR Centre for Fine Arts Brussels, 2016), Cologne: Verlag der Buchhandlung Walther König, 11–13.

Buchert, Margitta (2011): »Formen der Relationen: Entwerfen und Forschen in der Architektur«, in: Ute Frank/Helga Blocksdorf/Marius Mensing/Anca Timofticiuc, *EKLAT: Entwerfen und Konstruieren in Lehre, Anwendung und Theorie*, Berlin: Universitätsverlag TU Berlin, 76–85.

Buchert, Margitta (2014): *Reflexives Entwerfen. Entwerfen und Forschen in der Architektur / Reflexive Design. Design and Research in Architecture*, Berlin: Jovis.

Buchert, Margitta (2014): »Reflexive Design?«, in: Margitta Buchert, *Reflexives Entwerfen. Entwerfen und Forschen in der Architektur/Reflexive Design. Design and Research in Architecture*, Berlin: Jovis, 24–49.

Buchert, Margitta (2016): *Praktiken reflexiven Entwerfens. Entwerfendes Forschen/Forschendes Entwerfen in Architektur und Landschaft*, Berlin: Jovis.

Buchert, Margitta (2018): *Processes of Reflexive Design*, Berlin: Jovis.

Evans, Robin (2011[1995]): *The Projective Cast. Architecture and Its Three Geometries*, Cambridge, MA: MIT Press. Here, in particular, the last chapter »Conclusion. The Projective Cast«.

Fraser, Murray, ed. (2013): *Design Research in Architecture: An Overview*, Farnham: Ashgate Publishing.

Gänshirt, Christian (2021): *Tools for Ideas. Introduction to Architectural Design*, expanded and updated edition, Basel: Birkhäuser.

Jürgens-Kirchhoff, Annegret (1984): *Technik und Tendenz der Montage in der bildenden Kunst des 20. Jahrhunderts. Ein Essay* (Kunstwissenschaftliche Untersuchungen des Ulmer Vereins, Verband für Kunst und Kulturwissenschaften, 7), Gießen: Anabas.

Kienbaum, Laura (2016): »Zeichnen in der Forschung«, in: Margitta Buchert, *Praktiken Reflexiven Entwerfens. Entwerfendes Forschen, Forschendes Entwerfen*, Berlin: Jovis, 115–127.

Levine, Neil (1998): »The Significance of Facts: Mies's Collages Up Close and Personal«, in: *Assemblage: A Critical Journal of Architecture and Design Culture*, no. 37, 35–101.

MoMA (2014): »Cut 'n' Paste: From Architectural Assemblage to Collage City«, exhibition July 10, 2013–January 5, 2014; cf. https://www.moma.org/calendar/exhibitions/1343, accessed February 19, 2021.

Oechslin, Werner (2011): »Architekturmodell. Idea materialis«, in: Wolfgang Sonne (ed.), *Die Medien der Architektur*, Munich: Deutscher Kunstverlag, 131–155.

Polanyi, Michael (1966): *The Tacit Dimension*, London: Routledge & Kegan Paul.

Schneede, Uwe M. (2001): *Die Geschichte der Kunst im 20. Jahrhundert. Von den Avantgarden bis zur Gegenwart*, Munich: C. H. Beck.

Schön, Donald (1991[1983]): *The Reflective Practitioner. How Professionals Think in Action*, Abingdon: Routledge.

Schrijver, Lara (2014): »Architectural Knowledge: Method or Mystery?«, in: Margitta Buchert (ed.), *Reflexive Design. Design and Research in Architecture*, Berlin: Jovis, 50–71.

Shields, Jennifer A. E. (2013): *Collage and Architecture*, New York: Routledge.

Stauffer, Marie Theres (2007): *Figurationen des Utopischen. Theoretische Projekte von Archizoom und Superstudio*, Berlin/Munich: Deutscher Kunstverlag.

Stierli, Martino (2011): »Mies Montage: Mies van der Rohe, Dada, Film und die Kunstgeschichte«, in: *Zeitschrift für Kunstgeschichte* 74(3), 401–436.

Ursprung, Philip (2013): »Exponierte Exponate. Herzog & de Meuron«, in: Sabine Ammon/Eva Maria Froschauer (eds.), *Wissenschaft Entwerfen: Vom forschenden Entwerfen zur Entwurfsforschung der Architektur*, Paderborn: Wilhelm Fink Verlag, 289–305.

Weidinger, Jürgen (2013): *Entwurfsbasiert Forschen*, Berlin: Universitätsverlag TU Berlin.

Wehmeyer, Sarah (2018): »Collages Interactions«, in: Margitta Buchert (ed.), *Processes of Reflexive Design*, Berlin: Jovis, 124–140.

Embodied Knowledge, Tool, and Sketch: Intuitive Production of Knowledge in Architectural Design

Nandini Oehlmann

Editorial Summay: Entitled »Embodied Knowledge, Tool, and Sketch«, Nandini Oehlmann's contribution directs the focus to the »intuitive production of knowledge in architectural design«, also the subtitle of the text, and aims to trace the tacit, pre-reflective knowledge that plays a guiding role in the design process. As she defines design as having »an idea in mind as a vague notion«, her investigation is driven by the search for a profound understanding of the knowledge transfer of cognitive and manual knowing. She places an emphasis on the evolution of knowledge in the design process, from indistinct premonition to a specific concretization of the design. Tacit knowledge forms the core of this research, aiming to decipher this preconscious experience-based manual or bodily knowledge. [Katharina Voigt]

Keywords: Intuition; Design Process; Manual Knowledge; Tacit Knowledge; Language; Embodiment.

Introduction – On Design Processes

This research aims to investigate a topic that many designers, architects, and students experience in their everyday work: The process of how an idea, an intention or a design come into being. Designing entails having an initial idea in mind as a vague notion. This idea is then gradually formulated using the hand as an interface. In this setting, the hand has an autonomous function; it reexamines the previous idea and formulates it more specifically. At the same time, it can produce almost independently without cognitive intervention. This research is centered on examining the interface between cognitive and manual or physical knowledge when designing, with a specific focus on the notion of knowledge transfer.

Corresponding author: Nandini Oehlmann (Technical University Berlin, Germany); nandini.oehlmann@tu-berlin.de;
Open Access. © 2021 Nandini Oehlmann, published by transcript Verlag.
This work is licensed under the Creative Commons Attribution 4.0 (BY) license.

The thesis of the present research project asserts that there is a form of knowledge preceding cognitive knowledge; a knowledge before knowledge. It is manifested in the body and is therefore called manual or embodied knowledge. The present research investigates this form of knowledge as a special type of implicit knowledge, described by Michael Polanyi as »tacit knowing« (Polanyi 1966).

On one hand, this implies a knowledge of experience that can be used unconsciously. In terms of the design process, this is the knowledge of the pencil stroke made 1000 times, knowledge known inside and out. It is the manual knowledge described by Richard Sennett in his book *The Craftsman* (cf. Sennett 2008), and how many musicians, for example, experience their practice. On the other hand, it is a prior knowledge, an intuition that guides us when, for example, a line of thought is present as a premonition, but has not yet been specified.[1] Here, the sketch plays a crucial role as an approximation to an ideal state that has not yet been formulated; it is an essential tool in the cycle of making – acquiring – understanding.

The following article discusses aspects of several theories and thinkers that deal with the relation between body, language, and knowledge that can enrich and expand our knowledge of design processes.

Research Project: Design Process vs. Language Making

I will approach the aforementioned thesis by examining the relationship between language and knowledge. The discipline of cognitive linguistics precisely examines non-verbal and pre-linguistic thought. Moreover in language, this relationship between implicit and explicit knowledge and intuition and unconscious adaptations in everyday life is applied in a similar manner. Thus, I aim to transfer phenomena of language, how a thought takes shape as a word, to the process of architectural design – how an idea turns into form by means of the body.

Tacit knowing, as well as implicit knowledge, cannot be clearly put into words. It is less related to cognitive structures and more about mental processes; »We can know more than we can tell« (Polanyi 1966: 4). The key

---

[1] Heinrich von Kleist described this phenomenon in his text *Über die allmähliche Verfertigung der Gedanken beim Reden* (On the Gradual Completion of Thoughts During Speech) from 1805. In the process of speaking, thoughts reveal themselves that would not have been revealed by thinking alone.

research question therefore inquires: Does the hand know more than we can draw? Is there an embodied pre-knowledge that we can learn to retrieve? How can we make use of this implicit knowledge when we want to transfer knowledge?

The human use of language combines the direct interplay of cognitive knowledge and intuition. We use complex grammatical rules when speaking and writing, yet we can also intuitively form correct sentences without cognitively retrieving the corresponding rules. »Most of our knowledge of language is unconscious. However, this latent knowledge enables us to act as a recognized member of the language community« (Lutzeier 1985: 56. Translation: Nandini Oehlmann).

This notion additionally relates to the implicit acquisition of the mother tongue. Similarly, when designing, we can develop a »feeling« for joining individual parts into a whole. One could consider the practice of proprioceptive, embodied and lived experience as a pre-reflected knowledge: »Embodied organism-environment interactions [...] constitute our understanding of the world« (Lakeoff / Johnson 2002: 249). The experience gained is acquired casually in everyday life and remains available when designing space and construction. Vice versa, a rule can also be internalized by repetition until it is applied.

The verbalization of content occurs on different parallel process levels. At the same time, information is conceptualized, lexicalized, and a linear syntactic structure is generated and articulated in a motorized manner (Schwarz 2008: 210). Our statements are also generated incrementally. Conceptually, we do not completely plan our statements before we verbalize them. It is only in the process of articulation that utterances are conceptually completed (ibid.). »The subject applies these formal rules according to the situation and accurately reproduces patterns and contents of thought without explicitly and reflectively knowing them« (Seiler 2012: 126. Translation: Nandini Oehlmann).

In this context, the sketch – as a spontaneous visualization of a thought – plays an important role. Thus, the sketch exists as an interface between the incremental materialization and the formulation of knowledge in the world. The generation of knowledge by sketching is to be understood as a »tool situation«, because what is sketched eludes clear description and thus prevents a generic representation of the intended statement. The manner in which knowledge manifests itself in the world is always technology-based, depending on the tool selected. The sketch occupies a special position here; it manifests the characteristic of something still evolving.

The present work is particularly interested in the phenomenon of language due to its implicit acquisition and unconscious use, as well as the substantial amount of existing research in the field of cognitive science. Other than for the »linguistic turn« this is not about semiotic and semantic questions.

Congruence of Language and Thinking

Our use of language combines a fusion of cognitive knowledge and intuition. We subconsciously use complex grammar, formulate correct sentences, and reproduce content that has not yet been completed. The implicit acquisition of linguistic knowledge indicates that we can use this knowledge intuitively.

> »On the one hand it is clear that every sentence in our language ›is in order as it is‹. That is to say, we are not striving after an ideal, as if our ordinary vague sentences had not yet got a quite unexceptionable sense, and a perfect language awaited construction by us. – On the other hand it seems clear that where there is sense there must be perfect order. – So there must be perfect order even in the vaguest sentence.« (Wittgenstein 2009: 26).

In our use of everyday language, we constantly operate with imagined fuzziness and its linguistic description. The intended content is approached in gradual approximation during an ongoing process of conversation. Both communication partners trust that the other person will understand what they mean by an utterance (Bergmann 2005: 128). This elliptical peculiarity of language can be observed analogously in the sketch approach in designing, where images or spaces that have not yet been fully formulated are further conceptualized and developed in manual work.

Some theorists regard this intertwining of the structures of language on the one hand and thinking on the other hand as a process that, due to the close interrelation, cannot take place independently of one another.

Among those scholars is the cognitive psychologist Dietrich Dörner. He postulated that by creating a system that could understand language, one would also create a system that could think (Dörner 1998: 41). Regardless of the fact that language also has a social function, it first creates an event pattern, a kind of regulation for creating a picture. The process of understanding then devises a similar image for the recipient, but one that is less clear. In addition to that, the recipient can put together the meanings of the individual terms from the context of the statement. The ability to understand sentences includes the ability to construct schemas – and thus possible realities. If thinking is the construction of reality or of »possibility«, then simply understanding sentences is an activity that is difficult to separate from thinking (Dörner 1998: 47).

In his work *The Language and Thought of the Child* (cf. Piaget 1926), developmental psychologist Jean Piaget postulated the close connection between the ability to speak and to think. The child's intellectual, cognitive and linguistic development is based on the haptic-sensual experience of the environment. Accordingly, strong language ability is an indication of higher cognitive skills. The cognitive abilities he observed in children of pre-speaking age led him to conclude that thinking was independent of language.

Context

The context of this research is architectural education at the boundary between knowledge and ability. Designing is traditionally learned in studio work within a design project; here, methods and skills are imparted directly. A large part of the knowledge transfer consists of skills that cannot be formalized and is based on symbolic representations or sketches. Even many experts often fail to articulate which skills they have and how they use them.

Thus, the production of knowledge in architecture has little to do with practice because practice largely consists of implicit knowledge (cf. Heylighen/Martin/Cavallin 2006: 2); in this regard, tacit knowing, knowledge, and the knower form one entity. A comparison with the process of language acquisition is again worthwhile because this is also achieved through practice. Initially, individual expressions and rules are learned. The framework for using an idiom must first be internalized so that a virtuoso use of the language is possible. The artistic lingual expression in the sense of literature requires further involvement and skillfulness in dealing with language. This moment of »becoming literature« serves as a personal eye-opening moment when dealing with language. In architectural education, the search for this moment is often replaced with the search for a concept to illustrate a thought. With regard to knowledge transfer and communication, the discussions of situated cognition theorized by Jean Lave might be revealing. This notion concerns anchoring individual learning in context.

The Echo of Language in the Body

Recent neuropsychological findings demonstrate the strong connection between language and the body. Studies have shown that the sensorimotor system is activated in connection with language, even if it points to abstract connections (Boulenger et al. 2009: 1910–1919).

According to the neurobiologist and linguist Boulenger, abstract meanings in the human brain are not only generated by activation of the fronto-temporal cortex, i.e. the semantic center, but also by complementary activations of the sensorimotor system, which add to it (Boulenger et al. 2009: 1912). »These results establish for the first time the differential involvement of motor and premotor cortex in idiom processing and support theories that view abstract semantics as grounded in action-perception systems« (Boulenger et. al. 2009: 1910).

Knowledge of the Body

The tactile experience of the world forms our prior knowledge related to the world. In the overlap of experience and our imagination, we can use and apply it:

> »Our conception of a tree for example [...] arises by the tacit integration of countless experiences of different trees and pictures and reports of still others: deciduous and evergreen, straight and crooked, bare and leafy. All these encounters are included in forming the conception of a tree; they are all used subsidiarily with a bearing in the conception of a tree, which is what we mean by the word tree« (Polanyi 1969: 163).

Tacit knowledge is acquired through experience and practical action. Accordingly, it is also the result of failure and correction. It is comprehensively present in each person: »It is the skill of the hands, the knowledge of the skin, and of the deep layers of the brain« (Puusa/Eerikäinen 2010: 309).

Polanyi distinguishes tacit knowing from explicit knowledge. Explicit knowledge is characterized by the fact that it can be formalized and passed on, for instance in written form. Accordingly, it is independent of a knowing person (Heylighen/Martin/Cavallin 2005). Tacit knowledge can usually not be articulated, and it generally constitutes the necessary background knowledge to understand and handle the explicit knowledge. Furthermore, all knowledge is tacit knowledge or based on it (cf. Polanyi 1958; Polanyi 1966: 4). Therefore, it is not a separate form of knowledge, but an integral part of all knowledge.

The theory of the embodiment, which stems from recent cognitive science, describes the close integration of the body and mind when generating knowledge. Many aspects of cognitive processes depend heavily on the specific properties of a body, reaching beyond the cognition of the brain, in the interplay of perception – cognitive and motor skills (cf. Wilson/Foglia 2015). Thus only through the manifestation of the body in the world does knowledge become possible:

> »Mind is embodied, meaning is embodied, and thought is embodied in this most profound sense. […] According to such a view, there is no ultimate separation of mind and body, and we are always in touch with our world through our embodied acts and experiences« (Lakeoff / Johnson 2002: 249).

Under the influence of Merleau-Ponty and his explanations of the phenomenology of the body – the idea of overcoming the body as a mechanism-in-itself and consciousness as being-for-itself – sociologist Harold Garfinkel developed the theory of ethnomethodology. Garfinkel assumed that by observing the everyday and professional world, important actions and processes of knowledge generation could be examined. This school of thought later became known as »studies of work«. It examines the formal structures of practical processes. Textbook knowledge has a model character that cannot simply be transferred to everyday practical work. This gap between theory and practice, or between textbook and reality, exemplifies the everyday experience that can only be acquired through practical action in the social structure of the work context (Bergmann 2005: 132).

The knowledge of experience thus contains those contents of the human mind that arise while exercising the profession or in other contexts that enable people to act professionally. The »studies of work« explore this field of research in different occupations and work contexts. Even in (seemingly) context-independent activities such as performing a mathematical proof, it is shown how such an activity constitutes a craft in the interplay of blackboard, chalk, and hand.

A structure that contains knowledge, like a word or an action, is ambiguous in the sense that it can contain more than one state of knowledge depending on the context. Conversely, content can appear in various states or contexts. According to the ethnomethodological reading, common scientific language fails here. Rigid categorizations cannot reflect the rich, yet vague and ambiguous everyday language (cf. Garfinkel 1967).

Conclusion

With this text, I aim to further widen the broad field of questions concerning the specific knowledge contained in the design process. The phenomenon of language and implicit actions associated with tacit knowledge increase our awareness of the design process as a professional practice. A further step could entail generating new pedagogical frameworks for design education in architecture. Acknowledging and developing the specific knowledge impersonated in a designer is of great importance for the future of our profession. It concerns knowledge, which is hard to generalize, paraphrase, or formalize in an abstract process without the control of a person. Moreover, a discerning and educated personality who exercises the cycle of making – acquiring – understanding and who is enabled to do so by their previously accumulated knowledge, is irreplaceable in the design process, especially in the increasingly automated processes of generative design. Furthermore, new potentials emerge to intervene in the design process and to develop new methods. From the researched phenomena, new tools can be derived that could be used for the design process.

Concluding, this text constitutes a plea for understanding through doing. We cannot deny this ability by the increasing mechanization of the design processes, as it takes an educated personality to classify and transfer the generated content into a broader context.

References

Bergmann, Jörg (2005): »Ethnomethodologie«, in: Uwe Flick/Ernst von Kardorff/Ines Steinke (eds.), *Qualitative Forschung. Ein Handbuch*, Reinbek bei Hamburg: Rowohlt.

Boulenger, Véronique/Hauk, Olaf/Pulvermüller, Friedemann (2009): »Grasping Ideas with the Motor System: Semantic Somatotopy in Idiom Comprehension«, in: *Cerebral Cortex*, August 2009, 19(8), 1905–1914. doi: 10.1093/cercor/bhn217

Dörner, Dietrich (1998): »Sprache und Denken«, in: *Mannheimer Beiträge – Sonderheft 1998*, http://www-1v75.rz.uni-mannheim.de/ Publikationen/ MA%20Beitraege/Sh98/ Sonderheft98.pdf#page=41, accessed September 18, 2019.

Garfinkel, Harold (1967): *Studies in Ethnomethodology*, Englewood Cliffs, NJ: Prentice Hall.

Heylighen, Ann/Martin, Mike W./Cavallin, Humberto (2005) »How to Teach and Archive Tacit Design Knowledge«, in: *Design Intelligence* 11(6).

Heylighen, Ann/Martin, Mike W./Cavallin, Humberto (2006): »Building Stories Revisited: Unlocking the Knowledge Capital of Architectural Practice«, in: *Architectural Engineering and Design Management*, Volume 3, 65–74.

Kleist, Heinrich von [1805]: *Über die allmählige Verfertigung der Gedanken beim Reden.* – English translation: *On the Gradual Completion of Thoughts During Speech*, transl. by John S. Taylor, Amsterdam/Berlin/Stuttgart: edenspiekermann, [2006] 2011, https://spiekermann.com/en/wp-content/uploads/2008/11/Kleist_speech_ende.pdf, accessed January 17, 2021.

Lakoff, George/Johnson, Mark (2002): »Why Cognitive Linguistics Requires Embodied Realism«, in: *Cognitive Linguistics* 13(3), 245–263. DOI: 10.1515/cogl.2002.016

Lutzeier, Peter (1985): *Linguistische Semantik*, Stuttgart: Metzler.

Merleau-Ponty, Maurice [1945]: *Phénoménologie de la perception.* – English translation: *Phenomenology of Perception* [first transl. 1962 by Colin Smith], transl. by Donald Landes, Abingdon: Routledge, 2013.

Piaget, Jean [1923]: *Le Langage et la pensée chez l'enfant.* – English translation: *The Language and Thought of the Child* [1926], transl. by Marjorie and Ruth Gabain, New York/London: Routledge, 1959.

Polanyi, Michael (1958): *Personal Knowledge: Toward a Post-Critical Philosophy*, London: Routledge & Kegan Paul.

Polanyi, Michael (1966): *The Tacit Dimension*, London: Routledge & Kegan Paul.

Polanyi, Michael (1969): Marjorie Greene (ed.), *Knowing and Being: Essays by Michael Polanyi*, London: Routledge & Kegan Paul.

Puusa, Anu/Eerikäinen, Mari (2010): »Is Tacit Knowledge Really Tacit?«, in: *Electronic Journal of Knowledge Management*, Vol. 8, Issue 3, 307–318.

Schwarz, Monika (2008): *Einführung in die Kognitive Linguistik*, Stuttgart: UTB.

Seiler, Thomas Bernhard (2012): *Evolution des Wissens, Band 1: Evolution der Erkenntnisstrukturen*, Münster: LIT Verlag.

Sennett, Richard (2008): *The Craftsman*, New Haven: Yale University Press.

Wilson, Robert A./Foglia, Lucia (2015): »Embodied Cognition«, in: Edward N. Zalta (ed.), *The Stanford Encyclopedia of Philosophy*, https://stanford.library.sydney.edu.au/entries/embodied-cognition, accessed January 17, 2021.

Wittgenstein, Ludwig [1953]: *Philosophische Untersuchungen.* – English translation: *Philosophical Investigations* [first transl. 1953 by G. E. M. Anscombe] rev. fourth edition, transl. by G. E. M. Anscombe, P. M. S. Hacker and Joachim Schulte, Hoboken, NJ: Wiley-Blackwell, 2009.

Data-Driven Research on Ecological Prototypes for Green Architecture: Enabling Urban Intensification and Restoration through Agricultural Hybrids

Defne Sunguroğlu Hensel

Editorial Summary: In »Data-Driven Research on Ecological Prototypes for Green Architecture« Defne Sunguroğlu Hensel introduces a design research attempt to the field of environment design, landscape, architecture, and green technologies in the context of urbanization, questioning the interrelation of architectural buildings and ecological, agricultural, and natural free space. This research proposes their inclusive interplay, aiming to dissolve the notion of construction as a driving force of land degradation and instead emphasizing its potential to facilitate green infrastructures in the realm of the built environment. Green constructions are described as a reasonable interlocking of architectural basic structures and their agricultural or horticultural use. She analyzes historically proven examples, underlining their contemporary potentials for adaptation and transition. [Katharina Voigt]

Keywords: Urbanization; Environment; Green Construction; Data-Driven Design; Decision; Ecological Prototypes; Urban Agriculture; Urban Restoration.

Introduction

Environmental deterioration caused by rapid urbanization and climate change constitutes a major challenge for architecture in the 21st century. Construction is causing significant loss of agricultural and forest landscapes, degradation of ecosystems, depletion of natural resources, and decline in biodiversity and carbon stock as well as human-wildlife conflict (a trigger for pandemics such as Covid-19) (Salehi/Woodbridge/Arikan 2017; Groffman, et al. 2017; McDonald, et al. 2020; Güneralp, et al. 2013; World Economic Forum 2018). Humans depend on the services that nature provides for their health and well-being (Millennium Ecosystem Assessment, 2005). Land use and cover change and transformation through urban expansion and densification threatens the delivery of essential ecosystem services, i.e. food production

Corresponding author: Defne Sunguroğlu Hensel (Vienna University of Technology and Technical University of Munich); defnesunguroglu@lamolab.net; https://orcid.org/0000-0003-2968-6432
Open Access. © 2021 Defne Sunguroğlu Hensel, published by transcript Verlag.
This work is licensed under the Creative Commons Attribution 4.0 (BY) license.

and local climate regulation, as well as various other benefits derived from nature and human-nature relationship. Urban land take in Europe continues to exceed the target limit of 61,100 hectares/year to achieve »No Net Land Take« goal by 2050 (Science for Environment Policy, 2016). While construction and human intervention is often considered a major driver of environmental degradation, they are not necessarily always harmful. In fact, they can be vital for the protection, support, and enhancement of ecosystems and the delivery of services, as seen in historical agricultural systems for example (Pasta et al. 2017; La Mantia/Carimi/Di Lorenzo/Pasta 2011). Moreover, construction can even play a key role in sustainable intensification of urban agriculture and restoration to enhance ecosystems and service delivery in the urban environment.

Urban agriculture and land restoration can contribute to mitigating the negative environmental impact of rapid urbanization, and if integrated in architectural design and planning decisions even help reconcile urbanization with nature. In this context, urban agriculture and restoration is considered as a combined strategy to reverse past degradation that result from urbanization while avoiding and reducing new degradation in the continuous process of adapting and transforming the environment to protect and meet not only humans and their needs but also nature and the needs of other species. Some of these efforts are currently taking place at the landscape scale involving forest landscape restoration, restoration ecology, and ecological engineering. These include forestation, conservation, and sustainable management practices, as well as integrated land use planning, which goes beyond the classic agricultural intensification and land-sparing strategies. Other strategies, applicable at architectural and planning scales, include land recycling by building on brownfields, densification by filling gaps in the urban fabric, compensation for land taken by returning abandoned building land to agricultural, forest, or other types of semi-natural land cover, and minimizing buildings' negative environmental impact. Biodiversity, climate change, and human well-being challenges are drawing increasing attention to urban green infrastructure (UGI) and green architecture in terms of their potential to offer sites for incorporating plants in buildings and cities, i.e. vertical forests, green facades and roofs, or urban forests, urban agriculture, and green corridors (Rinaldi, Bianca; Tan, Puay Yok 2019).

Minimizing the environmental impact of land and resource consumption, construction and buildings through resource efficiency and boosting nature and agriculture in cities for climate change adaptation and mitigation, human well-being and biodiversity are some of the primary motivations for contemporary green construction (GC). This has already led to new green buildings, i.e. vertical forests like the Bosco Verticale in Milan by Stefano Boeri or the Biodiversity Tower M6B2 in Paris by Eduard Francois. There exists also a growing interest in ways in which the combination of green roofs and facades can act as green conservation tools, enhancing biodiversity, as well as more broadly, the integration of biotic and abiotic components of green buildings (Dover 2015). Buildings can make provisions for establishing vegetation on sites which have been lost to or cleared for construction. However, they are typically not designed for enhancing a habitat to increase its suitability for some target species and agricultural practices selected for their particular multiple ecological and service benefits. The latter is a substantially different approach compared with conventional approaches to green architecture that we are accustomed to see in cities. As a result, construction while being a mechanism for adapting the environment to suit human needs, is hardly conceived as a tool for intensification, by making it possible to achieve higher-level cultivation (both quantitatively and qualitatively) without dependency on unsustainable and resource intensive methods, and restoration, by introducing species and practices that are not only beneficial for humans but also local ecosystems. Therefore, while some buildings manage to integrate elements of green infrastructure, they can hardly be considered a means of ecological restoration and intensification. Achieving this goal requires a systematic and integrated design and planning approach, and coordinated, systemic and accumulative interventions at the architectural scale. Currently we lack the evidence base and design methods to adequately bring data and green construction intelligence into decision making processes.

In this context GC systems are characterized in terms of their capacity for agricultural intensification and ecological restoration, which determine the multifunctionality of green construction. The first attempt to mapping these systems show that at one extreme, GC typologies tend towards fully-enclosed systems of food production that are decoupled from their natural environment with detrimental environmental impact due to high input and no ecological significance. At the other extreme, they are structures and practices that enable extensive horticulture with either high or low external input. These types often provide ecosystem functions to a lesser extent. Historical agricultural constructions enable sustainable cultivation in challenging environments and provide solutions that work with local climatic and ecological conditions, available materials and renewable resources, and do not depend on external input, i.e. energy. These range from provisions for single plants, to extensive farming at the landscape scale, and urban farming with ecological value. Ecological prototypes, a notion introduced to refer to systems for architectural adaptation to facilitate agricultural intensification and ecological restoration simultaneously stand for a new type of GC. These novel systems are hybrid adaptive systems of design, construction, and practices that link architecture, horticulture and agriculture, landscape, and ecology. This is the area where research is most urgently needed. These novel systems are being investigated for their potential to enable high-value plants and farming practices in urban environments, which are otherwise challenging and unsuitable conditions for their cultivation. Special attention is given to developing systems with better capacity to balance and reconcile intensification, restoration and sustainability objectives in delivering ecosystem support and improved services in the built environment.

Data-Driven Research and Development of Ecological Prototypes

One of the objectives of ecological prototypes research is to learn from historical land systems that have evolved over generations. Solutions from the past can facilitate not only design innovation for next generation GC, but also help identifying questions that need to be asked to design better GCs for the changing needs of our time. These traditional agricultural land uses draw on natural and locally available resources and ecosystem services in an economic way to facilitate the cultivation of valuable crops in challenging environmental conditions. They also play a key role in the delivery of services like micro-climate regulation, which benefits plants and cultivation. In these examples, crop cultivation is facilitated through a combination of biotic means, i.e. introduction of a new species, plant manipulation (horticultural practices), and abiotic means, i.e. the dry-stone wall constructions that transform a slope into terraced landscapes and modify environmental gradients through added thermal mass to facilitate high quality vine production at high altitudes. The least intrusive systems include forest farming and forest gardening, as well as ancient methods such as *vite maritata* that utilizes trees as scaffolds for growing vine (Buono/Vallariello 2002). Systems with a slightly higher degree of intervention are characterized by modifications of the terrain. Examples are the funnel-shaped soil indentations for growing individual vine plants on the Canary island of Lanzarote, the terracing of slopes that can be found in many regions of the world, or structures that support plants in various ways. The latter include the use of scaffold-like structures for growing vine, lemon, or hop and linear constructions such as dry-stone or masonry walls, or Devon hedges made from earth banks faced with stone or turf with native trees and shrubs growing on it. More elaborate systems are dry-stone walls in conjunction with terraced landscapes, or as perimeter structures for walled gardens, such as the ones on the Italian island of Pantelleria (Lommatzsch/Brignone 2007). Dry-stone or masonry walls can be individual structures, such as the serpentine walls in England, or extensive systems spread over large areas, such as the peach gardens in Montreuil near Paris, France, that utilize so-called fruit walls. These types can either be open field systems or provide an enclosure such as the talut walls. Fully enclosed greenhouses originally evolved from the fruit wall with leaning glass surfaces, i.e. talut walls, later came to encompass three quarter span greenhouses, conservatories, orangeries, hothouses, and eventually contemporary industrial greenhouses to intensify and sustain production throughout the year. Significant progress in this regard emerged through the works of Louden, Paxton, and others (Hix 1974). Greenhouses can be further distinguished by the degree to which mechanical and electrical means are used to produce a controlled artificial interior climate.

Initial sets of data on historical agricultural/horticultural systems are currently being collected. This data comes from individual field surveys, literature sources, and various methods of analysis to be structured and integrated in a decision support system for research and development. This historically-derived information will include – but is not limited to – the following cases: (1) linear structures such as the dry-stone walls and terraced landscapes of Lamole in Italy, fruit walls of Thomery in France, and Serpentine walls in England; (2) perimeter structures such as the singular walled gardens of Pantelleria in Italy, and aggregated walled gardens such as the peach orchards of Montreuil sous Bois in France, and the volcanic vineyard landscapes of Lanzarote in Italy; (3) enclosed structures such as the lean-to and vaulted hot houses and early green houses; (4) transformable structures such as the lemon houses (limonaie) of Lake Garda; and (5) practices without structures such as Vite Maritata. Systematic and comparative analysis of diverse types of historical land systems is crucial for understanding the functional attributes that result in multiple benefits derived from these systems, including ecosystem services. Comparability of the performance of existing GC solutions from a multifunctionality perspective enables integrating historical knowledge in the implementation and adaptation of strategies and solutions to foster long-term persistence and resilience, and to changing requirements and conditions, which necessitate design innovation in order to be able to address complex GC challenges of our time.

Discussion

Historical data constitutes only a part of the necessary datasets for research, experimentation and development of novel GC systems. Another comes from research-by-design experiments which involves prototypical tests and full-scale constructions carried out as laboratory and field experiments. These design and construction experiments facilitate the generation of new data while at the same time using insights and information derived from historical data for experimentation and validation of theoretical results. Hence, a line of research on Ecological Prototypes focuses on earth-based materials and structures, which has a long history in the evolution of GC system typologies. A strong motivation for massive construction shaped by local materials (i.e. stone, soil, brick) was in particular to combine the advantages of structural and thermal mass. Therefore, these structures were often massive. In other contexts, heavy construction may be associated with significant trade-offs due to size and space occupied, material intensity and ground impact for which lightweight construction may be a better alternative.

The crinkle crankle or serpentine wall is an example for a historical technological innovation that shows one of the ways by which this trade-off was addressed in GC design. The serpentine is an undulating masonry wall system that is often only one brick deep, which is incorporated in walled gardens surrounding a house with the main purpose of training fruit trees across the sun exposed surface. It is a light-weight structural solution that provides stability without any additional supporting elements like the buttresses. Shape is a critical parameter as it provides stability while increasing the surface area of the wall. The change from flat to an undulating wall helps to generate more space for training fruit plants, optimize solar exposure and thermal energy storage, and protect the plants from cold winds.

Many architectural examples make use of the undulating wall principle, as for example seen in numerous projects of Eladio Dieste. However, these are rarely designed also to provide for the specific needs of plants and agriculture/horticulture. This strategy is being investigated in research focused on the development of a GC system called Nested Catenaries.

The first developmental phase of this research (Sunguroglu Hensel/Bover 2013), focused on questions of integrating spatial and structural design of an unreinforced masonry construction, a thin vaulted shell structure that can achieve large spans and resist dynamic loads. The next phase of development focuses on environmental questions including the modification of microclimate and environmental gradients to suit particular plant and agricultural practice needs. Nested Catenaries is one of the systems being developed in the context of ecological prototypes research.

Conclusion

This research introduces the concept of ecological prototypes, a novel type of GC system, and some aspects of the data-driven experimental and developmental design research framework. Ecological prototypes are described as the new generation GC and as integrated and adaptive design and construction systems. These systems link architecture, agriculture/horticulture, landscape and ecology to facilitate the protection, support, and enhancement of ecosystems and services in urban environments. The development of ecological prototypes for learning, adaptation, and application in environments with similar conditions and requirements necessitates bringing GC knowledge into data-driven design. This chapter focused on the historical case study research and the role of this dataset in experimental design research. It is important to note that the historical data is only a part of and not the only data-set that is being acquired, analyzed and structured for the purpose of ecological prototypes research. EPOC decision support system is currently being developed to model, manage, integrate, interrogate, and capture research relevant information through linking various computational methods and processes, including an expert database, where also the historical data is stored and collected (Sunguroglu Hensel 2020). Based on this approach, novel ecological prototypes can evolve with the aim to facilitate GC systems for architectural and context-specific adaptation, and sustainable construction that can enable ecological intensification of urban agriculture and restoration for enhanced ecosystem support and delivery of urban services.

References

Buono, Raffaele/Vallariello, Gioacchino (2002): »La vite maritata in Campania«, in: *Delpinoa* (44), 53–63.

Dover, John W. (2015): *Green Infrastructure: Incorporating Plants and Enhancing Biodiversity in Buildings and Urban Environments*. London/New York: Routledge.

Groffman, Peter M./Avolio, Meghan/ Cavender-Bares, Jeannine/Bettez, Neil D./Grove, Morgan J./Hall, Sharon J. et al. (2017): »Ecological Homogenization of Residential Macrosystems«, in: *Nature Ecology & Evolution* 1(7), 1–3.

Güneralp, Burak/McDonald, Robert I./Fragkias, Michail/ Goodness, Julie, Marcotullio, Peter J./Seto, Karen C. (2013): »Urbanization Forecast, Effects on Land Use, Biodiversity, and Ecosystem Services, in: Thomas Elmqvist/Michail Fragkias/Julie Goodness/Burak Güneralp/ Peter J. Marcotullio/Robert I. McDonald/ Susan Parnell/Maria Schewenius/ Marte Sendstad/Karen C. Seto/Cathy Wilkinson (eds.), *Urbanization, Biodiversity and Ecosystem Services: Challenges and Opportunities*, Dordrecht/Heidelberg/New York/London: Springer Open, 437–453.

Hix, John (1996[1974]): The Glass House, London: Phaidon.

La Mantia, Tommaso/Carimi, Francesco/ Di Lorenzo, Rosario/Pasta, Salvatore (2011): »The Agricultural Heritage of Lampedusa (Pelagie Archipelago, South Italy) and Its Key Role for Cultivar and Wildlife Conservation«, in: *Italian Journal of Agronomy* 6(2), 106–110.

Lommatzsch, Ines/Brignone, Francesco (2007): »Die Jardini von Pantelleria«, in: *Orangerien in Europa. Von fürstlichem Vermögen und gärtnerischer Kunst, ICOMOS – Hefte des Deutschen Nationalkomitees* (43), 86–90.

McDonald, Robert I./Mansur, Andressa V./Ascensão, Fernando/Colbert, M'lisa/ Crossman, Katie/Elmqvist, Thomas, et al. (2020): »Research Gaps in Knowledge of the Impact of Urban Growth on Biodiversity«, in: *Nature Sustainability* 3, 16–24.

Millennium Ecosystem Assessment (2005): *Ecosystems and Human Well-Being: Synthesis*, Washington, DC.: Island Press.

Pasta, Salvatore Claudio/Ardenghi, Nicola M. G./Badalamenti, Emilio /La Mantia, Tommaso/Console, Salvatore Livreri/Parolo, Gilberto (2017): »The Alien Vascular Flora of Linosa (Pelagie Islands, Strait of Sicily): Update and Management Proposals«, in: *Willdenowia* 47(2), 135–144.

Rinaldi, Bianca/Tan, Puay Yok, eds. (2019): *Urban Landscapes in High-Density Cities. Parks, Streetscapes, Ecosystems*. Basel: Birkhäuser.

Salehi, Pourya/Woodbridge, Michael/ Arikan, Yunus (2017): *Land degradation and cities. ICLEI Briefing Sheet* (3), 1–4.

Science for Environment Policy (2016): *No Net Land Take by 2050? Future Brief 14*, Bristol: Science Communication Unit.

Sunguroglu Hensel, Defne (2020): Ecological Prototypes: »Initiating Design Innovation in Green Construction«, in: *Sustainability, MDPI, Open Access Journal*, vol. 12(14), 1–17.

Sunguroglu Hensel, Defne/Bover, Guillem Baraut (2013): »Nested Catenaries«, in: *IASS Journal of the International Association for Shell and Spatial Structures*, 39–55.

World Economic Forum (2018): *Shaping the Future of Construction: Future Scenarios and Implications for the Industry*. Cologny/ Geneva: World Economic Forum.

Reflexions on the Plurality of Methods in Architecture

Oya Atalay Franck

Editorial Summary: With »Reflexions on the Plurality of Research Methodology in Architecture«, Oya Atalay Franck explores the plurality of methods in architecture, unfolding the broad variety of working fields in the discipline. She highlights the specificity of the design tasks, resulting in a unique challenge for each task with correspondingly individual answers and results, thereby framing designing as an adaptive creational process that corresponds to the distinct demands of the project. Although the design process here is outlined as interactive and feedback-dependent, including the interwoven use of different media and working methods, this contribution questions whether the discipline of architecture can actually be investigated according to proven procedures of research practice. [Katharina Voigt]

Keywords: Research Methods; Adoptability of Cross-Disciplinary Approaches; Research by Design.

Architecture is, first and foremost, the creation of spaces for human activity and habitat. In order for such space to be defined, the architect designs and constructs buildings and related structures. Architecture, in this sense, is also the product of this process: the buildings and man-made structures. The domain of the architect as »maker of spaces« extends to all areas of human presence and all levels of scale: from a single room in a herder's hut high up in the mountains to megacities with millions of inhabitants. Architecture thus also includes urban design and shall be used here in this encompassing sense.

The qualitative requirements of architecture as a human habitat are manifold, and they differ from place to place, from scale to scale, and from use to use. The Roman architect and theoretician Vitruvius summed them up in three main categories: firmness – a built structure has to be strong, hold its own weight and the weight that comes with its use, and withstand the elements; functionality – a built structure has to serve its purpose well,

Corresponding author: Oya Atalay Franck (ZHAW Zurich University of Applied Sciences, Winterthur, Switzerland); oya.atalay@zhaw.ch;
Open Access. © 2021 Oya Atalay Franck, published by transcript Verlag.
This work is licensed under the Creative Commons Attribution 4.0 (BY) license.

whether it is housing, trade, industrial production, services or leisure; and beauty – a built structure has to provide a worthy atmosphere and a satisfying experience for the senses and for the mind.

Architectural problems vary significantly – it is safe to say that no two are alike. In their professional careers, architects typically specialize in some category of task, designing for example schools, or houses, or hospitals, or city quarters. Each of these tasks has different requirements. Nevertheless, when we look at the process of solving architectural problems, we can identify certain analytical and synthetical phases and steps which are crucial for tasks at all scales and levels of difficulty.

First, the architect has to learn about the task at hand and understand its fundamental requirements. This includes getting to know the functional requirements and the means, wishes, and needs of the client and the user, understanding the conditions of the site – its geology, topography, climate – where the built structure is to be established, as well as learning about the social and cultural context. This is the analytical phase of the process.

The architect then has to develop spatial and technical solutions to this task, usually in variants which are discussed with the buyer and other stakeholders. This is the core of the architectural process and the key activity of the architect: the activity of designing and constructing. This encompasses the conceptual and synthetic phase of the process, where ideas regarding the solution to the problem come together in a vision of the final product.

Finally, the solution to the architectural problem has to be transformed from its merely theoretical state to its practical implementation through the planning of the construction process and its execution. This is the concretizing phase of the process, where that which was merely an idea is turned into solid matter.

These three phases of architectural production never follow each other in this »one-two-three« sequence. Instead, they overlap and interweave, for already during the first encounter with the client commissioning a work or the first visit to the site, the architect must consider the shape and structure of the final product. Ideas regarding materials and construction technology inform the process of shaping space as much as they are a result of it. Testing the feasibility of a concept sometimes results in backlash reaching all the way to the analytical phase, when certain findings may have to be critically reevaluated.

Designing architectural space is therefore always an iterative process, a process of feedback loops. Some design methods integrate this as a key element and actively work at different scales simultaneously: at the urban level, the level of individual spaces, and of the constructive detail – this is sometimes referred to as the »scenario method« (cf. Gerber/Kurath/Schurk/ Züger (eds.) 2018[2013]). Other methods approach an architectural problem much like using a zoom lens for photography, beginning with the broadest view and diving deeper and focusing more and more on the details of the situation at hand, trying to develop successful approaches to issues at smaller scales, quite like standardized patterns of a language (cf. Alexander/ Ishikawa/Silverstein 1977).

It should be mentioned that many architects may have a problem with the terminology used in this text. They may not like to think of their activity as providing solutions to problems in the way that an engineer might approach a typical task. Of course, thinking of architecture as mere »problem solving« is robbing it of its key element, the magical quality that architectural spaces and structures have when they become art, and which the German philosopher Schelling characterized as »solidified music« (Schelling 1859: 575).[1]

Such an objection is justified: Not everything about architecture can be rationalized and logically reduced to a »problem«. However, even if you exclude these »artistic« elements from the discourse on research and methodology, a large amount of substance regarding architecture and its process and products still remains and can be included. That is what is primarily discussed here: All of the components of the process and products of architecture, which can be analyzed and synthesized in a structured, systematical and methodological way.

Obviously, as areas of research, the first two Vitruvian qualities – firmness and functionality – are more open and welcoming to investigation, scientific and otherwise, than the third – beauty. Beauty is notoriously difficult to measure, to expose to empirical observation without killing it, and to logically reason and debate. David Hume, a leading thinker of the Enlightenment and one of the forefathers of empiricism and skepticism, wrote in 1742: »Beauty is no quality in things themselves: It exists merely

---

1 Translation: Oya Atalay Franck. German original: »Was also in dem Gebiet des Schematismus liegt, ist der arithmetischen Bestimmung unterworfen in der Natur und Kunst, die Architektur, als die Musik der Plastik, folgt also nothwendig arithmetischen Verhältnissen, da sie aber die Musik im Raume, gleichsam die erstarrte Musik ist, so sind diese Verhältnisse zugleich geometrische Verhältnisse.«

in the mind which contemplates them; and each mind perceives a different beauty.«[2]

But beauty may be the quintessential element of architecture, that which sets it apart from mere »construction«. »Beauty« in this context is a synonym for all that deals with aesthetics, with perception and emotion, and with the artistic element of architecture. If you ask an architect »what is architecture?«, you may get puzzling answers like these: »Architecture is masterly, correct and magnificent play of masses brought together in light« (Le Corbusier 1927: 29); or »Architecture is the will of an epoch translated into space« (Wedderkop 1924: 31–32);[3] or »Architecture is the reaching out for the truth« (Kries/Eisenbrand/von Moos 2012: 13).

This does not mean that the artistic element of a design is completely inaccessible to research. It is certainly open to reflection and critical thinking, which themselves are forms of research as well. But there is a similarity to alchemy or natural philosophy in the speculative unity of the natural and the spiritual in the concept of beauty, of that which can be explained and that which can not.

It's a banality to state that not all tasks of architecture pose the same difficulties and that not all architects are equally qualified to solve all tasks. This is not just a question of artistic creativity and talent, but also a question of experience and intelligence. Further – with the increasing complexity of a problem – it is a question of whether the architect tackles the process of learning about problems involved in a task and develops spatial and constructive solutions for this task in a systematic and methodical way.

One thing should be made clear: Architecture is a discipline that requires structured processes for problem solving. Through the centuries, architects have developed their own set of tools and methods for this systematic process. Some of these methods are analytical, some conceptual, but many are both: I think for example, of sketching and drafting, of mapping and model building, of plan and section, of perspective and axonometry, and of

---

2 https://oll.libertyfund.org/titles/hume-essays-moral-political-literary-lf-ed; based on: David Hume, (1987). *Essays Moral, Political, Literary,* edited and with a foreword, notes, and glossary by Eugene F. Miller, with an appendix of variant readings from the 1889 edition by T.H. Green and T.H. Grose, revised edition, Indianapolis: Liberty Fund, accessed April 6, 2020.

3 Translation: Oya Atalay Franck. German original: »Baukunst ist immer raumgefasster Zeitwille, nichts anderes«.

other standardized conventions of representation, yet also of morphological and typological study and classification.

Generally, large-scale tasks – such as developing a city neighborhood as opposed to designing an office building – are more complex than small-scale ones. This is certainly the case where the first two Vitruvian qualities are concerned, firmitas and utilitas. Quite a number of architectural problems are so complex, that they might be called »wicked«, as in mean or nasty. The term »wicked problem«, coined in the 1960s in the context of the social sciences and economics (Term coined by Horst Rittel, in: Churchman 1967: B-141), denotes a problem which is difficult to solve because of complex interdependencies between agents, muddled conditions and circumstances, and in general a resistance to resolution.

Difficult problems require stricter adherence to systematic analysis through research. There is a »natural inclination« of architecture – and of architects – toward research. I have heard many practicing architect-teachers at architecture schools claim, often a bit defensively, that the process of designing spaces and their defining structures is by its very nature a process of »research« and as such a quest for a specific kind of knowledge. However, these same architects would invariably say that the knowledge gained in an architectural process is highly specific, contextual and applicable only to a certain architectural, social or cultural setting, often only understandable to the »cognoscenti« and, in any case, difficult to communicate.

Unfortunately, because it does not benefit architecture as an academic discipline, there is a similarly strong disinclination toward applying the rules of scientific research to the design process. Rules such as careful and systematic observation, rigorous skepticism about what is observed and how the observed is understood, the formulation of precise hypotheses and of testable research questions, and in general, complete transparency and traceability of both process and results.

Practicing architects who also work in academia, who are therefore exposed to a scientific environment and who may be confronted with the demand for »scientific production«, are to some degree suffering under these demands. Architecture is in many ways an »intuitive« discipline that relies considerably on non-structured, improvisational processes. Typically, scientific research associated with architecture is exactly this: »associated« in the sense of »not located in its center« or in its »key process« – i.e. designing. Instead, research takes place at the »fringes« of the discipline, or – more precisely – at its intersections with other academic disciplines:

with engineering; with the natural sciences; with the humanities; or with the social sciences. This is a fundamental dilemma of architecture: how can methodological rigor and academic transparency be applied to a discipline which relies so heavily on intuition and on artistic creativity, on that which has to be felt but cannot really be explained?

As a panel member for the Swiss National Science Foundation and other funding agencies, I have reviewed quite a number of research grant applications from the fields of architecture and urbanism. Evaluations for scientific funding are usually based on certain key criteria, such as the scientific relevance of the project and the potential for the study's broader impact, the originality and topicality of the proposed project, the appropriateness of methods and the feasibility of the project plan. Many architect-researchers at schools and at institutes of architecture and urbanism face fundamental problems regarding third-party research funding for which they have to compete with other disciplines. I have observed a lower rate of success for grant requests from architecture than from other fields. This has often to do with certain »structural deficits« of the applications: a lack of clear definition of the research matter and of its delimitations; a lack in systematic preparation of the project according to scientific standards; and also a lack of stringency where processual structure and choice of methods are concerned.

There are several plausible explanations for these deficits, such as a lack of interest from the building industry in architectural research, no specialization in the scientific sense within the professional core of the architect-designer (the architect as »generalist«) and the artistic aspects of architecture. Additionally, and this may be the least noted but most important aspect: architects are not trained to conduct scientific research. I personally know of no school of architecture which has »Basic Research Methodology for Architects« or a similar course on its curriculum – not even as an elective. Like the tools developed by architects and builders for the professional practice of designing spaces and built structures, the scientists of the various academic disciplines have developed, tested and standardized their tools for research, and they continuously add new tools to the »methodological toolbox«. This »toolbox« is available for all: It has different sections, with for example different tools for qualitative or quantitative, experimental or observational studies. Some disciplines have a penchant for one group of tools or another. The social and the natural sciences as well as engineering like to gather quantitative data which can then be submitted to statistical analysis and other numbers-based methods. The humanities often use tools from the qualitative section of the toolbox, focusing on non-quantitative data and reflecting on the meaning that can be attributed to such information.

In my opinion, if architects want to be more successful both in academic work and in professional practice, they also have to invest in the »professionality« of the analytical components of the design process. This includes a higher sensitivity for the complexity of even relatively simple research tasks and what this means for the organization of the work process. Architecture does not take place in a laboratory, where agents and factors can be limited, but in the »dirtiness« of the real world.

This is a problem in other academic fields as well – think of sociology or anthropology, or medicine.[4] Furthermore, architects cannot subtract themselves from a problem as more or less neutral observers, because it is their objective and task to transform that which they study.

Architects have learned to work in teams including specialists from other fields, such as systems planners and engineers, sociologists and ecologists, and others. This must be twice true for architect-researchers. Some architectural tasks – especially at larger-scale levels: a neighborhood, a city, a metropolitan area – pose very complex, even »wicked« problems. Think, for example, of developing concepts for urban housing in noise-polluted areas, where you have to be able to reconcile such contradictory claims as density, light, noise-protection and community life. To understand these problems and to evaluate possible solutions for them, architects have to engage in even more careful and systematic research than usual. These complex and at times »wicked« problems often require knowledge from other disciplines, such as sociology, cultural studies, history, ecology and economics. Solving such problems, or – in the case of »unsolvable« wicked problems – finding the best possible compromise approaching a solution – requires

---

4 Think of the difficulties of a general practitioner who has to treat patients in all of their dimensions of health – biological, psychological and social – and not just as (for example) a »kidney problem«. The field of research dealing with basic health services is – appropriately called – health services research. It is to be differentiated from basic, translational and clinical research. Health services research faces similar problems as architectural research in that it deals with the highly complex and »dirty« situations of reality, with no possibility for randomized controlled trials. And, unlike basic and clinical research, where huge amounts of money are poured in, it is notoriously difficult for this field of medicine to get recognition and research funding.

interdisciplinary work. Only interdisciplinary collaboration, both in the analysis of the problem at hand and in the synthesis of solutions, will provide resilient and durable results.

The various disciplines each contribute not only with their experience and their factual knowledge, but also with their methodological skills. Architects, who often understand themselves as »generalists«, might be tempted to use such »foreign« methodologies for their own analyses. This is usually not a successful strategy, for unlike sociologists and cultural anthropologists, historians and natural scientists, architects are not usually trained in working with these tools of scientific inquiry. Generalists are not universalists, they are not the master of all trades, and they do not need to know all the facets of a problem and its solution. The task of the architect as a generalist is instead the organization of the interdisciplinary analytical and synthetical process and the translation of the knowledge gained from this interdisciplinary work into spatial manifestation.

References

Alexander, Christopher/Ishikawa, Sara/Silverstein, Murray (1977): *A Pattern Language. Towns, Buildings, Construction*, New York: Oxford University Press Inc.

Gerber, Andri/Kurath, Stefan/Schurk, Holger/Züger, Roland, eds. (2018[2013]): *Methodenhandbuch für das Entwerfen in Architektur und Städtebau*, Zurich: Triest Verlag.

Churchman, C. West (1967): »Wicked Problems«, in: *Management Science*, Vol. 14, No. 4, Application Series.

Kries, Mateo/Eisenbrand, Jochen/von Moos, Stanislaus (2012): *Louis Kahn – The Power of Architecture*, Weil am Rhein: Vitra Design Museum.

Le Corbusier [1923]: *Vers une architecture –* English translation: *Towards a New Architecture*, transl. from the 13th French edition by Frederick Etchells, London: John Rodker, 1927, repr. Oxford: Architectural Press, 1989.

Schelling, Friedrich Wilhelm Joseph von (1859): »Philosophie der Kunst«, in: *Sämtliche Werke. Abt. 1, Bd. 5*, Stuttgart, 1859. www.deutschestextarchiv.de/book/show/schelling_kunst_1859; accessed April 6, 2020.

Wedderkop, Hermann von (1924): *Der Querschnitt* 4(1); https://www.arthistoricum.net/werkansicht/dlf/73143/43/0/; accessed April 6, 2020.

Reflexive Research

Katharina Voigt

As opposed to pure design-based research – which, seeking to exploit the design process and outcomes themselves as a basis for knowledge, is independent from superordinate reflection and consideration against the background of a theoretical embedding – reflexive research interlocks the manifold processes of creation, reconsideration, testing, analysis, and reflection. Here, making and thinking are considered to be interrelated; the tracing of the processes of architectural knowledge creation and knowing forms the core of this approach. Within this reflexive pursuit, the process of designing and the process of research are considered equal. Moreover, design proceedings and intellectual research insights are even assumed to be outcomes of the very process of investigation. Action knowledge is understood as an integral part of theoretical knowledge constitution, and vice versa, while both are considered to be interrelated.

Reflexive research methodologies investigate the intertwining intellectual and applied, theoretical and practical, abstract and specific discourses in the field of architecture; these otherwise rather opposite counterparts are here addressed in regard to their mutual interconnections. In this regard a holistic and all-encompassing attempt to investigate this notion broadens the field of research as an integrated practice of questioning, exploration, and reflection. The exploration of how findings and insights are developed in conjunction with the reflexive approach grants access to their mutual interconnection and directs the focus of investigation particularly to the process instead of the resulting outcomes.

On the one hand, this form of examination is applied as a methodology of scientific research in architecture. On the other hand, it not only reveals the procedural character of the constitution of knowledge in the discipline of architecture, but also establishes a perspective on the research process as a processual procedure, which, for its part, can be examined and verified by means of reflexive practice. Reflection thus connects to the dimension of reflecting as well as to that of the interrelation of knowledge, knowledge constitution and design practice. The object of research, the research itself and the processes of research are not only equally suitable to be examined with procedures of reflexive work, but also emerge from them. Precondition, condition, and the corresponding results and insights are additionally considered as a network of mutual conditionality. Thus, the reflective approach to architectural research reveals a profoundly dynamic way of working, which is just as suitable for analyzing processes of architectural thinking and design as it is and corresponds to those in its own procedural structure.

In order to bridge the alleged gap between theory and practice, reflexive research as well as reflexive design aims for the interdependent, reciprocal fusion of both. They are driven by the intention to learn from one another, to integrate research into design and design into research, and further, to consider both as equal contributors to knowledge creation in architecture. Sharpening design and research against one another, emphasizing their commonalities as well as their differences, he argues that systematic approaches in design are more closely related to scientific research and have the potential to solve a rage of tasks.

Reflexive, Reflexivity, and the Concept of Reflexive Design

Margitta Buchert

Editorial Summary: In her contribution »Reflexive, Reflexivity, and the Concept of Reflexive Design« Margitta Buchert frames the notion of reflexive design and research, pitting the various underlying concepts against one another and forming the framework for reflexive design research. As such, she emphasizes the punctuated distinction of reflection as an integrated component of research and of design and reflexion as alignment and attitude. In this sense she highlights the reciprocal interdependence of theory and practice as well as of the thinking and the making. Buchert introduces reflexive research in an attempt to investigate processes of architectural creation and design as well as their proceedings. »Reflexive Design« forms an open method to allow practices and processes of design and research to intertwine. [Katharina Voigt]

Keywords: Design Research; Reflexive Attitude; Sur-Réflexion; Knowledge Generation; Openness.

Starting Points

Reflexive approaches as research perspectives in architecture reveal their nuances when, initially, the reflexive is considered along with the reflection. It is unlikely that anyone would consider architecture to be a »pure« practice without reflection. Although (as well as due to) being the first known reference to reflective dimensions in architecture, the authority of Vitruvius' *Ten Books on Architecture* seems unquestioned. He postulated architecture as a science (scientia), with the components of production and reflection, fabrica and ratiocinatio (Oechslin 2009: 26–28). Vitruvius conceived »fabrica« and »ratiocinatio« as knowledge forms of the architect. »Ratiocinatio« is linked to intellectual work, theoretical attentiveness and conception, and it is seen as a foundation for the specific architectural actions and as possibility to explain, show, and develop in relation to production.

Yet, is reflection the essential element that turns search into research, as the British architect and philosopher Ranulph Glanville put forward, who

Corresponding author: Margitta Buchert (Leibniz University Hannover, Germany);
m.buchert@igt-arch.uni-hannover.de; https://orcid.org/0000-0002-1355-3670
Open Access. © 2021 Margitta Buchert, published by transcript Verlag.
This work is licensed under the Creative Commons Attribution 4.0 (BY) license.

with Leon van Schaik etsablished an innovative and international renown Practice andf Research PhD at the RMIT in Melbourne, Australia in the 1990s? (Glanville 2010: 93) Or, do we have to distinguish issues and intensities, perhaps in combination with methodological concerns and/or values, qualities and meaning? (Friedman 2003).

Glanville addressed »design research«, which can be described as being guided by the intertwining of theory and practice in different variations with the purpose of generating knowledge. When examining the workflow of both the design and the research processes, they appear iterative when dealing with complex tasks and targets. Diverse moments and phases of reflection in design and research alike can be observed, which may trigger the process, yet additionally require intensity and extension to present it as a recognizable knowledge form (Cross 1999: 5).

An opportunity to step aside from specific expectations and requirements of given definitions of science – thus providing a base for specificities of architectural research – has been proposed with the concept of »Reflexive Design« (Buchert 2014). In reference, for example, to the theoretical concepts of the French anthropologist Pierre Bourdieu, the reflexive with »x« and reflexivity as a practice, which owes its specific seductiveness to the notion of radicality, can trigger ways of research leading to a broad variety of creating knowledge (Bourdieu/Wacquant 2001: 174–184).

By going beyond the widespread tripartite of »research for, into and through design«, as suggested in the 1990s by the dean of London's College of Arts, Christopher Frayling, and opening up diverse mixing of research-based design, design-oriented research, as well as of self-inquiry and »common ground«, this concept is characterized by a high degree of openness and by increasing individual and collective abilities to handle complexity (Frayling 1993: 5).

»Reflexive Design« highlights a Western and international tradition that views the specific strength and potential of architecture in the capacity to combine art and science, theory and practice, thoughts and feelings, analysis and imagination in exceptional synthesizing ways. This notion should also characterize methodological implications of research. In the realm of the reflexive and reflexivity, this basis can obtain a certain systematicity, an approximation to objectivity, and the potential to generate discourse.

Simultaneously, the artistic creative forces are kept alive by sur-réflexion, as conceived by the philosopher Merleau-Ponty (Merleau-Ponty 2012: 75–76). Thus, the diverse interplays create impulses for continuous active renewal of the discipline with innovative ideas and high-quality concepts and projects. This can ultimately generate changes in the built environment through the spaces and places shaped by architecture. The reflexive emerges as an important source of perception and understanding, as a particular type of interplay between conception and production, as well as of insight and cognitive content.

Reflection, Reflexivity, Sur-Réflexion

The Reflective Practitioner. In the 1980s, the American scientist and urbanist Donald Schön presented the theoretical idea of the »Reflective practitioner«. He explored forms of knowledge in practice that were not only based on technical rationality or on logical transparency. Rather, his concept of the reflective was a knowledge-based and at the same time improvisatory approach to complex situations (Schön 2003: 39–69). In reference to the Hungarian-British polymath Michael Polanyi, Schön highlighted that the iterative design process also encompasses tacit knowing, which can only be partially described (Buchert 2011: 80–81). It is influenced by continuously changing degrees of awareness, is often perceived as an intuitive or serendipitous action for those involved, and it focuses on problems and design results.

Furthermore, Schön indicated that there usually exists a base concept of the designer or collective (Schön 1987: 31–35). Such a base concept can be conceived as a direction and attitude that accompanies the various project designs (Lawson 2004: 95–98). It forms a relative constant and interacts with the prevailing situational circumstances in each case, which evolves from the knowledge base within the discipline, as well as from biographical, social and cultural contexts, and which can be enhanced and qualified by research phases (Buchert 2014: 33). As expert research shows, such a background determines professional competence to a significant degree (Lawson 2006: 299–301).

Reflexivity. This context also plays a central role in the concepts developed by the French anthropologist Pierre Bourdieu, who discussed it using the term »habitus« and a primary interest in relationships (Bourdieu 2006: 88). Furthermore, in his ambition to uncover how human action could be understood, Bourdieu qualified reflexivity as a modality of asking questions on dispositions, frameworks, and patterns of thinking and action. Moreover, reflexivity is also seen as a penetrating critique of established forms of science from a collective of researchers supporting and strenghtening each other and developing instruments that comply with the kind of knowledges they seek. This concept disregards disciplinary boundaries, crossing theory and practice, ideas and materiality as well as subjective and objective ways of knowing (Bourdieu/Wacquant 1992: 3). Freed from a set of pre-determined conditions, autonomy and invention as well as general insights may be triggered.

There exists a broad field of discourse on reflexivity, which addresses relations between knowledge and the ways of creation through careful interpretation, and by using multiple lenses for stimulating critical awareness. It reveals creativity in the theory and practice of research and the understanding of practices of worldmaking (May/Perry 2017). Moreover, this field encompasses interpretations of contemporary conditions of risks, being postulated as »Reflexive modernization« by Ulrich Beck, Anthony Giddens, and Scott Lash (Beck/Giddens/Lash 1996). In connection with reflexivity, these views not only advocate the role of questioning and reforming the objectives and ideals of modernity, but also the imaginative powerful trigger that reflexivity can be.

Thus, the reflexive and reflexivity act as generators in both epistemological and empirical pursuits. The generation of knowledge in interaction with design practice or even as part of the design process is a specific variation of this alignment. They are in many ways an indication of the reciprocal nature of the perception of, and references to, the world and the self. They can also reveal the foundations, premises, and potentials of design and research practices in architecture, as well as landscape and urban design with projective ambitions.

Sur-Réflexion. A further relevant idea of the reflexive can be found in the work of the philosopher Maurice Merleau-Ponty, who described the factual existence of a human being – perceived on a sensual-physical level – as fundamental for raising awareness. (Merleau-Ponty 1994: 153–159; Merleau-Ponty 2012). The unfolding experience is based on the embodied presence in a field of relations, which serves as an instrument to be anchored in the world, to configure with it and to make it accessible over time through the dynamic emergence of understanding. Hereby, Merleau-Ponty opted for a plurality of being and recognized the sense of identity and meaningful qualities of an active and contextually embedded perception and its continual reset and revitalizing character (Merleau-Ponty 1994: 273–274; Merleau-Ponty 2012: 102, 186). Current research in neuroscience and cognitive science has produced insights that underline such models of the confluence of body and mind (Buchert 2021: 43–44).

Furthermore, Merleau-Ponty's objective was not only to reveal grounds for experiencing, but also to highlight the capacity of reaching beyond existing structures in order to generate others (Merleau-Ponty 1963: 47, 175; Merleau-Ponty 1994: 137–138, 154). Because Merleau-Ponty embraces the ability to surmount the immediate environment and to settle between real and possible worlds, his studies are useful in the 21st century in terms of fluid definitions of the individual and of balancing orientation and disorientation, and at the same time of differentiation (Buchert 2006: 57). In the end, he invited the understanding of vagueness as a positive phenomenon and linked it to artistic ways of producing alterity – to extend, challenge or change perceptions of realities; a competence, which he denoted »sur-réflexion« (Huber 2013: 142–152).

Reflexive Design

Concept. The concept of »Reflexive Design« draws insights from all of these ideas and discourses on the reflexive and reflexivity. It concerns questions of design research as a practice and its specificity in relation to other practices of world creation. As a mediating concept and by combining reflexivity and design, the aim is to create a more open setting compared to methodically restricted ways of researching. Practices and processes of research and design can interlink in multiple ways, and knowledge forms can appear in different interplays. The concept of »Reflexive Design« was established at the Faculty of Architecture and Landscape Sciences at the Leibniz Universität Hannover as a research topic and is a part of the overarching research focus »Future Habitats«. It is not a method in the first place, but an attitude, an alignment, a modality.

Conceived to reveal and understand individual, collective and overarching features and impacts of the relations between perception, thinking and action, »Reflexive Design« opens up possibilities for exploring the superordinate routes of a wide variety of research questions and procedures. It thereby provides a platform for what they create, for innovative ways of reflection and action corresponding to the complexity of the 21st century, and for connecting rational and intuitive attentiveness. It is meant to trigger collective ways of exploring variations of what design research might uncover, working back and forth in a dynamic relationship. Finally, this concept was developed to broaden the knowledge base on best-practice design research projects and to foster the exchange of academia and diverse practices of the disciplines connected to design living environments. Moreover, especially forward-looking conceptions of locally and globally effective, viable contributions to tasks and developments in the design of future habitats should be explored. In sum, this research field encompasses projective activities that focus on the world as it could be.

Setting. Annual international symposia on design and research in architecture and landscape (DARA) and selected publications on the topic constitute the research setting. The essential identity of this framework resides in the inquiring and inventive creation of knowledge. Since 2011, changing subjects and questions have brought office practitioners, professional theorists, PhDs and postdocs as well as experts from diverse disciplines together, with the objective of developing qualities of design and research, which could be described as fitting for architecture, urban design and landscape architecture in specific ways and features. The practice of reflexivity and the diverse entanglements of design and research thereby unfold as a collective undertaking.

To reveal understanding and a set of tools of and for design research, which can be used from all interested in the »Reflexive Design« field, would be a strong factor for the autonomy of architectural design sciences and act as a starting point for uncovering a particular type of insight and cognitive content without being forced into the aims of a strict methodology. By glancing at Merriam-Webster's definitions for »method«, the descriptions of the enumerated include: a systematic plan, a way, a process, a body of skills, an orderly arrangement, a habitual practice or orderliness and regularity, all of which can be interpreted as elements of systematicity. (Hoyningen-Huene 2013: 25–30; Merriam-Webster 2019). Reflexivity evokes a process of on-going ordering and can be supported by conscious comparison, including a mixture of well-known methodological tasks, approaches and medias.

Sequence. Each of the tentative subtopic was an experiment in the field of »Reflexive Design« and therefore a research pragmatic instrument, which could simultaneously help outline a theory of practice. One of the objectives entails understanding the manifold realms of practice and their development potentials for revealing resources of knowledge. For office practitioners as well as for theoreticians, it additionally opens up the possibility of understanding one's own position in the process of cognitive production. As such, each symposium was explorative and extremely iterative between research-based, design-based, and various combinations of these approaches. Each topic created the possibility for evaluation and further consideration in the awareness of absences and exclusions. At the same time, it became apparent that there are many ways to apply variations of this approach.

The first book, titled »Reflexive Design. Design and Research in Architecture«, presents the concept using different lenses, thereby revealing and discussing its foundations and theories as well as reference fields and the range of the concept as an approach, alignment and attitude. In this regard, the terminology has been contoured as a topological field based on a combination of disciplines and discursive and designerly realms that work together to better understand the concept as a mediating in-between realm (Buchert 2014).

The second publication on the subtopic »Practices« opens up a spectrum and varieties of research possibilities specific to architectural, urban, and landscape design in relation to well-known research foci and the current discourse on them (Buchert 2016). One of these approaches is to be found within the heuristic manner of searching and finding in relation to real-world contexts to reveal new knowledge on practical and theoretical issues. Finding as an assumption becomes a making according to a directing alignment. Experimenting is a second well-known research practice that tests the boundaries of an established field of knowledge as well as a new concept, and reveals specific ways of knowing in the discipline. A third approach resides in catalysing in the sense of initiating and accelerating a reaction by providing a mediating step and leading it in a certain direction. It is linked to teaching practices and research formats as well as to exhibition concepts for uncovering different forms of knowledge, transmission, and communication.

With »Processes« as a further subtopic, specific features and grades of the reflexive stance begin to further crystallize (Buchert 2018). Architects, urban designers and landscape architects are trained to cope with complex questions and to shift between scales, tasks, tools, medias and actants, to act and reflect in multiple ways and to grasp uncertainty by imposing a kind of systematicity. A spectrum of tools, hybrid procedures and decision-making come into focus as well as driving forces in the context of questions such as how to start, stop and develop. These aspects outline a path to configure and understand research, and finally, a way of handling both the entanglement of design and research as well as transformations in different realms.

These are exemplary descriptions. The generation of further topics and inquiry remains viable, such as concerning values, relationality or projections. Moreover, the discussions at the symposia as well as within other academic discourse fields like, for example, the EU-funded project »Communities of tacit knowledge: Architecture and its ways of knowing« (TACK 2019), provide possibilities to critically discuss and evaluate the reflexive and reflexivity, and test its intersubjective potential. Thus, such contextualization also contributes to a refining of the concept of »Reflexive Design«.

Ongoing

Reflexive approaches at their best entail a broad range of methodological engagement. For the development, articulation and communication of design knowledges, the notion of »Reflexive Design« emerged with a surprising power and with new realms of creative exploration. As a concept, it serves as a kind of binding and structuring alignment and trigger, capable of generating ideas and new directions. The peculiarity resides within the many different versions of combining research-oriented design approaches and design-oriented research that may co-exist. The knowledge it generates – concerning designerly ways of knowing and acting as well as the formation and configuration of artefacts and further concepts – has the potential to be injected back into the realities it describes.

References

Beck, Ulrich/Giddens, Anthony/Lash, Scott (1996): *Reflexive Modernisierung. Eine Kontroverse*, Frankfurt am Main: Suhrkamp.

Bourdieu, Pierre/Wacquant, Loïc [1992]: *Réponses: pour une anthropologie réflexive*, Paris, Seuil. – English translation: *An Invitation to Reflexive Sociology*, Chicago: Chicago University Press, 1992.

Bourdieu, Pierre/ Wacquant, Loïc (2001): *Science de la science et réflexivité*, Paris: Éditions Raisons d'agir – English translation: *Science of Science and Reflexivity*, Cambridge: Polity Press, 2004.

Bourdieu, Pierre [1980]: Le sens pratique, Paris: Les Éditions de Minuit. – English translation: *The Sense of Practice*, Athens: Alexandreia, 2006.

Buchert, Margitta (2006): »Spielräume im Unbestimmten«, in: Margitta Buchert/Carl Zillich (eds.), *Inklusiv. Architektur und Kunst*, Berlin: Jovis, 54–59.

Buchert, Margitta (2011): »Formen der Relation. Entwerfen und Forschen«, in: Ute Frank et al. (eds.), *EKLAT*, Berlin: TU Universitätsverlag, 76–86.

Buchert, Margitta (2014): *Reflexive Design. Design and Research in Architecture*, Berlin: Jovis.

Buchert, Margitta (2016): *Praktiken Reflexiven Entwerfens*. Berlin: Jovis.

Buchert, Margitta (2018): *Processes of Reflexive Design*. Berlin: Jovis.

Buchert, Margitta (2021): »Design Knowledges on the Move«, in: Lara Schrijver (ed.), *The Tacit Dimension. Architectural Knowledge and Scientific Research*, Leuven: KU Leuven University Press, 83–96.

Cross, Nigel (1999): »Design research. A disciplined conversation«, in: *Design Issues* 15(2), 5–10.

Frayling, Christopher (1993): »Research in Art and Design«, in: *Royal College of Art Research Papers* 1(1993/94), London: Royal College of Art, 1–5.

Friedman, Ken (2003): »Theory Construction in Design Research. Criteria, Approaches and Methods«, in: *Design Studies* 24(6), 507–522.

Glanville, Ranulph (2010): »Reflection«, in: Adam Jakimovitz/Sarah Martens/Johan Verbeke (eds.) *Reflections+13*, Gent: ARC, 92–102.

Hoyningen-Huene, Paul (2013): *Systematicity. The Nature of Science*, Oxford: Oxford University Press.

Huber, Lara (2013): *Der Philosoph und der Künstler. Merleau-Ponty als Denker der réflexion*, Würzburg: Königshausen und Neumann.

Lawson, Bryan (2004): *What Designers Know*. Amsterdam et al.: Elsevier.

Lawson, Bryan (2006[1990]): *How Designers Think. The Design Process Demystified*, 4th edition, Amsterdam et al.: Elsevier Architectural Press.

May, Tim/Perry, Beth (2017): *Reflexivity*, London et al.: SAGE.

Merleau-Ponty, Maurice [1942]: *La Structure du comportement*, Paris: Presses Universitaires de France. – English translation: *The Structure of Behaviour*, London: Beacon Press, 1963.

Merleau-Ponty, Maurice [1964]: *Le Visible et l'invisible*, Paris: Gallimard. – German translation: *Das Sichtbare und das Unsichtbare*, 2nd edition, Munich: Wilhelm Fink Verlag, 1994.

Merleau-Ponty, Maurice [1945]: *Phénoménologie de la perception*. – English translation [1962]: *Phenomenology of Perception*, London: Routledge, 2012.

Merriam-Webster (2019): Dictionary. »Method«, www.//merriam-webster.com/dictionary/method, accessed June 22, 2019.

Oechslin, Werner (2009): »Lost, but thus of even graver Concern: The Orientation of Architectural Theory to Practice«, in: Luise King/Stiftung Städelschule für Baukunst (eds.), *Architecture & Theory. Production and Reflection*, Hamburg: Junius, 22–45.

Schön, Donald (2003[1983]): *The Reflective Practitioner. How Professionals Think in Action*, 3rd edition London: Ashgate.

Schön, Donald (1987): *Educating the Reflective Practitioner*, San Francisco: Jossey-Bass.

TACK (2019–2023): »ERC, Communities of Tacit Knowledge: Architecture and its Ways of Knowing«, Project no. 860413.

Wacquant, Loïc (1992): »Toward a Social Praxeology«, in: Pierre Bourdieu/Loïc Wacquant [1992]: *Réponses: pour une anthropologie réflexive*, Paris, Seuil. – English translation: *An Invitation to Reflexive Sociology*, Chicago: Chicago University Press, 1992, 1–59.

Architecture Schools and Their Relationship with Research: It's Complicated

Jan Silberberger

Editorial Summary: In »Architecture Schools and Their Relationship with Research: It's Complicated«, Jan Silberberger describes the problematic divide between practicing architects that teach design at architecture schools and scholars investigating the practices of designing from a theoretical or social scientific perspective. Identifying three recurrent misunderstandings between these two groups, he stresses the lack of awareness about genuine research approaches within the discipline of architecture. Emphasizing the interconnectivity of research and practice, Silberberger highlights the potential for further development of the discipline that thorough reflections on the methodologies applied in architectural design afford. [Katharina Voigt]

Keywords: Design; Research; Studio Teaching; Theoreticians; Practitioners; Misunderstandings.

> »We have taken science for realist painting, imagining that it made an exact copy of the world. The sciences do something else entirely – paintings too, for that matter.« (Bruno Latour 1999: 78–79)

It remains unclear whether Bruno Latour hinted at the work of Paul Feyerabend with this statement. Feyerabend, a philosopher of science, has famously and meticulously elaborated on the parallels between the sciences and the arts, showing that the former are in fact much more creative than many people like to admit – and the latter, in turn, far more rigorous in terms of their methodologies than is commonly supposed (1975; 1984). Most likely, Latour did not. Nevertheless, we may interpret the quote as an indication that corresponding to the distinctively wide variety of painting (in terms of, e.g., objectives, techniques, scale, and audience / market), there is an equally recognizable variety of ways of »doing« science. The notorious contrasting pairs »basic versus applied«, »quantitative versus qualitative«, »government funded versus private« should suffice to prove this point.

Corresponding author: Jan Silberberger (ETH Zurich, Switzerland); silberberger@arch.ethz.ch; https://orcid.org/0000-0002-4427-3487
Open Access. © 2021 Jan Silberberger, published by transcript Verlag.
This work is licensed under the Creative Commons Attribution 4.0 (BY) license.

Architecture – as an academic field – seems to echo the ambiguities related to these binary polarities in an almost exemplary manner. At an architecture school, students not only encounter an astounding broadness of thematic fields, methodological approaches, knowledge bases and objectives, but are simultaneously faced with characteristic »ontological« ambivalences:

1. Affected by the economization and new regimentation of higher educational institutions (Braun/Merrien 1999; Schimank 2008), architecture schools developed an increased research orientation during the last ten to fifteen years (Ammon/Froschauer 2013) – more and more so with regard to its core discipline, architectural design (Gethmann/Hauser 2009). While this development is in itself far from problematic (quite the opposite, it should be welcomed), it is bound to become so, if it leads to the somewhat paradoxical target of transferring assessment criteria and procedures from the hard sciences (or the humanities) – without or with only very little scrutinizing – to an »epistemic culture« (Knorr Cetina 1999) that has hardly any intrinsic or genuine hard science experience (Gisler/Kurath 2015). Such attempts often lead to highly erratic combinations of concepts, functions, perceptions, and effects – which do neither help to practice nor to teach architectural design in a comprehensible, verifiable, non-arbitrary manner.

2. Design architects rarely publish in scientific journals, as the manner in which they are accustomed to presenting their findings is hardly text-based. (It should not be forgotten that the TU Delft has successfully started to tackle this issue by setting up peer-reviewed magazines, such as »SPOOL« or »Writingplace«, which specifically respond to the demands of design architects.) Failing to comply with the expectations and requirements of the established scientific community, most architecture schools nowadays exhibit a characteristically defensive and deficient self-conception. Remarkably though, outsiders often share a completely different perspective of architecture as an academic field. For them, architectural design – and especially the way it is taught – presents itself as a highly advanced field of study. Scholars from management science (Boland/Collopy 2004), for instance, appreciate design for its methodologies that allow for adequately dealing with the uncertainties, ambiguities and non-linearity that govern our complex world. Seen from their point of view, architecture schools constitute sophisticated training grounds for the exploration and manipulation of complex adaptive systems.

»Practitioners« and »Theoreticians«

Looking back at the »Research Perspectives in Architecture« conference, one of its most remarkable achievements, to me, was that so-called practitioners – practicing architects that teach design at architecture schools – and so-called theoreticians – scholars investigating the practices of designing, for instance from a social scientific perspective – exchanged their views on the issue of research in architecture in a rather engaging debate. This debate, once more, laid bare the problematic divide between practitioners and theoreticians. Truly remarkable, though, is the fact that it brought the two antagonistic groups together in a way that facilitated the identification of specific sources of conflict and misunderstanding, and indicated, in the end, that their views on architectural design and its methodologies may not be so different.

In particular, the discussions relating to the keynote lecture given by Dietmar Eberle, who runs offices in several countries with more than 250 employees, has taught design at a variety of architecture schools and can be considered an ideal-typical representative of the above-mentioned group of practitioners, pointed to an explicit and significant misunderstanding. Eberle began his talk by pointing out that designers and scientists perform entirely different functions and that therefore, we should simply forget about »research by design«. The longer he spoke, however, the more he conveyed the impression that his work is in fact rather closely related to common definitions of research: for instance, when Eberle presented his publication *9 x 9 – A Method of Design* (2018), he argued that the methodology he taught is characterized not only by a high degree of comprehensibility and traceability, but also by its transferability and applicability to a wide range of problems.

Unfortunately, when arguing that a design project or a finished building respectively should be regarded as architecture's true equivalent to a peer-reviewed publication in the hard sciences, Eberle did not go into detail – although he could have provided telling examples from his practice. His head office in Lustenau (Austria), for example, perfectly corresponds to the criteria expected for scientific research. It addresses a question – »What is the role for human intervention in an office building that is dispensed with all its heating, ventilation and cooling technology?« (see https://www.baumschlager-eberle.com/en/work/projects/projekte-details/2226/). Furthermore, it builds on a clear-cut hypothesis – »Though modern buildings tend to use less and less energy, the cost of servicing and maintaining them is growing ever higher« (ibid.), and its analysis is presented in a publication (Eberle/Aicher 2015) that is far from the ill-founded architecture coffee-table book.

As a matter of fact, it can be argued that Eberle's »2226« building contributes to all three categories of design research developed by theorists: »research for design«, »research through design«, and »research about design« (Frayling 1993). First, it clearly incorporates knowledge from related fields such as building physics or thermal comfort. Second, we can assume that during the design phase, knowledge (e.g., with regard to the structure of the exterior walls) had been created through »reflection in action« (Schön 1983); moreover, we can state that this practice-based conduct had been combined »with a research question specifically related to research« (Schneider 2007: 216) leading to an »applicability of the knowledge gained [that] is not restricted to the product on which research is being conducted« (ibid.). And third, we could argue that the analysis of the building's use constitutes a sociological inquiry about design. In this sense, it does not seem too far-fetched to claim that Eberle, despite condemning the terminology (and the conception), evinces picture-perfect examples of research for, through, and about design in his practice – thereby proving that the topic of the conference as well as the subsequent observations made may in fact not be all that irrelevant for design architects.

Methodology, Scope and Objectives

The contribution at hand is based on an analysis of data that had been obtained by means of an ethnographic study investigating the teaching of architectural design. Within this study, my colleague, PhD candidate Kim Helmersen, and I visited selected studios at five architecture schools (ETH Zurich, Technical University of Munich, University of Stuttgart, AA London, KADK Copenhagen), ranging from technical universities to art schools. Although our focus had been on methodologies of designing as they become discernible in studio teaching, we frequently touched upon the issue of »research in architecture«. While our study adopts an approach from Science and Technology Studies (Latour/Woolgar 1979; Knorr Cetina 1981) and primarily aims to provide particular, idiosyncratic and localized accounts (Latour 2005), this contribution constitutes an attempt to form generalizations on the basis of a range of similar observations across our cases.

Observations and Provocations

Referring to the sources of confusion addressed in the introduction, in what follows I have compiled three concise descriptions of observations, which I will then combine in a somewhat provocative statement:

a) Most architects (practitioners as well as theoreticians) agree that design methodologies should be non-deterministic and foster a certain degree of freedom – while disagreeing on whether a method should be understood as something rigorous and formalized that possesses precisely defined characteristics or as something supple that can, and has to be, tweaked and adapted to the case at hand.

b) In line with Kurath (Kurath 2015), who argues that knowledge production in architecture can be characterized by a traditional orientation toward ideals such as individuality, singularity and non-reproducibility, the knowledge creation within the studios we observed was related to the development of a particular solution to a (site-)specific task or problem at hand. However, attempts to deduce reproducible, universally applicable answers, insights or theories from this site-specific problem-solving approach were often frowned upon. At the same time, teachers and students drew heavily on references; that is, they searched for projects dealing with a similar problem and/or comparable conditions and thought about ways of applying them to the task at hand (Silberberger 2021). While this conduct cannot be considered a universalization, it nevertheless clearly represents a form of generalization (Flyvbjerg 2011).

c) Almost everyone working at an architecture school seems to concur with Denise Scott Brown that there is a need for »ways of being rational about uncertainty« (Scott Brown 1999: 379). There is, however, a lot of dissent with regard to the degree of traceability, comprehensibility, and verifiability that »these ways« should exhibit. From the perspective of the ethnographer, one cannot help but wonder if those who argue for a small degree, might not just hide behind Cross's famous but also vaguely defined slogan »designerly ways of knowing« (Cross 2007), claiming that designers depend on tacit knowledge and rarely produce formal or explicit knowledge.

It seems safe to say that, despite significant efforts, architecture's core – designing – is (still) far from being considered mainstream research, and that the findings it produces rarely function in the sense of marketable products within a global academic system. Hence, it is realistic to anticipate that the economization and harmonization of higher education and the corresponding trend toward an ever-increasing »commodification of academic research« (Nordmann et al. 2011) is likely to impair architectural education. But maybe – and this is the somewhat provocative proposition I would like to make – maybe, the fact that the discipline of architecture is forced to challenge its self-conception, is forced to reflect on its role in relation to other research-based academic disciplines and is forced to think about its (teaching) methodologies is not such a bad thing after all. Maybe it is long overdue.

Conclusion and Outlook

Perhaps some readers are familiar with the National Endowment of Science, Technology and the Arts (NESTA), an innovation foundation based in the UK. I was not, until I attended a talk by RIBA president Alan Jones in 2019. In this talk, Jones presented an extensive report entitled *The Future of Skills: Employment in 2030* issued by NESTA in 2017 (see https://www.nesta.org.uk/report/the-future-of-skills-employment-in-2030/). As its title already suggests, this report deals with the question of which skills remain or become relevant in the course of the rise of artificial intelligence. For the field of architecture, the report reveals either very bad or relatively good news – depending on one's understanding of the discipline.

Out of the 120 skills which NESTA has assessed, designing is ranked 68th in terms of relevance, which suggests that one should think about cutting down on its education. This obviously does not sound too good. Interestingly though, skills such as »Judgment and Decision-making« (ranked 1st), »Fluency of Ideas« (ranked 2nd), »Complex Problem Solving« (ranked 8th) or »Critical Thinking« (ranked 11th) are considered most important. Yet wouldn't we – almost naturally – associate these four skills with designing? Wouldn't we say that these four top-tier skills constitute an integral part of every design process?

To conclude, I would like to pose three interconnected questions:

- Will the field of architecture be able to understand (and communicate) its core practice – designing – in relation to these future core skills?
- That is, will it be able to produce descriptions of its methodologies that go beyond singular cases without losing density and specificity?
- And will it be able to systemize and frame the complex proceedings undertaken within the design studio as effective processes of knowledge transfer and creation?

References

Ammon, Sabine/Froschauer, Eva Maria, eds. (2013): *Wissenschaft Entwerfen: Vom forschenden Entwerfen zur Entwurfsforschung der Architektur*, Paderborn: Wilhelm Fink Verlag.

Boland, Jr., Richard J./Collopy, Fred, eds. (2004): *Managing as Designing*, Stanford, CA: Stanford University Press.

Braun, Dietmar/Merrien, François-Xavier, eds. (1999): *Toward a New Model of Governance for Universities? A Comparative View*, London: Kingsley.

Cross, Nigel (2007): *Designerly Ways of Knowing*, Basel: Birkhäuser.

Eberle, Dietmar/Aicher, Florian, eds. (2015): *be 2226_Die Temperatur der Architektur/ be 2226_The Temperature of Architecture*, Basel: Birkhäuser.

Eberle, Dietmar/Aicher, Florian, eds. (2018). *9 x 9 – A Method of Design*, Basel: Birkhäuser.

Feyerabend, Paul (1975): *Against Method*, London: New Left Books.

Feyerabend, Paul (1984): *Wissenschaft als Kunst*, Frankfurt am Main: Suhrkamp.

Flyvbjerg, Bent (2011): »Case Study«, in: Norman K. Denzin/Lincoln, Yvonna S., eds., *The Sage Handbook of Qualitative Research*, Thousand Oaks, CA: Sage, 301–316.

Frayling, Christopher (1993): »Research in Art and Design«, in: *Royal College of Art Research Papers* 1, no. 1, London: Royal College of Art, 1–5.

Gethmann, Daniel/Hauser, Susanne (2009): *Kulturtechnik Entwerfen. Praktiken, Konzepte und Medien in Architektur und Design Research*, Bielefeld: transcript Verlag.

Gisler, Priska/Kurath, Monika (2015): »Architecture, design et arts visuels: les transformations des disciplines après la Réforme de Bologne«, in: Gorga, Adriana/ Leresche, Jean-Philippe, *Disciplines académiques en transformation: Entre innovation et résistance*, Paris. Editions des Archives Contemporaines, 165–179.

Knorr Cetina, Karin (1981): *The Manufacture of Knowledge: An Essay on the Constructivist and Contextual Nature of Science*, Oxford: Pergamon Press.

Knorr Cetina, Karin (1999): *Epistemic Cultures: How the Sciences Make Knowledge*, Cambridge MA: Harvard University Press.

Kurath, Monika (2015): »Architecture as a Science: Boundary Work and the Demarcation of Design Knowledge from Research«, in: *Science & Technology Studies* 28(3), Helsinki: Finnish Association for Science and Technology Studies, 81–100.

Latour, Bruno/Woolgar, Steve (1979): *Laboratory Life: The Social Construction of Scientific Facts*, Princeton: Princeton University Press.

Latour, Bruno (1999): *Pandora's Hope: Essays on the Reality of Science Studies*, Cambridge, MA: Harvard University Press.

Latour, Bruno (2005): *Reassembling the Social: An Introduction to Actor-Network-Theory*, Oxford: Oxford University Press.

Nordmann, Alfred/Radder, Hans/Schiemann, Gregor, eds. (2011): *Science Transformed? Debating Claims of an Epochal Break*, Pittsburgh: University of Pittsburgh Press.

Schimank, Uwe (2008): »Ökonomisierung der Hochschulen: eine Makro-Meso-Mikro-Perspektive«, in: Karl-Siegbert Rehberg (ed.), *Die Natur der Gesellschaft. Verhandlungen des 33. Kongresses der DGS in Kassel 2006*, Frankfurt/New York: Campus, 622–635.

Schneider, Beat (2007): »Design as Practice, Science and Research«, in: Ralf Michel (ed.), *Design Research Now*, Basel: Birkhäuser, 207–218.

Schön, Donald (2003[1983]): *The Reflective Practitioner. How Professionals Think in Action*, 3rd edition, London: Ashgate.

Scott Brown, Denise (1999): »The Hounding of the Snark«, in: Peter Galison/Emily Thompson (eds.), *The Architecture of Science*, Cambridge, MA: MIT Press, 375–383.

Silberberger, Jan (2021): »Referencing in Architectural Design«, in: Jan Silberberger (ed.), *Against and For Method: Revisiting Architectural Design as Research*, Zurich: gta Verlag.

Thinking the Transformative

Steffen Bösenberg

Editorial Summary: Steffen Bösenberg's contribution »Thinking the Transformative« reflects the dynamic momentum of reflexive design and research. In reference to the working process of his doctoral thesis, he highlights the procedural circularity of reflexive, concept-driven research approaches, tracing the »circular motion of constant reflection and rethinking«. Hereby a transdisciplinary concept of »plasticity« is explored as a productive tool in the analysis of design methods in adaptive reuse. Decision-making, reconsideration, comparison or evaluation thereby become considerable as reciprocally interlinked processes, which equally depend upon and shape each other. Most interestingly, the transformation and plasticity of the process mirrors the dynamic dimension of the investigated case studies. [Katharina Voigt]

Keywords: Adaptive Reuse; Transformation; Plasticity; Design Methodology; Reflexive Design; Post-Industrial Design; Concepts.

The Circular Motions of the Reflexive

Reflexive research as a discursive topic of recent decades is an intentionally iterative mode of approaching the world as a not entirely rationalizable complex. From a position of acknowledging the entanglement of the implicit and the explicit, it hereby tries to gain access to a body of knowledge otherwise hidden within the individual practices of design. This entanglement is particularly noticeable in the field of architecture, where it is both inherently tasked with shaping multiple layers of our physical reality, and – as a scientific practice – finds itself in a position where field-specific modes of research are still being explored. Here, as a circular motion of constant reflection and rethinking and open to a multi-methodical research design, reflexiveness provides insightful notions on the contexture of the »vagueness and clarity« within the swerving process of creativity (Buchert 2014: 20–25). The reflexive is hereby more than a retrospective reflection; rather, it entails a prospectively directed mode of thinking that not only excavates knowledge from within the creative, but strives for creative research output as well.

In the often chaotic, or at least ambiguous, process of designing, reflexiveness serves as an evaluating force. For »reflective practitioners«, an insight that can be evaluated against underlying or superimposed theoretical concepts is directed not only at the development of their own individual creative acting, but also renders practically gained knowledge accessible to others (Schön 1983; Visser 2010). The reflexive, as a sociological mode of thinking as it appears toward the end of the 20th century, subsequently introduces a layer of explicitly self-conscious reflection, critical to one's own position or field (e.g. Bourdieu/Wacquant 1992). Within these notions, reflexivity in research asks both for prospective as well as retrospective motions in the research design, which consequently gains a more developmental, dynamic, and ultimately self-transformative momentum (Attia/Edge 2017). Potentially, this retains the malleability of the research that opens it up to different methodical approaches of research and positions adjacent to architecture's established practical tools, such as drawings and diagrams. In connecting modes of designing with modes of research, especially with an output of specific design methods in mind, it seems insightful not only to reflect on theoretical concepts on the practice, but also to explore the tools of practice for the theoretical (Buchert 2014: 8–14). Within these circular motions, the research project underlying this short exploration of the reflexive seeks to intertwine both concepts from outside the field as well as tools from within the practice.

As discussed further in the context of the author's own research, where the choice of methods can be a developmental process, the question arises of if, and how, an overlaying conceptual framework can stabilize these multi-directional motions of the research to coherently synthesize the obtained insights as transferable knowledge.

Plasticity as Reflexive Concept in Research on Adaptive Reuse

Strategies of adaptive reuse that reintroduce industrial structures as spatial resources play a vital role in current and future developments of our urban habitat (Hassler/Kohler 2004: 6–9; Eisinger 2013). Gaining conceptual access to evaluation and transformation of these seemingly alienated typologies is an architectural task that has yet to be framed explicitly as a design-methodical topic. In the context of the described circular motions of reflexivity, the author's research project »Plasticity. Strategy of post-industrial transformation« iteratively attempts to frame specific notions within a theoretical research background and best-practice case studies, reflecting an overlaying concept of »plasticity« in order to generate design-methodical knowledge.

Hereby, conceptualizing the transformative as a way of organizing knowledge is critical, as adaptive reuse is neither a mere contemporary nor isolated phenomenon but complexly interwoven with multiple discourses and practices. Countless examples of anonymous architecture, such as the many famous conversions of ancient theaters, showcase specific spatial and iterative design strategies that rely on the morphology of the structures and their entanglement within an urban context, rendering the spatial as a resource (Jäger-Klein 2013). However, as examples mainly outside a theoretical reflection, their qualities and underlying strategies tend to be implicit.

Explicit concepts of the adaptive, on the other hand, have been explored in architectural theory with varying degrees of depth. As a topic of preservation and methodology, adaptability emerges during the 19th century in the work of architects and thinkers such as Viollet-Le-Duc or John Ruskin (Scott 2007: 44–61). As a notion of sustainable usage of resources, it surfaces as a partially explicit, partially implicit topic within the discourses on »obsolescence« as they surface in the early 20th century in the New World metropolises of New York and Chicago (Abramson 2017: 14–20). To some extent, the two discourses both intertwine and divert; the mid-century preservationist movements argue retrospectively for a conservation of the old, while discourses of obsolescence seek prospectively for new forms of adaptability in the buildings of the future (Cairns/Jacobs 2017: 119–124). Subsequently, strategies in between the two emerge – with Rowe and Koetter's *Collage City*, modern takes on the ruin such as in the work of Arata Isozaki, or Aldo Rossi's notion of »permanence« (Rowe 1978; Isozaki 1968; Rossi 1984: 57–61). As an explicit method of designing, it is reflected upon more precisely toward the end of the 20th century, as seen in the works of Hermann Czech or Vittorio Gregotti (Czech 1989; Gregotti 1991). In contemporary architecture, such explicitly transformative strategies have become distinct features in the positions of numerous high-profile practices like EM2N, Lacaton & Vassal or the recent critical theoretical and practical reflections on preservation by Rem Koolhaas (Carver et al. 2014). As such, the topic of transformation, in its multivalent forms scattered across its long but mostly unreflected practical continuity and diverse theoretical understanding, is challenging to frame. Where there is neither typological nor programmatic commonality, the research project thus seeks to frame a commonality in their design strategies. It hereby turns to a term that has its own history as a possible tool for rethinking transformation – plasticity.

Plasticity – at its core – focuses on the act of transformation, instead of its mere products, hence becoming a potential way to look at specific strategies within adaptive reuse as well. Other fields have already argued a comparable potential – as recently explored in the work of philosopher Catherine Malabou (e.g. Malabou 1996; 2009), but most instructively in neurobiology. Within the latter, after a lively and critical discourse in the 1970s, it continues to be a driving force in neuroscientific research. (Buchtel 1978; Berlucchi/ Buchtel 2009). But even though architecture seems so closely related to the term and the morphogenetic qualities it describes, plasticity lacks a comparably distinct and complex definition within the field. Its ability to link temporal factors to morphological systems might therefore be illuminating when explored.

Within the research design, this conceptualization follows up on the theoretical baseline of the project. In a hermeneutic-phenomenological tradition, the research background of conversion and the specifics on the reuse of industrial typologies is hereby approached as an exegetical, historical research that is reflected upon specific lines of thought regarding transformation within architecture. This broad framing serves as a first lens in analyzing and reducing the relatively heterogenous context of adaptive reuse.

A transdisciplinary reading of the term »plasticity« further acts as a tool of structuring found aspects. In phenomenological terms, the notion of plasticity is consequently explored as a way of sharpening intention as a directedness of thought. In a reflexive manner, it is not seen as a fixed framework but is constantly evaluated and reshaped throughout the research.

A case study on best-practice-built projects such as the Toni Areal in Zurich or the Fondazione Prada in Milan then tries to iteratively refine this framework by applying it as an analytic device. To evaluate the found aspects, a diagrammatical analysis explores a more explicit understanding of the concrete spatial dependencies, merging the transdisciplinary approach with a more commonly elaborated architectural medium. The diagram hereby serves as an explicitly reflexive and thus knowledge-generating tool, as it has been explored in the past few decades by several theorists and practitioners (Frichot 2011). In a final step, the outlined architectural approach to

»plasticity« is revisited to extract and exemplify specific aspects as a transferable design method. It is thus seen as a malleable tool in itself.

Transformative Research on Transformative Strategies

The notion of reflexiveness – as presented in this research – is utilized to make sense of an underlying, partly implicit understanding of the practice within the transformation of the built environment, which, in this case, entails the obsolete industrial structures of a post-industrial society.

As shown, adaptive reuse hereby presents itself as a widely researched and, as a development of the last few decades, extensively publicized topic (e.g. Petzet/Heilmeyer 2012; Baum/Christiaanse 2012, et al.). Yet in terms of understanding the underlying notions of the transformative from the perspective of the designing architect, knowledge is scattered, sometimes hidden, within a field that spans from preservationist discourses over technical guidelines to philosophical endeavors on the fixity of architecture itself, and across a wide range of individual architectural projects.

Approaching an idea within this field requires not only a focus that can be laid upon the body of knowledge within creativity and built like a magnifying glass to extract one isolated set of aspects. Rather, it requires an additional tool that can grasp at and then extract the widely branched aspects of an idea and provide the means of disentanglement accordingly.

In the case of the presented research, the concept of plasticity as a specific notion of the transformative has serendipitously already been explored in multiple discourses across scientific fields. This equips it with some level of agency but more importantly with an established framework of rules and critiques (Paillard 1976).

It hereby generates two circular motions within the research: First, an inner reflexive motion that sharpens the strategies understood through the notion of plasticity by finding, extracting, and analyzing topics of architectural theory and practice. Second, the iterative evaluation of the alignment against the exterior conceptions of plasticity to question their transferability to the architectural field. It also addresses the condition of architecture as an »open work«, as could be argued in reflection of Umberto Eco's writings on the openness of art (Eco/Robey 1962) – not a fixed monument but a continuous flux of intermediate states. The inherent challenge of the concept of authorship is thereby, and arguably, also a reason for the long-term invisibility of adaptive reuse in avant-gardist and high-profile positions in the field (Scott 2007: 1–19).

Conveying a self-aware perspective of the field and the subsequent reflection of its own context, the research project additionally attempts to impart a reflexive view on architecture's basic notions of flexibility, adaptability, transformability and whether they might be complimented by distinctive definitions of plasticity as a template for thinking transformatively in a more general fashion. This veering motion between the content of the research background and its underlying intentions seems to enforce a reflexive stance in order to thoroughly make sense of the subject.

The research design is ultimately tasked with inquiring about the existence of commonalities in architectural transformation – despite the inherently different tasks within industrial adaptive reuse which span across distinct typologies, individual programmatic challenges, and their respective unique contexts (Hassler/Kohler 2004: 59–66). What does the transformation of a late-1970s dairy plant in Zurich by EM2N have in common with Diller Scorfidio + Renfro's reconfiguration of the 1930s New York High Line or O.M.A.'s partly additive, partly intertwining reconfiguration of the Fondazione Prada in Milan? Here, distinct strategies of contexture and transformation create a comparability, and therefore transferability, where without a reflexive approach, an overarching understanding of the transformative may be difficult to develop. At its core lies a specific way of thinking the transformative, not merely the adaptive. As such, it also looks past the adaptation of the object reflecting its impact on its context.

While this presented research introduces a tool of framing the transformative from outside the profession, architecture itself also provides its distinctive tools of analysis and synthesis. Plasticity – as a complex idea of how matter, form and function intertwine – here finds a possibly surprising similarity in its motives concerning the method of the diagram. This notion is especially relevant as it has been explored in connection to Gilles Deleuze and Félix Guattari's ideas on the diagrammatic throughout the late 20th century. This discourse was transposed into the realm of architecture by several practitioners and theorists such as Stan Allen, Ben van Berkel or Caroline Bos (e.g. van Berkel/Bos 1998).

Among other aspects, they posed the question of whether a focus on matter and its generative potential – instead of just »imposing« form onto matter – accesses a new thinking about the nature of the built (DeLanda 1998). Although the diagrammatical discourse of the late 1990s and early

2000s stood in the light of the novelty of computational parametric design, and the notion of matter has not been understood as industrial bricks and mortar but as parameters, forces, and rules, this notion seems relatively close to the presented ideas on transformation. The conceptual similarities to the intended overcoming of »form« in favor of exploring the forces underlying »transformation« are notable. As a generative force, the diagram in this sense appears to be a suitable tool to steer the conceptual framework of plasticity closer to the actual process of designing architectural transformation. The complementary disposal of such different concepts and tools requires a constant adaptation in which different aspects are evaluated against each other without dismantling the overall structure. It is here where the circular motion of the research design itself helps to react to these interchanges.

Malleable Frameworks

In the complexity of the built – the partial implicitness of the act of designing and the wide range of notions connected to the topic of adaptive reuse – a research method is needed that does not only frame a section of, but sifts through, a broad field of notions. In this research, the aim is to turn to other fields and try to transfer their supposed means of conceptualization, and incorporate them – specifically the concept of plasticity – within a reflexive design strategy aimed at an outcome directed at designing practitioners. A reflexive approach, that is able to react – but also constantly needs to be investigated – to the multi-layered body of knowledge it approaches, be it theoretical positions, built objects, or underlying concepts, can offer an insightful research framework through its own malleability. It helps in diluting a framework that is ultimately not superimposed as an external concept of plasticity but implemented as a reactive interplay between conceptions within a transdisciplinary reading of the term.

Herein lies the ambition to explain the found phenomena of transformation in their complexity, meaning to grasp architecture as a multifaceted realm in which the virtual ideas of designing and the physical reality of the built intertwine in manifold ways. The transformative, after all, does not manifest itself in isolated aspects but as a combination of different qualities and intentions, such as form, material, program and structure, among many others.

In addition, the connectiveness of a reflexive design that can be linked to its circular motion that provides a constant force of evaluation makes it a viable instrument for exploring the arsenal of both architectural and scientific tools. It, of course, remains to be seen and evaluated how transferable the aforementioned strategies will be; it should be noted, that the represented notions of reflexivity pose their difficulties in exactly this heterogenous, sometimes ambivalent and constantly veering movement. The conceptualization of a term from outside the profession, as presented here, can therefore also be seen as an attempt to steer this process, not only as a conceptual framework.

Plasticity is thus a proposal for a tool beyond architecture's usual means and attempts to add a more conceptual and strategic instrument that, within a reflexive approach, provides both a pro- and retrospective force. It potentially gives access to a rich field of expertise hidden in individual positions and the built products of architectural practice, possibly creating a transferable output for others to build upon, where it would otherwise remain in the realm of the unique. Thus, it can hopefully serve as a starting point for further research on transformative design methods, as well as their application in practice, which extend further than just the obsolete industrial.

References

Abramson, Daniel M. (2017): *Obsolescence. An Architectural History*, Chicago: University of Chicago Press.

Attia, Mariam/Edge, Julian (2017): »Be(Com)Ing a Reflexive Researcher: A Developmental Approach to Research Methodology«, in: *Open Review of Educational Research* 4(1), 33–45.

Baum, Martina/Christiaanse, Kees (2012): *City as Loft. Adaptive Reuse as a Resource for Sustainable Urban Development*, Zurich: gta Verlag.

Berkel, Ben van/Bos, Caroline eds. (1998): »Diagram Work«, in: *Anyone Corporation, Any Magazine*, no. 23 (June).

Berlucchi, G./Buchtel, H. A. (2009). »Neuronal Plasticity: Historical Roots and Evolution of Meaning«, in: *Experimental Brain Research* 192(3), 307–319.

Bourdieu, Pierre/Wacquant, Loïc [1992]: *Réponses: pour une anthropologie réflexive*, Paris, Seuil. – English translation: *An Invitation to Reflexive Sociology*, Chicago: Chicago University Press, 1992.

Buchert, Margitta (2014): *Reflexive Design. Design and Research in Architecture*, Berlin: Jovis Berlin.

Buchtel, H. A (1978): »On Defining Neural Plasticity«, in: *Archives Italiennes de Biologie* 116 (3–4), 241–247.

Cairns, Stephen/Jacobs, Jane M. (2017): *Buildings Must Die: A Perverse View of Architecture*, Cambridge: MIT Press.

Carver, Jordan/Koolhaas, Rem/Otero-Pailos, Jorge/Wigley, Mark (2014): *Preservation Is Overtaking Us*, New York: Columbia University Press.

Czech, Hermann (1989). »Der Umbau«, in: *Umbau. Theorien Zum Bauen Im Bestand*, UMBAU 29 Basel: Birkhäuser, 10–13.

DeLanda, Manuel (1998): »Deleuze, Diagrams, And the Genesis of Form«, in: *ANY Diagram Work. Data Mechanics for a Topological Age* (23), 30–34.

Eco, Umberto/Robey, David (1989 [1962]). *The Open Work*, Cambridge: Harvard University Press.

Eisinger, Angelus (2013): »The Social Value of Transformation«, in: Baum, Martina/Christiaanse, Kees: *City as Loft. Adaptive Reuse as a Resource for Sustainable Urban Development*, Zürich: gta Verlag, 67–71.

Frichot, H. (2011): »Drawing, Thinking, Doing: From Diagram Work to the Superfold«, in: *ACCESS. Critical Perspectives on Communication, Cultural and Policy Studies* 30 (1), 1–10.

Gregotti, Vittorio (1991): »Von Der Modifikation (Della Modificazione)«, in: *Umbau. Theorien Zum Bauen Im Bestand*, UMBAU 29, Basel: Birkhäuser, 10–13.

Hassler, Uta/Kohler, Niklaus (2004): *Über das Verschwinden der Bauten des Industriezeitalters: Lebenszyklen industrieller Baubestände und Methoden transdisziplinärer Forschung*, Tübingen: Wasmuth & Zohlen.

Isozaki, Arata (1968): *Re-Ruined Hiroshima. Ink and gouache with cut-and-pasted gelatin silver print on gelatin silver print*, Museum of Modern Art, New York.

Jäger-Klein, Caroline. 2013. »Conversions in Urban History«, in: Baum, Martina/Christiaanse, Kees, *City as Loft. Adaptive Reuse as a Resource for Sustainable Urban Development*, Zürich: gta Verlag, 59–66.

Malabou, Catherine (1996): *L'Avenir de Hegel. Plasticite, Temporalite, Dialectique*, Paris: VRIN.

Malabou, Catherine (2009): *Plasticity at the Dusk of Writing: Dialectic, Destruction, Deconstruction*, New York: Columbia University Press.

Paillard, Jacques (1976): »Réflexions sur l'usage de concept de plasticité en neurobiologie«, in: *Journal de Psychologie Normale et Pathologique*, no. n° 1, 15.

Petzet, Muck/Heilmeyer, Florian (2012): *Reduce, Reuse, Recycle*, Ostfildern: Hatje Cantz Verlag.

Rossi, Aldo (1984 [1966]): *The Architecture of the City*, London: MIT Press.

Rowe, Colin (1978): *Collage City*, Reprint, Cambridge: MIT Press.

Schön, Donald (2003[1983]): *The Reflective Practitioner. How Professionals Think in Action*, 3rd edition, London: Ashgate.

Scott, Fred (2007): *On Altering Architecture*, London/New York: Routledge.

Visser, Willemien (2010): »Schön: Design as a Reflective Practice«, in: Collection, *Parsons Paris School of art and design. Art, Design & Psychology*, 21–25.

Qualitative Research

Ferdinand Ludwig

When we discuss architecture, we usually speak about qualities. It is therefore immediately obvious that qualities – or qualitative aspects and approaches – also play an important role in architectural research. Qualitative research methods are widely used in sociology, anthropology, political science, psychology or e.g. educational research (Alasuutari 2010). They can be defined as an analytical procedure that uses a wide range of conditions as data to be evaluated and examines them against the background of as broad a spectrum of perspectives as possible, without setting criteria for evaluation from the outset.

The use of this data is informed by methods such as discourse analysis or interpretative phenomenological analysis (Creswell 2002). Such a transfer of qualitative research methods to the field of architecture can strengthen design and research methods and offers great opportunities for architectural research, as they are comparably open, flexible, and process-based in the field. The hypothesis is developed from the empirical material (induction) and, if necessary, re-examined (abduction). The flexibility allows for the adaptation of the methodological design, the methodological procedure, and the theoretical references to the requirements of the field or the research situation.

In contrast to this generally accepted approach, which is defined by a specific method, qualitative research can also be defined by the object of research. In this case, qualitative aspects – in contrast to quantities – are investigated, but this very often involves quantitative, empirical methods. This approach to qualitative design can be described as science-informed design, while the first approach often forms the basis for research through design. Thereby, the first approach aims to gain new, intrinsically architectural knowledge (see chapter design based), whereas science-informed design locates research and thus knowledge gained outside of the field of architecture and design.

Despite the fact that designers sometimes claim that research through design is the most exciting form of research in architecture, it is important to note that the different relationships between research and design are all legitimate, as Uta Graff explains in the chapter »Research Perspectives in Architecture«. For architectural research, however, it is problematic if the term »qualitative research« is used to describe completely different methodological approaches. A clarification of the terms is essential here in order to make the diversity of approaches more distinguishable.

References

Alasuutari, Pertti (2010): »The Rise and Relevance of Qualitative Research«, in: *International Journal of Social Research Methodology* 13 (2), 139–155.

Creswell, John W. (2002): *Educational Research: Planning, Conducting, and Evaluating Quantitative*, Upper Saddle River, NJ: Prentice Hall.

Research through Design under Systematic Quality Criteria: Methodology and Teaching Research

Sören Schöbel, Julian Schäfer, Georg Hausladen

Editorial Summary: In their contribution, Sören Schöbel, Julian Schäfer and Georg Hausladen ask how architectural design can be used as a method of gaining scientific knowledge. They state that this is only possible if architectural design, which is generally characterized by a specific, creative, subjective and case-by-case process, is embedded into a methodical framework that enables general, i.e. transferable and verifiable knowledge. By stating that qualitative research in the disciplines in which it was developed is essentially based on a creative but nevertheless systematic interpretation of data in search of new, previously unknown structures the authors see a proximity to design in architecture, and therefore suggest transferring the quality criteria of qualitative research to research-based design. They describe three basic principles – regularity, relevance, and universality – and illustrate how research through design can be carried out using these principles with the example of different teaching formats. [Ferdinand Ludwig]

Keywords: Landscape Architecture; Ecology as Technology; Qualitative Research; Abduction; Research Quality Criteria.

Quality Criteria of Research through Design

The most exciting form of research *in* architecture is research *through* architecture – thus through architectural design itself.

A distinction can be made here between research on the spatial model, research through structural realization and research through design – designs that remain only ideas on paper for the time being. For questions where the first two architectural research approaches are not applicable, the remaining possibility is to draw conclusions from the design process itself. This entails using architectural design as a method of gaining scientific knowledge. To do this, we must embed design, which is first and foremost a specific, creative, subjective and case-by-case process, into a method that enables general, i.e. transferable and verifiable knowledge.

Research through design, in this sense, is a systematic process in which knowledge is gained from experience – from empirical data. In the sciences, two different methods are known with which insights can be gained from empirical data. These are the quantitative and the qualitative methods. Both are justified if they are used in the right place, that is, for the right question. For example, if we want to know why architects are interested in pursuing a doctorate, we could conduct a survey here using a quantitative method. From literature, we could derive four classical main reasons (deduction): 1. a higher income is expected from a doctorate; 2. their parents have a doctorate; 3. the professor requires it for employment; 4. another reason.

It might be useful for the Faculty of Architecture to find out the percentage of the reasons among the scientific staff to promote doctoral studies particularly effectively.

But if we want to know which deep motives, attitudes and orientations lead to this desire, then we would have to use a qualitative method. Without pre-fabricated categories, we would only let the participants explain what moves them and which values they associate with architectural research. This, too, would provide data, which would not be put into pre-defined boxes, but used rather to search for something new. This discovery of new information through critical and creative interpretation of data is called abduction. In this way, we could describe different types or milieus of doctoral candidates, whose existence we cannot prove nor measure, but whose existence can be described. For the faculty, this may be even more interesting.

To be able to recognize both methods as scientific, there are rules or »quality criteria« for both.

If we now want to define research through architectural design as a systematic process in which knowledge is gained from experience, we must also be able to describe this process and establish rules – quality criteria.

Qualitative research is essentially based on a creative but nevertheless systematic interpretation of data in search of new, previously unknown structures. It therefore has a proximity to research through architectural design. And it is thus beneficial to transfer the quality criteria of qualitative research (cf. Steinke 2000) to our methodology.

We can classify the quality criteria into the six »classic« areas in the philosophy of science (cf. e.g. Steinke 2000). For a method to be considered scientific, it must be systematically structured and follow rules (*regularity*).

The applied method must match the research question, the object (*relevance*). And it must have general validity that extends beyond the individual case or be clearly delimitable to a certain area (*universality*).

These first three criteria are indivisible. We need to take a closer look at the other three, objectivity, validity and reliability, as here differences are already being made between quantitative and qualitative research. Even more so in the case of design research where we must encounter special features.

Objectivity means that the findings are not influenced subjectively, culturally or by the method itself. In qualitative research, this criterion cannot apply because the power of interpretation comes from the personality of the researcher. Therefore, it is important here to disclose this subjective content as comprehensibly as possible.

The next criterion for quality is that research results are valid. The »what« and the »how« of the investigation must fit together, i.e. the method of investigation must correspond to the object of investigation. In quantitative research, this can be proven by statistical tests of representativeness or correlation. In qualitative research, this is more likely to be substantiated by arguments. Does the research result match reality, the real world? In our example: Do doctoral students talk openly and profoundly about their motives when asked about them? Only then does such a survey make sense.

This criterion can also be tested for designs. Can general knowledge resulting from a design solution be translated spatially and into the real world? Is the design authentic in this sense?

The final quality criterion is *reliability*. Can a result of the investigation be repeated? And is the investigation structured in such a way that it can be disproved because the exact process can be traced? Is there certainty that there are no errors? In quantitative research, experimental procedures can be repeated identically. This is not possible in qualitative research; therefore, several methods are juxtaposed here that investigate the same phenomenon in different ways. Returning to our example we could evaluate their private Instagram posts in addition to questioning the doctoral candidates, which would certainly be revealing.

This is even more difficult in *research through design* because creative processes are never exactly the same. However, if not just one, but many designs are included in an architectural competition, collection, or assemblage, they can be compared. Another possibility is to evaluate whether a design can be thought of as the basic type of a typology, a model, or an architectural convention.

So, there certainly are ways to operate *research through design* not only systematically, but also with regard to general knowledge. The precondition is that researching architects bring as much light as possible into the *black box* of the creative core of their research processes.

Topics of Our Research

When designing landscapes and cities on a regional scale, we address topics that are largely determined by the conditions and constraints of industrial structures and infrastructures. We thereby operate between functional requirements, everyday usage and aesthetic impact. The banalities of modern society are reflected in structures that enter our lives in an equally banal way: energy production and transmission, highways and by-pass roads, commercial and residential areas and, as their compensation, areas for the protection of species, ecosystems, and eventually for »recreation«. For each of these concerns, there exist standard approaches that are safe, can be approved in planning practice, and which one becomes accustomed to in the end. The result is a landscape in which everything works, but no coherent whole is created. In our research, we are looking for new solutions off the beaten track, to think unconventionally, and thus to display possibilities of what new, generalizable solutions can look like.

Teaching Research

In the first seminars since 2008, we investigated how new knowledge is produced in landscape architecture and what methods are suitable for this. We have established a rule-guided procedure that is revised and adapted with each seminar and which meets the quality criteria of qualitative research. A group of students develops specific solutions to a research question by designing short-term proposals. In preparation for this step and to create an »abductive attitude« (cf. Reichertz 2000), the participants are introduced to state of the art and generally accepted good engineering practice of the topic. We then discuss the short-term proposals with the whole group. The focus is always on the basic idea of each group explaining the essential core of their design. These ideas or concepts, represented in both written terms and drawn shapes, constitute the data collection. To scan the data collection of hidden structures, such as basic types or categories, a cluster analysis is performed. »Cluster analysis or clustering is the task of grouping a set of objects in such a way that objects in the same group (called a cluster) are more similar (in some senses) to each other than to those in other groups (clusters)« (Wikipedia).[1] This process of building clusters is also done in the group, creating a collective understanding. The developed clusters of terms or shapes lead to abductive reasoning, which can be tested in the subsequent designs or textual analyses (reliability).

Research through Design Seminars since 2013

In the next sections, we give an overview of the content and methodology of various topics that have been used to run research seminars in recent years. We would like to briefly describe the relevance, i.e. the extent to which the chosen method produces results that allow new interpretations and explanations for the particular question, and the universality that relates to the research question itself. In the first mentioned seminar, the validity and in a further step the reliability are demonstrated – i.e. whether the results found can be reproduced with another experimental procedure.

Social Flow Generator (2019/20)
Lecturers: Julian Schäfer, Parisa Vaziri

As part of an ongoing research project[2], we are investigating how renewable energy plants and facilities in the landscape can fulfil a social purpose in addition to their energy aspect. Whether they are accepted by people as social places depends largely on their atmosphere, on the interaction of the constellations of a place with the mood of those who perceive the place. Such local moods cannot be measured, but they can be described, interpreted and designed by visual images.

In the biennial competitions of the Land Art Generator Initiative, such spatial concepts are designed according to the motto »Renewable Energies can be beautiful« as qualities of a place and its perception. Such concepts are part of our cultural reality as spaces of possibility. Research through design is therefore the appropriate method of systematically investigating

---

[1] https://en.wikipedia.org/wiki/Cluster_analysis, accessed July 31, 2020.
[2] Parisa Vaziri: »Resilient Trans(action) through Landscape and Urban Design«.

this phenomenon (relevance). Since the question of the social impact and designability of renewable energies arises in practically all contemporary and future landscapes, it also has a general validity (universality). In the seminar, all contributions to the LAGI competition of 2014 (Copenhagen) were evaluated with respect to designed atmospheres and summarized into general types in a two-step cluster analysis.[3] The validity was verified by not only describing the atmospheres in the visualizations, but also by examining the competition texts for atmospheric terms as a parallel test. To test the reliability of such energetic-atmospheric concepts, test designs were finally created by the researching students at other locations.

Collage Landscape (2018/19)
Lecturers: Sören Schöbel, Julian Schäfer

In *Collage City*, their groundbreaking 1978 work, Rowe and Koetter called for urban development to reconnect both rational-scientific[4] and poetic-contextual thinking and planning. Since not only the city, but also the landscape is essentially negotiated by society as an image (universality), the development of ecologically differentiated forms of land use (Schöbel 2017) requires both rational and poetic thinking. Here, too, it is a matter of a spatial synthesis of the functionally separated, for which only methods of research through design can be considered in a systematic way (relevance). In the seminar, the students designed differentiating structures of agriculture in short-term architectural proposals. For each concrete location, they started with a rational-ecological and a poetic-contextual idea and connected them according to other approaches. In this way, 13 teams created a total of 78 impromptu, ecologically differentiated and aesthetically legible agricultural structures for three locations, which were then clustered into types of similar ideas or »attitudes«.[5]

---

3   The clusters found by one student in our seminar, J. D. P. Murcia, are: Diffuse limits, Ludic interactivity, Marvellous analogies, Entangled particles, Dramatic tragedy, Dizzy attraction, Paranoiac vastness.

4   Rowe and Koetter also use the term »utopian« for this, but in doing so mainly refer to urban tabula rasa planning of modernity.

5   M. Wang, another student, described the attitudes to aggregate, to integrate, to separate, to differentiate.

Production of Urbanity (2017)
Lecturer: Sören Schöbel

The Leonrodplatz in Munich has a high degree of traffic use, but at the same time, too little urban life. The directly adjoining surroundings with the criminal justice center and the »creative quarter« are currently being radically transformed. The square is thus released from its peripheral location and converted into a center. The question arises of how it will not only allow passage as a connecting element, but also promote rest and social encounters (universality). The seminar examined the role of dynamics, primarily traffic, in this process. By designing 40 alternative scenarios, a range of possible reconfigurations of the square were examined in equal measure. The research through design process then described which basic approaches to a stronger interaction of the dynamics on Leonrodplatz could lead to a production of urbanity (relevance).

B15 Neu – A New Federal Highway (2016/17)
Lecturers: Sören Schöbel, Julian Schäfer

Expansion projects on federal roads can result in completely new routes. For the renewal of the B15 between Landshut and Rosenheim, a new line parallel to the old route is chosen, which largely avoids the previously connected villages as a by-pass. Following the established transportation planning paradigm as well as the principle of vehicle dynamics, the space is thus rapidly and safely crossed, but at the same time, the villages are cut off and the landscape is cut through. This is a common consequence of such expansion projects, but also of village by-passes (universality). The National Tourist Routes in Norway show that roads can also be designated as »appropriate« for the landscape. To show the diversity of possible relationships between landscape and road, research through design explores the opportunities offered by highway construction (relevance). The question was tested using a real-life example of a major section of the route. The designs produced by the students were clustered according to their principles, which in return can be applied to comparable cases of highway projects (reliability).[6]

---

6 M. Groos, another student, found the following principles: take the inventory into account, change, entertain the driver, enrich the environment, in contact with elements, efficient and useful, no time pressure, design discreetly.

Sören Schöbel, Julian Schäfer, Georg Hausladen

Overhead Power Lines (2015/16)
Lecturers: Sören Schöbel, Julian Schäfer

The energy transition requires electricity to be transported inland from the large wind farms in the North and Baltic Sea. On one planned route, energy is to be delivered to Landshut via a so-called »high-voltage direct current« transmission line. The seminar focused on the question of how the high-voltage line from there to Munich could be designed more appropriately and, therefore, be more readily accepted by society – conceptualizing real alternatives instead of provoking citizen protests with an inescapable master plan (universality). The openness of this research aim required a designing approach, so the research through design method proved to be useful. The design results could best be explained as a picture, but here too we can also rely on established categories.[7]

Alpine Reservoirs (2014/15)
Lecturers: Sören Schöbel, Michael Schmölz, Andreas René Dittrich

The Alps are currently being discussed as a source and space for the production, but also for the storage of renewable energies. New pumped hydroelectric energy storages could serve as a kind of battery to secure the electricity supply in Europe, used for load balancing. This is opposed by the fear that these storages would disturb sensitive ecosystems on the one hand and local recreation and tourism on the other. So which landscape-related typologies of Alpine reservoirs can be developed that enable new methods of water retention and storage as well as energy production (universality)? In the first step, the ideas for new energy storages are elaborated and their complexity is illustrated in synthetic designs. The clustering of the designs identified the different levels of possible new categories. One group of students, for example, analyzed the »ideals« underlying the designs and differentiated these into objects, complex systems, and moods.[8]

---

7 For example, the two students L. Schmied and I. Hoffmann describe the approaches exaggerating (übertreibend), tracing (nachzeichnend), inventing (erfindend), guiding (geleitend), emphasizing (betonend) and subdivide them in play (spielen), strengthening (stärken) and ignoring (ignorieren).

8 The students E. Egerter, Q. H. Le and M. Hölzl named alluvial forest (Auwald), cascades (Kaskaden), unspoiled nature – hiding (unberührte Natur – verstecken), natural lakeshore (natürliches Seeufer), swimming pool (Schwimmbecken), path across water (Weg übers

Designing Landscapes by Ecological Systems (2014/15)
Lecturers: Georg Hausladen, Sabine Kern

Landscapes are always also ecological systems, understood as systems of interacting populations and species. The ecological system, however, is only one dimension of the landscape, which has manifold relationships with other dimensions, e.g. social or economic. Therefore, addressing the ecological dimension of the landscape cannot be reduced to questions of nature conservation and environmental protection. Although these fields represent key socio-political tasks, the concrete implementation of the associated objectives (e.g. the protection of a species) always also has effects on various social, economic and, not by the least, further ecological systems in the landscape (other species, agricultural or forestry systems, energy and material flows). The design of landscapes by ecological systems should take this into account. Based on an ecological object, e.g. a certain species, an interaction system or a material resource (water, air, soil), we ask for possibilities that arise from concrete realizations in relation to the other dimensions of landscape. The methodical starting point here is the fact that functionally equivalent systems (e.g. certain habitats) can be realized through different spatial designs that vary in social and economic terms. The aim is to break through conventional and dogmatic ideas of nature conservation through to the use of a design approach.

Ecology as Technology (2013/14)
Lecturers: Daniel Czechowski, Georg Hausladen

Ecology is generally understood as a biological natural science, which is »applied« above all in certain socio-political fields of problems, nature conservation and environmental protection. However, a reduction of

---

Wasser), industry (Industrie), skywalk (Skywalk), lid (Deckel), adventure playground (Abenteuerspielplatz), aquarium (Aquarium), botanical garden (Botanischer Garten), island (Insel), water terraces (Wasserterrassen), walk in fog (Nebelwanderung), Alpenglow (Alpenglühen), skater bowl (Skater Bowl), Atlantis (Atlantis), boat trip (Bootsfahrt), reed landscape (Schilflandschaft), lake district (Seenplatte), waterfall (Wasserfall), amphitheater (Amphitheater), cage (Käfig). On the other hand, another group, F. Gutmann and T. Mezger, named the possible connection more broadly as emancipation, integration, composition, dominance, camouflage and harmony (Emanzipation, Integration, Komposition, Dominanz, Verschleierung, Harmonie).

ecology to the academic-scientific field and the few classical »application areas« obscures the understanding of its overall potential as a technology. As a natural science, it has a technological potential which by no means only serves the above-mentioned problem areas, but can be activated for the design of urban and landscape spaces. The aim of the seminar is to establish an understanding of ecology as a possible technological basis for design. Based on freely chosen examples, the students elaborate spatially varying solutions (designs), i.e. solutions that function technically in relation to the chosen task, but have different aesthetic and, ultimately, multifunctional landscape and urban impacts. Again, the methodical approach is derived from the aesthetic divergence of functionally equivalent solutions. Ecology as a technology is thus to be freed from the constraints of nature conservation and environmental protection and to be considered as a possible field for general spatial design.

Knowledge Produced through Architectural Design

Research as the »production« of new knowledge needs both creativity and system. Architectural design as a form of research entails extensive singular solutions to general assumptions. A systematic approach of dealing with creative conclusions has been called »abduction« in the philosophy of sciences and has been acknowledged in many social disciplines (among others). Abduction is the base of all kinds of »qualitative research«, representing systematic and transparent approaches to overcome preconception and creating new clusters of coherences of phenomena. Research through design in architecture as a germane method can benefit from the generally accepted quality criteria of qualitative approaches. Research comprises »creative and systematic work undertaken to increase the stock of knowledge, including knowledge of humans, culture and society, and the use of this stock of knowledge to devise new applications« (Organisation for Economic Co-operation and Development 2015). Architects produce knowledge in unique built forms. To turn specific solutions into general conclusions, a systematic and replicable methodical procedure is required. Thus, to discover or condense general knowledge from unique phenomena, social and many other sciences (maths, economics etc.) use the potentials of abductive reasoning and apply a systematic approach called qualitative research. Qualitative abductive reasoning is a systematic collection and interpretation of phenomena (e.g. design solutions or built forms) as data, that intellectually interprets and critically scrutinizes their proper meaning and combines – clusters – unique with related phenomena into categories. Such categories or clusters are quite close to what architects call typologies – interpreted relations between phenomena.

For these qualitative approaches, quality criteria, following fundamental postulations of philosophy of science and theory of cognition, have been developed in the mentioned sciences. We claim that the similarity between qualitative research and architectural typologization can be used in the design-specific approaches if we do the same – accept, adopt, and adjust quality criteria of systematic research in what we call »Research through Design«.

The authors as head, research fellow and lecturer at the professorship of Landscape Architecture and Regional Open Space (LAREG) at the Technical University of Munich (TUM) have been teaching and conducting research in landscape architecture together for many years at the TUM.

References

Flick, Uwe/Kardorff, Ernst von/Steinke, Ines eds. (2000): *Qualitative Forschung. Ein Handbuch*, Reinbek bei Hamburg: Rowohlt.

Legewie, Heiner: »Gütekriterien und Qualitätssicherung qualitativer Methoden«, in: *Vorlesungen zur Qualitativen Diagnostik und Forschung*, http://www.ztg.tu-berlin.de/download/legewie/Dokumente/Vorlesung_12.pdf, accessed January 28, 2021.

Mayring, Philipp (2002): *Einführung in die qualitative Sozialforschung: Anleitung zu qualitativem Denken*, Weinheim: Beltz.

Organisation for Economic Co-operation and Developmen, OECD (2015): »Frascati Manual 2015: Guidelines for Collecting and Reporting Data on Research and Experimental Development«, in: *The Measurement of Scientific, Technological and Innovation Activities*, Paris: OECD Publishing. doi: 10.1787/9789264239012-en

Reichertz, Jo (2000): »Abduktion, Deduktion und Induktion in der qualitativen Forschung«, in: Uwe Flick/Ernst von Kardorff/Ines Steinke (eds.), *Qualitative Forschung. Ein Handbuch*, 2nd edition, Reinbek bei Hamburg: Rowohlt, 276–286.

Schöbel, Sören (2017): »Differenz der Landschaft. Im Gespräch mit Wolfgang Haber«, in: Sören Schöbel (ed.), *Landschaftsvertrag*, Berlin: Jovis, 85–93.

Steinke, Ines (2000): »Gütekriterien qualitativer Forschung«, in: Uwe Flick/Ernst von Kardorff/Ines Steinke (eds.), *Qualitative Forschung. Ein Handbuch*, 2nd edition, Reinbek bei Hamburg: Rowohlt, 319–331.

Architects as Public Intellectuals: How Far Beyond Can We Go?

Hannah Knoop

Editorial Summary: The research of Hannah Knoop is methodologically based on political theory, extended by fundamental methods of art history and the humanities. The starting point of her work is the presumption that the work on the design, the architectural activity, also inherits an intellectual dimension and that both the architect as a person understands, and represents the challenge, expectation, and dimension of the so-called intellectuality, as well as that the public grants her this quality. She observes that the quantitative research method in political science is based on three principles: contextuality, processuality, and reflexivity; terms that are quite familiar within the discipline of architecture and which have corresponding connotations. In doing so, she stresses that a critical examination and constant review of this transfer from an established research science to the architectural research field is essential. [Ferdinand Ludwig]

Keywords: Hannah Arendt; Space of Appearance; De-Civilization; Medial Public; Plurality; Contextuality; Processuality; Reflexivity.

On Qualitative Research

Looking at qualitative research methods in social science, they can be roughly summarized as being primarily concerned with collecting and evaluating non-standardized data, and thus proceeding methodologically interpretatively and hermeneutically. In particular, the actor's perspective is of decisive importance for the evaluation of the data. It contains the aim of gaining deeper insights into decision-making criteria and motivational structures.

The results and answers have to be interpreted explicitly based on context; thus, this method can also be regarded as reflexive in itself and indicates an inductive approach.

Qualitative research methods in general are extensively used, researched, and further developed, especially in the social sciences. The decisive question is: How to transfer them to architectural research and strengthen

Corresponding author: Hannah Knoop (Karlsruher Institut für Technologie (KIT), Karlsruhe, Germany); hannah.knoop@kit.edu; https://orcid.org/0000-0001-6086-5768
∂ Open Access. © 2021 Hannah Knoop, published by transcript Verlag.
This work is licensed under the Creative Commons Attribution 4.0 (BY) license.

its methods? From the architectural-research perspective, the following aspects of qualitative research are of particular importance: a dynamic research process; the inherent deliberate openness about the results; the exploration of unknown phenomena, resulting in the development of new theories and models, i.e. an inductive approach and the interpretative approach, in which a subject-related understanding is the focus of attention.

The latter aspect, in particular, resonates within architecture and the debate on the perception of users: the basic assumption for research following the interpretative paradigm is that of an interpretative understanding of human experience.

In this sense, interpretative research follows diverse theoretical lines of tradition, stretching from philosophical hermeneutics and phenomenology to Max Weber's concept of an understanding sociology and American pragmatism, to symbolic interactionism, ethnomethodology, and social constructivism (cf. Blatter et al. 2018: 34).

The Concept of Intellectuality

An intellectual person places herself in the cross-hairs by resuming and delivering again. In this sense, architectural activity is an intellectual activity par excellence. In particular, the absorption of what exists is an essential part. The giving away – after a process of production and creation – is then expressed as strikingly visible in the medium itself. In order to produce architecture, it is therefore necessary, on the one hand, to take an intensive look at social themes with an almost seismographic feel for current and future challenges, and, on the other hand, to wisely reproduce precisely these questions in the form of spatially concrete offers or even solutions.

At this moment, it is significant to note the reason why the term »Public Intellectual« is consciously used in this research project.

Architects as Public Intellectuals

The aim of the research project is to investigate the influence, interaction and interrelation of social, political, and intellectual dimensions in architectural discourse and architecture itself.

It invariably concerns the reflection of the spatially concrete space as a fixed reference point. Thus, this space is also the moment of examination for all theoretical aspects. Beyond an introduction and discussion of the concept of intellectuality, it is necessary to transfer the concept mainly used in the discipline of the humanities into architecture. Within the discipline of architecture, the concept of the Public Intellectual is appropriate, since it expands it through the crucial component of the public sphere.

What is meant when speaking of the public sphere today? – a functional concept, i.e. to »define the public sphere without defining it« [Adorno]; »an ideal; a spatially concrete place; a condition of knowledge« [Arendt]?

The public sphere is regarded as the indispensable foundation of any democratic system, functioning as a political collective and as a political corrective. If we look at this concept today, we cannot avoid asking who creates the public sphere, to whom does its performative power serve, and to what extent is the public sphere created and structured by media technology?

Even in current times, can political movements be observed that have developed their social impact out of an impulse to mobilize a so-called critical mass – especially in the spatially concrete public.

The dimensions of the public sphere that can currently be identified have an immense influence on architectural creation and architects, but how can it be grasped?

In order to approach these questions, it is necessary to build a theoretical framework as a link between the individual phenomena, and to question historical theories to enable reflection on one's own present:

In *The Human Condition*, Hannah Arendt pursues several consequent distinctions. In addition to the three basic human activities of Labor, Work, and Action, she analyzes public and private space; natality and mortality; the social and the private; and so on. Looking at the phenomenon of the public, it is noticeable that within Arendt's work »dimensions of the public« exist. The public sphere, which is specifically addressed in *The Human Condition* as a space in which people move, speak, and act, is a »political public«. On the other hand, the public as a precondition for judgement is rather a criterion for perception – thus an »epistemological public« (cf. Bajohr 2011: 8; cf. also McCarthy 1981).

Another important distinction that Arendt explains precisely and summarizes in its historical context, is the original separation of the social and the political (cf. especially »The Rise of the Social«, in: Arendt 1998: 38–49). It is from these distinctions that the interrelations between social and political norms of architecture, and the allocation of space for social and political action and thought in the scopes of architecture and in architectural discourse emerge.

The Medial Public Is Not an Agora

The electronic media offers an unforeseeable possibility for encounters and individual communication on digital platforms as an anteroom of the places of assembly, i.e. the spatially concrete places of the public. In agreement with the sociologist Armin Nassehi, however, it is also important to note that the low-threshold nature of digital spaces has simultaneously led to the de-civilization of communication (cf. Nassehi 2019). At present, it can be observed that this de-civilization, previously explicitly attributed to digital public spaces, is now being retransferred to social space in physical space.

Political theorist Hannah Arendt maintained an idealized idea of the public sphere as a Greek agora: an arena of discourse in which the free and the equal compete with each other in the competition of words, and in the presence of their whole person, so that they are judged by those physically present. This ideal can by no means be transferred to the media public sphere; it is not structured along the lines of the agora. In actual Internet communication, speakers do not appear as whole personalities who could be dismantled by the civilized reference to their self-contradictions. Rather, their speech exists in the form of freely floating fragments of language that are instrumentalized for political purposes.

This leads to the compelling conclusion that the task and activity of the architect must be understood as the action of a public intellectual.

How Far Beyond Can We Go?

The research topic has to be explored in exchange with other disciplines. In addition, it is a topic that questions our common notion of theory and practice, written or spoken word versus built architecture, in this clear distinction. The concept of the word »language« must be understood as broadly as possible, namely in its actual sense as a »form of expression«. At this very moment, built architecture as a form of expression is to be placed on an equal level with the word expression – and of course vice-versa.

This approach additionally encompasses a specific perspective: namely that of the architecturally reflected search for a meaning, in order to be able to penetrate the aesthetic expressiveness of architecture with an intellectual architectural approach.

Methodologically, the research is based on political science and the methods of qualitative research, extended by fundamental methods of art history and the humanities. It is therefore a presumption that the work on the design, the architectural activity, also inherits an intellectual dimension and that both the architect as a person understands and represents the challenge, expectation, and dimension of the so-called intellectuality, as well as that the public grants her this quality.

The Understanding of Meaning as a Core-Category

One of the theories upon which this research is particularly based, is Hannah Arendt's political theory, as it provides a thought-provoking basis with a definite architectural-theoretical relevance for the discourse on the built, spatially concrete space. This is the case, as there is no question that the public cannot be thought of without the dimensions of the political and social. They are the point of origin for the interrelation of social and political norms of architecture opposed to giving space to social and political action and thinking in the spaces of architecture and in the architectural discourse. With Arendt's understanding of the concept of plurality, she also offers a base for our contemporary debate on coexistence, as the diversity of people in their respective uniqueness is guaranteed precisely by the reality of the common world: in the political space, the Arendtian space of appearance. This space is spatially concrete: people meet each other in speaking and acting. In doing so, they not only communicate the content of a message, but themselves as well. If this plurality is destroyed, a loss of the world and a radical isolation within a mass society inevitably follows, in which the Arendtian animal laborans dominates as way of life.

The fact that the intellectual dimension is to be included in the survey can initially be justified with the hope that, as much as the concept of intellectuality in general, and even more so in the specific case of architecture requires a critical introduction, it could be the connection between politics, sociology, and architecture. In light of the fact that the question of architectural research appears more topical than ever, it is being discussed in a variety of ways and in the context of various methodological and programmatic issues; a look at the intellectual dimension of architecture holds the potential to fruitfully complement the artistic, creative, technical or processual view of the discipline and its research. In addition, it is important to dare to build a bridge across disciplines to philosophy, political science, and sociology.

Furthermore, the term also attracts attention in the general discourse and its various levels of meaning. In particular, the current political and social debate seems to have taken a like or dislike to this term, from which further stimulating potential for a discursive and conceptual debate in all the sub-areas used for consideration can be derived; the relevance and explosiveness of the topic presented becomes apparent.

On Qualitative Research in Political Science

There are well-established methods to follow and, within qualitative research, precise definitions on how, where, and when to collect data. Yet on closer inspection, there arise methodological challenges, such as a low number of cases. This leads to interviews that go into much more detail and reach a depth that would not be possible within quantitative research. The advantage is that results can be better generalized.

However, there is no doubt that a research structure and argumentation must be repeatable and comprehensible. This is, of course, a precondition for all research work and ultimately serves the purpose of traceability in connection with the legitimate question of relevance.

The qualitative research method within political science can form a meaningful foundation for research projects in – historically speaking – young architectural research. A prerequisite for this is the critical examination and constant review of this transfer from an established research science to the architectural research field. The qualitative research method in political science is based on three principles: contextuality, processuality, and reflexivity. These terms are quite familiar within the discipline of architecture and have corresponding connotations. As such, they can also be transferred to the political-theoretical context – and again, vice-versa.

Contextuality: The meaning of social and political phenomena can only be understood by including the context in which they occur – context is key. In this respect, we often speak of a naturalism of interpretative research, which aims to investigate phenomena in their »natural« environment, and systematically considers the contextuality of statements and actions.

Processuality, Openness, and Flexibility: Interpretative research usually follows a circular research strategy in which – instead of starting with hypotheses which are then tested – theses and theories are developed from the empirical material (induction) and, if necessary, are re-examined (abduction). This sometimes requires »on-site flexibility«, i.e. the competence to adapt the methodological design, the methodological procedure and the theoretical references to the requirements of the field, the research situation in the course of the research process, or to change.

Reflexivity: The researcher is seen as a constitutive part of the research field. The researcher is significantly involved in the production of the data (Blatter, et al. 2018: 37).

Epilogue

How far beyond can we go? It is possible to go beyond – and it is necessary to do so in the case of a broader survey with a broad understanding of architecture as a discipline.

The traceability of any investigation is and remains crucial. In this context, it is helpful to take a close look at the methods of qualitative research and to draw conclusions about the case studies in one's own research on the basis of the numerous case studies within the discipline of political science. In this context, it is of decisive importance that vague or even subjective views are critically evaluated.

If this starting point is made consciously within the research design, the potential that qualitative research holds can be fully developed, and the deliberate openness in the methodology can be applied.

References

Arendt, Hannah (1998): *The Human Condition*, Chicago: University of Chicago Press, 38–49.

Bajohr, Hannes (2011): *Dimensionen der Öffentlichkeit. Politik und Erkenntnis bei Hannah Arendt*, Berlin: Lukas Verlag.

Blatter, Joachim/Langer, Phil C./ Wagemann, Claudius (2018): *Qualitative Methoden in der Politikwissenschaft. Eine Einführung*, Wiesbaden: VS Verlag für Sozialwissenschaften. doi: 10.1007/978-3-658-14955-0

McCarthy, Mary (ed.) (1981): *Hannah Arendt, The Life of Mind*, New York: Harcourt.

Nassehi, Armin (2019): *Theorie der digitalen Gesellschaft*, Munich: C. H. Beck.

Nassehi, Armin: »Die Grenzen des öffentlichen Raumes«, in: *Bundesstiftung Baukultur*, https://www.bundesstiftung-baukultur.de/magazin/audio-nassehi, accessed February 23, 2020.

Playing Seriously: An Introduction to Corporeal Architecture, Neuroscience, and Performance Art

Maria da Piedade Ferreira

Editorial Summary: With a focus on experiential qualities Maria da Piedade Ferreira distinguishes her research object from classical (rather technical) quantities such as load-bearing capacities. In her text she illustrates how she employs methods, techniques, and instruments from performance art and neurosciences to investigate the effects of spatial conditions on the human body. In doing so, she explores a mix of qualitative and quantitative approaches, namely by experimenting with emotion measurement: Qualitative research, by including methodologies which attribute measurable values to the felt experience, might help us better understand the effects of the built environment in the human body during the design process itself, and after building. Accordingly, her aim is to integrate art and science methodologies that allow us to design spaces as intelligent extensions of the human body and positively impact how this feels and acts in the world. [Ferdinand Ludwig]

Keywords: Corporeal Architecture; Neuroscience Performance Art; Embodiment; Emotion Measurement; Human Centered Design.

On Qualitative Research

A broad definition of »qualitative« defines this adjective as relating to, measuring or measured by the quality of something rather than its quantity. In the context of the research project, *Corporeal Architecture*, the term »qualitative« additionally acquires the meaning of the procedure which, by adopting a wide scope of analytical tools, allows us to evaluate and extract conclusions on the effects of architectural spaces and design objects in the human body and mind. By including methodologies which attribute measurable values to the felt experience, qualitative research might help us better understand the effects of the built environment on the human body during the design process itself and after building (Mallgrave 2010: 133–144).

Corresponding author: Maria da Piedade Ferreira (Hochschule für Technik, Stuttgart, Germany); m.piedade.ferreira@gmail.com; https://orcid.org/0000-0002-8433-7705
Open Access. © 2021 Maria da Piedade Ferreira, published by transcript Verlag.
This work is licensed under the Creative Commons Attribution 4.0 (BY) license.

Performance for the Design Project »Tricky Tables«.
Maria da Piedade Ferreira, FATUK Kaiserslautern, 2017/2018.
Photographer: Maria da Piedade Ferreira, 2018.

Investigating a qualitative approach to research, the *Corporeal Architecture* project integrates performance art, qualitative methods, psychophysiology, and self-assessment tools in the teaching of architecture (Ferreira 2017). The aim is to understand how to create spaces which may improve the quality of the built environment and use these tools to observe in real-time how body, space, and movement are interdependent.

Qualitative research methods have a long tradition of being used in psychology, mathematics, medical sciences and more recently, neurosciences, thereby revolutionizing many other disciplines. Architecture and design are no exception, and a growing community of individuals and institutions are embracing the potential of qualitative research to analyze how the existing built environment can be improved to address contemporary health concerns characteristic of urban settings (Goldhagen 2017: 2–41). This offers us the possibility of creating design methodologies that are science-informed. A building, home or office can then be designed or adapted as an intelligent extension of the human body and positively impact how we feel and act in the world in the world (Sussman and Hollander 2015: 1–9).

Qualitative research offers many possibilities but also poses challenges and ethical concerns. It is important that while working with such tools, one clearly has in mind the current limitations of technology and understands that the measurements collected should not be seen as deterministic but as indicators of how, body and space/design objects affect each other. Moreover, architects must learn to develop the sensitivity to deal with the consequences of looking so deeply into the bodies and lives of others. Therefore, integrating such practices in the context of design and teaching also poses the challenge to architects, as seen in medical professions, of learning how to respect boundaries and privacy, and use the information collected with the highest ethical standards.

Research Project – Introduction

The artistic research project *Corporeal Architecture* takes place in the context of design education and explores the relationship between body, space, and object, in particular taking into consideration the contemporary scientific view of the body and mind as a whole – generally addressed as the embodied mind theory (Varela et al. 1991). It is my proposal that the integration of the somatic techniques of performance art and neuroscience in architectural design have the potential to develop corporeal awareness and stimulate the creativity of future designers.

Supported by experimental work, which includes methodologies from psychophysiology and neuroergonomics, the doctoral thesis *Embodied Emotions: Observations and Experiments in Architecture and Corporeality* argues that advances in fields related to the study of the brain shouldn't be ignored by architects, since they present an opportunity for the discipline to rethink its approaches to design and teaching (Ferreira 2016).

The methodology it proposes combines the somatic practices of performance art (Marshall 2008) with emotion measurement tools (Kim et al. 2015: 10–12) in design education and encourages the active creative participation of students regarding the design, fabrication, and performance with body extensions, body restrictions, pieces of furniture, and installations. The performances are documented on camera and film and are archived in the YouTube channel *Corporeal Architecture* as well as the website corporeal.persona.co.

Hypothesis of Research

The present hypothesis is that by training students to be able to tune into their own corporeal awareness using techniques from performance art and technology, their spatial, sensorial and perceptual skills will expand, develop, and refine and, consequently, their creativity and sensitivity as designers will improve. Such approaches are not new; the outcomes of the pedagogy at the Bauhaus, which integrated performance, philosophy, and science as a teaching method, are still a living testimony (Mallgrave 2013: 128–139). Therefore, *Corporeal Architecture* aims to retrieve a tradition that has always been important in the teaching of architecture and design: learning directly through the body and experience, and extending it through technology.

Methodologies, Approaches and Alignments

Each human body carries a history and a story. When working with human bodies, especially in states of vulnerability as often occurs when applying the somatic techniques of performance art and psychophysiology measurement tools, it is paramount to create a place where each student does not feel coerced to expose or participate, but has the space and the time to choose the level of participation which feels appropriate and meaningful. This is a golden rule in my practice, especially since most students of architecture and interior design have never been exposed to performance art, and have only used emotion measurement technology in a medical context.

Students of architecture often legitimately ask – what does this have to do with architecture? So it is also my intention that they can get the most out of the classes and understand how the exercises develop their skills as designers.

Furthermore, when teaching performance art, for example, as usually happens in an art academy, students are challenged to overcome inhibitions and certain forms of cultural conditioning which might present limitations for their creative development. Here, the same dilemma applies as in theatre, for example, where a director might use aggressive strategies to break the passivity of the actor (Marshall 2008: 100–102). It is my position instead, that positive reinforcement and encouraging each student to choose their own themes for reflection and their own level of expression and participation bring out the best of their creative potential. Joy, pleasure and play are conscious strategies which I employ in my classes in all stages of the design process – design, building, and performance. These strategies are not permissive – my role as teacher is to ensure that the atmosphere is playful but that there are rules that always include the respectful treatment of oneself and one's colleagues, and privacy regarding the data obtained.

Aims and Objectives

The *Corporeal Architecture* project aims to explore the affective influence of architectural space and design objects on the human body, whether empathy/attunement between the user's body and its surroundings can take place (Pérez-Gómez 2016: 165–196), and how affordances are expressed in action (Noë 2004: 103–106). Through this methodology, students experience main interlocking strands: an introduction to the somatic techniques of performance art, which is undertaken through practical exercises that directly work with the body in movement and basic notions of neuroscience, (Eberhard 2009), behavioral sciences, (Bradley et al. 1994: 49–59) sensorial design, (Pallasmaa 2005: 70–71) affective science (Lang et al. 1998: 1248–1263) and psychophysiology tools (Kim et al. 2015: 10–12).

Designed to make students aware of their own body's relation and reaction to space, such experiments are taken in the context of seminars and workshops with the aim of developing their own corporeal awareness.

Questionnaires and other self-assessment tools are often also employed, taking into consideration that the information collected is most important as direct feedback on bodily states under certain conditions, and not necessarily a deterministic analysis of effect.

Context: Qualitative Research

Now, more than ever, is a designer also someone who conceives a space, taking into account the well-being of its users and aiming to provide places where meaningful experiences happen (Ruggles 2017: 89–97). Physiological measures recorded from the body, such as heart rate, skin conductance, and blood pressure, which have been applied in experiments for the *Corporeal Architecture* project, have previously been used in psychological studies (Lang 1998: 1248–1263) and in neuroergonomics.

Both psychophysiology and neuroergonomics share one goal – the design of safe and efficient technologies and systems for human effort. Therefore, such methodologies offer a very fertile ground for designers and architects to conduct research, particularly when integrating performance art. Although the technology still has more limitations than possibilities, I stand by the position that an integrated design practice that includes such methodologies and developments will not only radically change the way we design but, most importantly, how we live.

Such approaches also offer problems like, for example, the question of »data bias« which is not only a contemporary concern, but has been a constant historical reality, as statistics and histories have mostly been written from a male gendered perspective. Data bias has for centuries guided how we think, design and act in the world, and established ideas on comfort and usability. Historically, and especially after the Industrial Revolution, design objects were mostly adapted to generalized male standards based on the averaged collected data from male-gender humans (Criado Perez 2019: 29–66). Such a built environment shaped cultures and identities, forcing everybody, regardless of one's naturally imperfect humanity, to adapt to such standards. And although the 21st century has definitely seen improvements in this regard, most of the spaces we live and work in are mostly adapted to the efficiency-driven ideal of the »car-driving healthy male standard«, a residue of Taylorism.

There are also fundamental aspects of being human and of the creative process that are not measurable or translatable as data, such as play, which develops with improvisation and intuition. Another non-measurable human feature has to do with our innate interest in ritual and need for introspection (Mallgrave 2018: 155–175). In a century when religion has less importance than before and human beings' instinctual need for community and ritual is increasingly met by commercial experiences, it is architecture that has the responsibility to create typologies where such needs are met; Alberto Pérez-Gómez (2016: 165–196) refers to architecture as a place for free enjoyment or catharsis, which can take place where humans individually and collectively feel a sense of attunement.

The *Corporeal Architecture* project aims to act by integrating playing in teaching as a creative strategy characteristic of performance art, while also taking reference from ritualistic traditions that address the movement of the human body, the breath, and the interaction with objects and other bodies. By learning, for example, to observe how the rituals of everyday life develop, such as cleaning the house, preparing a meal or taking a walk in a park, and how the placement and order of the objects and buildings which support such rituals allow humans to achieve goals and create a sense of placement and feel situated, students can understand their importance but also how, at the same time, such conventions might equally in time become obstructive or even un-desirable.

I work with performance art to introduce the idea of protocol in the interaction between body and space or body and object, as well as one's own body and the bodies of others, and to question through direct interaction where the protocol comes from and why, and which narratives are performed in such patterns of behavior. In this way, students are sensitized to their own habits, and by observing their own movement, learn how such protocols are shaped by cultural identities (Marshall 2008: 97–99). When working with students, I also try to find in the mix of all these conditionings the subtle idiosyncrasies that make each student a creative individual. By becoming aware of one's patterns of thought and interaction with the world, students become conscious of their agency and limits, their possibility of choice, and their potential to become active participants in shaping and transforming the world.

Conclusion

Working between the seemingly different worlds of art, architecture and research brings forth questions, as my work is not always understood by students and peers. My research is dedicated to the conscious exploration of this situation of liminality, as the capacity to relate different ways of conceiving and addressing the same topics, across disciplines, and between worlds. Therefore, my approach to technology and specifically emotion measurement takes advantage of what we can learn about the interaction of the body and space through data, but does not accept it as the full picture of the felt experience. Rather, it is understood more as an abstraction that is conditioned by the architecture of the machines used and their own form of artificial sentience. In this regard, I approach technology (as well as design and architecture) as an extension of the human body's sensorium. It is important to note that just like human bodies, machines are prone to failure. This is especially the case when working with emotion measurement tools, which from my experience, pose many problems. Bio-markers require direct contact with the body and do not respond well to continuous or sudden changes of movement. This alone considerably restricts the range of motion and situations which can be explored by analyzing a body performing in architectural space. So my experiments with emotion measurement took place in minimalistic settings which explored basic human actions, such as sitting at different heights and positions for different periods of time and performing simple daily actions such as eating dinner, reading the newspaper, dressing and undressing. Another aspect, which is especially relevant in my practice and is influenced by the presence of digital media and social networks in our lives, is privacy. This is particularly important since my work with performance explores improvisation, and in such situations, it is not uncommon for unconscious patterns to take expression. Another strategy I consciously employ in my practice is to perform myself with the group. I develop the same task, show how the preparatory exercises are done, and perform. Here, I work again in liminality, as performer and director, often also documenting. This requires a high level of presence. It is often the biggest challenge in a performance with students of architecture to create an atmosphere where, for a certain amount of hours, the entire group is fully present. The preparatory exercises encourage this, but it is not always possible or successful and the outcomes are unpredictable. However, working within this paradox is also the source of many creative opportunities.

References

Bradley, Margaret M/Lang, Peter J (1994): »Measuring Emotion: The Self-assessment Manikin and the Semantic Differential«, in: *Behavior Therapy and Experimental Psychiatry* 25(1) 49–59.

Criado Perez, Caroline (2019): *Invisible Women: Exposing Data Bias in a World Designed for Men*, London: Penguin Random House.

Eberhard, John Paul (2009): *Brain Landscape. The Coexistence of Neuroscience and Architecture*, Oxford: Oxford University Press, doi: 10.1093/acprof:oso/9780195331721.001.0001

Ferreira, Maria da Piedade (2016): *Embodied Emotions: Observations and Experiments in Architecture and Corporeality*, PhD thesis, Lisbon: FAU Lisboa.

Ferreira, Maria da Piedade (2017): »Corporeal Architecture: Teaching future Architects to think through the Body Using Neurosciences and Performance Art«, in: Itai Palti/Anne Fritz (eds.), *Conscious Cities Journal 2 – Bridging Neuroscience, Architecture and Technology*, doi: 10.33797/CCJ.02.05

Goldhagen, Sarah Williams (2017): *Welcome to your world – How the built environment shapes our lives*, New York: HarperCollins Publishers.

Kim, Mi Jeong/Cho, Myung Eun/Kim, Jeong Tai (2015): »Measures of Emotion in Interaction for Health Smart Home«, in: *IACSIT International Journal of Engineering and Technology* 7(4), 10–12.

Lang, Peter J./Bradley, Margaret M./Cuthbert, Bruce N. (1998): »Emotion, Motivation, and Anxiety: Brain Mechanisms and Psychophysiology«, in. *Biological Psychiatry* 44(12), 1248–1263.

Mallgrave, Harry Francis (2010): *The Architect's Brain: Neuroscience, Creativity and Architecture*, Hoboken, NJ: Wiley-Blackwell.

Mallgrave, Harry Francis (2013): *Architecture and Embodiment: The Implications of the New Sciences and Humanities for Design*, New York: Routledge.

Mallgrave, Harry Francis (2018): *From Object to Experience: The New Culture of Architectural Design*, London: Bloomsbury Publishing.

Marshall, Lorna (2008): *The Body Speaks: Performance and physical expression*, London: Methuen Drama.

Noë, Alva (2004): *Action in Perception*, Cambridge, MA: MIT Press.

Pallasmaa, Juhani (2005): *The Eyes of the Skin: Architecture and the Senses*, Chichester, UK: John Wiley & Sons.

Pérez-Gómez, Alberto (2016): *Attunement: Architectural Meaning After the Crisis of Modern Science*, Cambridge, MA: MIT Press.

Ruggles, Donald H. (2017): *Beauty, Neuroscience & Architecture: Timeless Patterns & Their Impact on Our Well-Being*, Denver, CO: Fibonacci LLC.

Sussman, Ann/Hollander, Justin B. (2015): *Cognitive Architecture: Designing for How We Respond to the Built Environment*, New York: Routledge.

Varela, Francisco J./Thompson, Evan/Rosch, Eleanor (1991): *The Embodied Mind – Cognitive Science and Human Experience*, Cambridge, MA: MIT Press.

Perception-Based Research

Uta Graff

Trained perception and architectural design are inseparably intertwined. The future experience of a building is already anticipated in its design. Architectural design and creation anticipate the experience of architectural spaces to the extent that it is already conceived in the design process. The imagination of future buildings additionally includes the dimension of the spatial experience. It is based on perception, memory and sensory experience – the already familiar is transformed into something new, and starting from well-known spaces, future ones are developed as resembling them, as comparable in a certain way or as different from existing references. The concreteness of architecture requires a distinct imagination. In order to transmit the knowledge embedded in the design, suitable and adequate forms of representation are required.

The more attentively one feeds one's own imagination, the more precise a design and its representations can be. Precise in this case does not mean refining with pristine distinction, but signifies thought and being made with care. Representation, presentation technique, and architectural conception are reciprocally interlinked. As architecture itself, as well as its manifold ways of presentation are all forms of aesthetic expression, they ought to meet the atmospheric, sensory, attentive or substantial qualities of one another.

Hence, the design is integrated into a complex time structure of memory and projection: Ideas and concepts for perspective architectures are developed from the memory of past experiences, and the present sense of spatial exploration. Accordingly, the cultivation of perception also enhances design competences. The more precise the perception of the experiencer, the more differentiated the collection of experienced architectural encounters and memories becomes, which are further refined into architectural ideas through association and combination. Design is a core competence of the architect, which involves clarifying and specifying the idea of the architecture one is working on. In this superordinate, integrative process, the architectural design with its contextual and typological, its spatial and structural, its constructive and technical, and its material and atmospheric characteristics is conceived and specified. Concretizing what is conceptualized is an integrated part of the architectural design.

Focusing on lived experience as an essential for the perception and conception of architectures enables an attentive approach to the merely intuitive and unconscious elements of both processes. By placing perception at the center of attention, the individual, subjective experience and personal event of the architectural encounter acquire greater significance: Internalized knowledge about space is constituted by more or less consciously lived spatial impressions, comprising one's memory of spaces. Architectural ideas and conceptions are thus conceived from this incorporated archive of spatial knowledge. Any architectural design is inseparably interwoven with the personal archive of spatial memory and experiences of its author. Accordingly, the subjective dimension of spatial experiencing and architectural conception must be taken into account, as this dimension – beyond the general validity of certain essential principles of spatial formation and perception – is formative for the experience of the built environment.

These Are Only Hints and Guesses

Francesca Torzo

Editorial Summary: In »These Are Only Hints and Guesses« Francesca Torzo explores experience, conscience, and culture as territories to reflect on architecture. Tracing back the narratives and stories from the past as a basic foundation of knowledge, she unravels the resonance of history and knowledge within contemporary experience and design in architecture. Based upon what has been, the thinking and making of architecture is always embedded in the stream of memory and tradition, referring to what was there before. Proceeding from this basis, the personal archive of memories fuels the processes of association and imagination. Any idea is integral to a cultural context, while culture is considered to be this stream of consciousness, forming the background to recent lived experience and its projection into future conception and design. [Uta Graff]

Keywords: Time; Spatial Relations; Memory; Vision; Allusions; Perception; Observation; Experience.

>»Go, go, go, said the bird: human kind
>Cannot bear very much reality.
>Time past and time future
>What might have been and what has been
>Point to one end, which is always present.«
>T. S. Eliot: 1935.

>»J'ai beaucoup reconstruit : c'est collaborer avec les temps sous son aspect de passé, en saisir ou en modifier l'esprit, lui server de relais vers un plus long avenir; c'est retrouver sous le pierres le secret des sources. Notre vie est brève : nous parlons sans cesse des siècles qui précèdent ou qui suivent le nôtre comme s'ils nous étaient totalement étrangers; j'y touchais pourtant dans mes jeux avec la pierre. Ces murs que j'étaie sont encore chauds du contact de corps disparus ; des mains qui n'existent pas encore caresseront ces fut de colonnes.«
>Marguerite Yourcenar: 1958.

Corresponding author: Francesca Torzo (Bergen Architecture School, Bergen, Norway); mail@francescatorzo.it
Open Access. © 2021 Francesca Torzo, published by transcript Verlag.
This work is licensed under the Creative Commons Attribution 4.0 (BY) license.

134 Francesca Torzo

»Layering of Time, Presences and Sensations«,
Carlo Scarpa: Renovation and Addition of Castelvecchio, Verona, 1958–1964.
Photographer: Francesca Torzo, 2020.

At the age of eight, Heinrich Keller, son of a baker from Zurich, suffered a very serious leg fracture and was confined to bed for years. On the eve of the march on Versailles and the establishment of the first French Republic yet immobilized by his confinement, Heinrich began to draw landscapes that he had never visited, but imagined with precision and an abundance of detail. It was the year 1786, the time when Natural philosophers, namely the mathematicians, were divided in debates about Newton's laws, Northern European writers started to travel through Italy, and Count Gaspard Monge began his invention of descriptive geometry. It was during this time that the Paris Constituent Assembly voted for the meter – a submultiple of the Paris meridian – as the new unit of measurement. While the most skilled artisans migrated from city to city and country to country, crossing wars deploying makeshifts, as was the case of the peculiar journey from the Prussian Neuchatel through the courts of Madrid, Paris, London, and all the way to China for the invention of the first three mechanical dolls: the Writer, the Designer, and the Harpsichord Player.

As an apprentice for more than 20 years at Henri Füssli atelier and later at his own publishing shop – which he had opened at about the age of 40 – Heinrich meticulously recreated the Swiss Alpine landscapes on cartographic maps and plates burnished by the candles' smoke, moving his gaze afar to Lake Maggiore and Milan. The topography of the Alps, the streets, the cities, the human artefacts, and the detailed scenes of daily life are portrayed like the characters of one unitary landscape, a fresco most probably just imagined by this unusual engraver who did not travel much but collected the tales of contemporary voyagers. The minimalism of his panoramas magnifies the details that inhabit the landscape, whether they entail a thickening of lines portraying a couple on a walk along a countryside path or small rural buildings up on a mountain pasture, Zurich bell towers or the outstretched profile of the Alps. The panoramas that Keller imagined, or reconstructed, depict landscapes that were formed with millenary slowness: the Alps' chains that have been inhabited by individuals and communities for centuries and the cities, and villages that are still part of everyday life.

When we look out of an airplane window today, we can observe the movements of the mountain chains and valleys and see how the roads, railways, and bridges were largely built with a pragmatic intelligence that reflects the topography. We can also see how the configuration of villages and cities changes, hinting at a memory of the topography. Similarly, when walking down the streets of historical cities, the flow of the roads and the arrangement of the facade walls express the memory of the first settlements, and we are able to sense if we are in a place formed by meandering rivers and sand, by the clash of the plates of Africa and Europe, or by the deposition of volcanic ashes. Cities and houses recount thousands of years of geology as well as how humans decided to settle in a landscape and how, over the centuries, the various communities made the decision to confirm, or transform, parts of these cities.

The transformation of cities, at least until after the First and Second World Wars, rarely contradicted the initial settlement decisions. Rather, they more often confirmed the pre-existing urban and architectural structures, building and evolving them, inhabiting them with new signifiers, and demolishing parts and adding others. This was likely a result of the slowness of the processes that made necessary and inevitable an economics of the act of building, in the sense of a wise »home administration«, aiming for a maximum result with a minimum expenditure of means. If the character, that is the cultural expression of the city, has been deeply transformed over time, seeing that construction is an instrument that represents culture and the communication – as well as the festivity – of the political power around which a community converges and finds agreement for a finite period of time. Nevertheless, it is possible to detect the permanence of a »cultural structure« of cities, phrasing that attempts to name the ensemble of characteristics that has survived over centuries and that makes an anthropic location unique.

As architects, we are always confronted with an area that has already been inhabited, whether it is a landscape or an urban context. It is never a tabula rasa. The underlying question of our profession is perhaps how to successfully observe and recognize the »cultural structure« of a place, meaning those permanencies that cannot be ascribed to a language or a form, though they inevitably express the cultural cipher, as well as the technique and availability of the means and materials specific to a historical period that therefore cannot be reproduced, and consists of spatial relationships that are specific to each place. These relationships, between human constructions and a topography, as well as among the constructions themselves, are not parametric nor linguistic. Indeed these spatial relationships can be identified and measured, but they do not address univocally a set of ratios nor a deterministic parametric rule; they seem to be the result of building gestures being repeated over centuries, even with different phrasing, and they convey the idea and the perception of a place. The loggia, for example, is the expression of a Mediterranean life, not so much due to the figure of the loggia itself, but as a result of the culture of living that they allude to and dispose. If we visit a masonry loggia veiled with a thin layer of plaster, or a loggia built of wood or concrete, our mind recalls a memory, together with a vision, of the sun.

The question of »how do we know what we know« arises.

In his notes on painting, Leonardo da Vinci observed how difficult it was to paint the »concept in the mind of man« because unlike the portrait of a man as a body, which can be easily parametrized, the »concept«, or the culture, must be drawn through gestures and movements; it is alive. Even buildings and cities are alive. They continue to live in the spaces that human beings are able to inhabit with new meaning.

It seems to me that the mind of people is »hungry«, it needs continuous nourishment and an imperceptible unaware swing between distraction and concentration. Our senses constantly recollect flakes of experience and store them in our mind; then, unpredictably though precisely, our mind recomposes these fragments into wholes, which orient our perception and our communication of the world. This continuous movement of associations and allusions is paradoxical. Somehow, we may find solace in imagining that our mind has space to host contradictions and store them, awaiting a time for them to become a new entity of perception, which may be a memory, a vision, or both.

Observing these human phenomena instils a kind of empathy for beings which soothes impatience. It does take patience and an open-minded curiosity to overcome one's own individuality and to be able to read the contradictory experiences of others' lives and cultures as well as to learn from them. The privilege of our profession is that it offers us the possibility of arranging spatial dispositions that reflect these experiences, thus belonging harmoniously to the slow phenomena of human culture that unravels far beyond the lifetime of a human being.

I interpret the architect's profession as a director of fiction, meant as a weaver of narratives at the disposal of people's experiences; hence, observing is an ineffable source of collecting experiences and imaginaries that belong to individuals as well as to a collective. We trace these narratives by stitching together the primary spatial relations, training a clarity in formulating questions, and then it is our responsibility to ensure that the promises are not compromised, so that people may live the authenticity of an experience, while we leave the scene.

Measures reveal and trace orders among living beings, things, spaces. I recall Vitruvius's enthusiasm in describing how the square and compass – in Latin straight lines, euthygrammi, and constellations, circini – were the utensils of geometry addressed as the mental tool in charge of tuning harmony of the parts with the whole.

Geometrical drawings are hence open maps which note the potential orders, rhythms, and harmonies of spaces. It seems that there is not one dimension better than another, nor a proportion more compelling than another. Dimensions do not have a value on their own but exist out of relations with other dimensions, and their meaning or scale perception changes throughout time. Therefore, the proportional systems investigated throughout centuries by mathematicians, philosophers, and architects resemble folk tales, beautiful ones, that express the everlasting human need to obtain the secret rule of the universe, and we find ourselves among contradictory theories that are equally true.

The main concern of my daily work is exactly this observation of the »cultural structure« of a place and the search for consonance and decorum, which are not figurative, but rather an expressive morphology with the hope of weaving a cultural continuity that is able to include contrasts between those who lived before us and those who will come.

References

Eliot, Thomas Stearns (1935): »Burnt Norton«, in: *Four Quartets*, 1937–1942.

Yourcenar, Marguerite (1958): »Tellus Stabilita«, in: Marguerite Yourcenar, *Mémoires d'Hadrien*, Paris: Gallimard.

Corporeality of Architecture Experience

Katharina Voigt

Editorial Summary: In »Corporeality of Architecture Experience« Katharina Voigt examines the embodied knowledge in the perception and the exploration of architectural spaces. She highlights embodiment, experience, and sensation as primary fields of investigation. The interrelation of architecture and the human body is described as dependent on bodily ways of knowing and movement as access to sensory encounters with architecture. Relating to the practice of contemporary dance and particularly the work of Sasha Waltz, she regards the body as an archive, generator, and medium of pre-reflexive knowledge, emphasizing its resonance with the space. She exploits the potential which an investigation of the body-based, sensory experience holds when being explicitly addressed and regarded as an integrated part of both, the perception and the design of architecture. [Uta Graff]

Keywords: Corporeal Experience; Embodied Knowledge; Bodily Archive; Contemporary Dance; Sensorimotor Perception; Reciprocity of Space and Movement; Sensuality; Sasha Waltz & Guests.

Research Based upon Perception

As architecture constitutes the built environment of the living world, it forms the context of our physical access to the world of matter. The process of creation and anticipation in architectural design and the actual exploration of architectural situations are equally dependent on past and present lived experiences. Setting perception at the core of research in architecture, the corporeality of the perceiver becomes an inevitable concern of investigation: Spatial perception is an enactive process of movement, exploration, sensual effects, and the sensorimotor encounter of the individual with the physical realm. The perception of space is bound to the body and is preconditioned by both the self-awareness of the body and the perceptual sensation through the body. Therefore, body consciousness and the corporeal outreach into the world condition and direct spatial perception. As according to Maurice Merleau-Ponty, »my whole body for me is not an assemblage of organs juxtaposed in space. I am in undivided possession of it and I know where each of my limbs is through a body image in which all are included« (Merleau-Ponty 2003/1962 [1945]: 112–113). Proprioception is a given condition of our embodied existence. Accordingly, the investigation of the perception of space and architecture is inseparably linked to the body, as it is its indispensable prerequisite. The more differentiated the sensorimotor capacity of the body and the corporeality of movement in space are exploited, the more precise the knowledge of *how* we perceive architecture can be gained:

> »If bodily space and external space form a practical system, the first being the background against which the object as the goal of our action may stand out or the void in front of which it may come to light, it is clearly in action that the spatiality of our body is brought into being, and an analysis of one's own movement should enable us to arrive at the better understanding of it. By considering the body in movement, we can see how it inhabits space and, moreover, time, because movement is not limited to submitting passively to space and time, it actively assumes them [...].« (Merleau-Ponty 2003/1962 [1945]: 117)

Against the background of perception, research in architecture concerns the interrelation between space and body, based upon their respective feasibility to resonate with one another and the reciprocity of their interaction. The choreographic techniques and procedures in contemporary dance serve as tools for an in-depth understanding of the corporeal effect that architectural spaces have on the human body. They enhance the phenomenological horizon of architectural space and the corporeality of the body as a connection to the world of the living. The sensual dimension of architecture experience, as well as its impact on the corporeality of its perceiver, becomes therefore intelligible and attainable to be included in the process of architectural design.

Architectural Encounter as Corporeal Experience

This research pursues the question of how to find a deeper understanding of the corporeal impact architectural spaces have on the human body. Contemporary dance has the potential to serve as an effective technique to increase corporeal awareness and body-knowledge. In this respect, it is crucial to inquire how it can be made accessible as a tool to comprehend the sensory and corporeal agency of architectural spaces and the anticipation of their perception in the architectural design.

Theoretical and experiential examinations of the reciprocal interaction of architecture and corporeal spatial perception form the objective of this research. For a procedural and multisensory experience of space, the corporeality of the perceiver appears to be an indispensable prerequisite, as »there would be no space for me at all, if I had no body« (Merleau-Ponty 2003/1962 [1945]: 117). Moreover, this space only emerges to me when I conduct movement within it or refer to the memory of prior sensorimotor experience. Contemporary dance is a rich source to foster knowledge and understanding of the interdependence of body and space:

> »As a medium, dance needs the body, but its true media are space and time. Space and time are articulated for human beings by the medium of the body. Dance literally embodies space and time or rather the unity of space and time.« (Weibel 2014: 11)

In order to transition the bodily knowledge from contemporary dance into the discipline and discourse of architecture, the role of the body in the architectural realm needs to be specifically addressed. Key questions regarding the embodied dimension of perception and experience in architectural research are: How is the sensual and sensorimotor experience of architectural spaces constituted? How can the associative and tacit body knowledge of (previous) spatial explorations be made accessible for the architectural design? How can contemporary dance practices contribute to the anticipation and integration of future embodied, sensorimotor architecture experiences in the design process?

Hypothesis

In reference to the last question, the hypothesis of this research claims: The immanent knowledge of the body enables the anticipation of future architectural experience in the design process. Contemporary dance – and in particular the choreographic work and oeuvre of Sasha Waltz – exemplifies an attempt to make this tacit embodied knowledge explicit and available as a design tool. The tacit body-knowledge we bear in our memory from prior architectural encounters and tangible spatial contexts can be made available and accessible for the anticipation of architectural perception in the design process if we conceive the body as a medium and integrate body-based working methods into the discipline of architecture.

Methodologies, Approaches and Alignments

This research project is essentially divided into three sections: the theoretical framework of phenomenology and perception theory, the examination of Sasha Waltz's working methods and oeuvre as a case study, and the transfer knowledge from contemporary dance as a constituent component of the architectural design.

Phenomenological theory and concepts concerning the interrelation of body, movement, and space are reflected. The French movement in phenomenology is specifically referred to, as – opposed to its German counterpart – it accentuates fluid and motion-dependent interrelations between the individual and the living world, advocating an enactive and embodied approach to their reciprocal interconnection. Furthermore, recent findings from cognitive sciences, philosophy of embodiment, arts theory, and performance studies frame the project's theoretical horizon.

Sasha Waltz's oeuvre serves as an artistic exemplum to substantiate the theoretical considerations. Waltz's working method and selected works of hers with explicit relation to space are examined in regard to their adaptation of architectural spaces, both in-situ and on stage. The respective spatiality of their repertory of gesture and movement is explored correspondingly. Waltz's procedures of creation and her working methods are specifically addressed to extract a superordinate understanding of her choreographic investigation of space. Her work is examined with a particular emphasis on its emerging relationship with space. In addition, her genuine choreographic techniques are compared with design methods in architecture, to which they have a close affinity, as both draw from the visual arts, using drawings and sketches in the conception and to develop ideas. While the experiential, sensual, and corporeal knowledge of architectural spaces emanates from the means of contemporary dance and the work of Sasha Waltz & Guests, this research aims to reach further, incorporating the practices of contemporary dance and their respective embodied knowledge into the process of architectural design.

Aims and Objectives

Despite the transdisciplinary nature of this research project, the investigation is led with the expertise and from the perspective of an architect. The overarching aim is to consider the dynamic and enacting potential of architecture and the built environment and to integrate embodied knowledge and corporeal memory into the anticipation of future architectural experiences in the design process. Working methods and procedural techniques from contemporary dance are applied to architecture, seeking a profound understanding of sensorimotor perception. Thus, it is intended to align the spatial experience with an architecture that is conceived, designed, and created as an experiential space.

Embodiment, Experience, and Sensation

Research in architecture in regard to its perception depends upon a changing understanding of architecture itself. As it is regularly considered to constitute the matter framework of the man-made built environment – which serves as a vessel containing human action, adaption, and appropriation – its investigation under the premise of perception takes more elusive, immaterial phenomena into account. Considering the embodied, lived experience, and sensual effects of architectural spaces, the concept of architecture as the manifest world of solitary objects falters and is replaced by the subjectivity of the individual experience. Hence, the seemingly objective access to the architectural context becomes questionable.

Experience does not appear as a singular momentary incident, but is integrated into a superordinate context of individual memories, associations, and imaginations. The present sensations and perceptions evoked by an encounter with a specific space are interwoven with a lively and ever-changing assemblage of fragments from previous experiences. They correlate in imaginary projections, so that perceiving emulates an inventive and creative act of mental associations. »People say that life takes place. It is architects who make place. The architect's role is to give existence, or presence to the spaces that are the acts of our lives and the foundation of our memories. The very nature of such interactions with the world forms culture, cities, and dwelling« (Condia 2019: 183). Therefore, the architectural context is to be considered as an invitation for exploration and interaction, rather than the condition for adaption and appropriation, as it is considered in a static, vessel-like understanding of architecture. In this sense, architecture and its perceivers appear to be mutually dependent, as an interresponsive resonance is evoked between the two.

According to Harry Francis Mallgrave, this lively interaction draws reference to the philosophical term of the *Vita Activa,* which »in this sense entails not only making things but making experiences, which is the hallmark of our vital natures« (Mallgrave 2018: 130). This literal activation of architectural perception exposes the corporeality of the body as its medium:

> »The existentially most important knowledge of our everyday life [...] does not reside in detached theories and explanations, but in a silent knowledge that lied beyond the threshold of consciousness fused with the daily environmental and behavioural situations. [...] We experience a work of art or architecture through our embodied existence and identification.« (Pallasmaa 2001: 14–16)

The body-knowledge contributes to the conscious memory of the mind, as accordingly, »the experienced, remembered, and imagined are qualitatively equal experiences in our consciousness«, which is evident in the fact that »we may be equally moved by something evoked by the imagination as by the actually encountered« (Pallasmaa 2001: 18–20). Through the inscribed traces of previous experiences, the body becomes a lively archive that preserves past perceptions, integrates present sensations, and – against the background of this accumulated knowledge – constitutes the anticipation of future experience. It forms a bodily archive of experiences from encountered spatial situations. Through a deepened awareness of this corporeal repertory of pre-noetic memories, our bodies have the potential to become tools of anticipation. Architectural design requires preconceived knowledge to imagine its abstract conception on a one-to-one scale. Through our capacity to resonate and to empathize with our surrounding world, we are able to imagine its experiential appearance. The reference to prior lived experience, contained in our bodily memory, enables us to read architectural plans and to imagine their respective spatial qualities. Furthermore, the enactive attempt at a physical model – the sensual touch of its surfaces or moving about this scaled object of the intended spatial sequence – triggers a corporeal interaction, inviting the spectator to take up a position in relation to the object.

Taking into account the practice, work, and oeuvre of Sasha Waltz requires the personal archive of her spatial memory as well as her contribution to the constitution of future spatial and corporeal encounter. For Waltz, dance inevitably relates to space – on one hand in etymological sense of choreography as a corporeal engraving of space, and on the other hand in the sense in regard to the actual space within which the dance takes place and where certain aspects of an architecture are revealed by the means of dance. »Spaces, says Sasha Waltz, are the basis of her work, the starting point, the beginning« (Schlagenwerth 2008: 7); spatial gestures and figures of movement are inseparably interconnected and affect each other as interrelating counterparts. This intertwining between body and architecture, expansion and compression, is essential for the anticipation during the conceptual process. Unless we evoke actual experience, the architectural concept remains an abstract approximation outside of reality. A holistic attempt at architectural design requires the integration of its phenomenological qualities and its impetus for movement, interaction, and adaption as intrinsic aspects of its conceptual creation.

Conclusion

Often, the interrelation of architectural spaces and the human body remains unnoticed, as it affects us in a pre-noetic manner. Beyond our conscious recognition, it might even remain unaware. Despite the all-encompassing sensual experience of actual architectural encounter, it is a demanding challenge to highlight its constitutive parts in order to make them accessible for the design process. According to Alban Janson and Florian Tigges, spatial experience is an interplay between corporeal expansion and the impact of space on the body, as upon entering a space »our personal sphere, seeks to engage with the space« and we become aware of »how it expands either hesitantly or instantaneously, taking in the space and feeling it out or filling it up in its various directions and forms through the spatial extension of our own subjectivity.« (Janson/Tigges 2014 [2013]: 107).

In regard to the conceptual creation of architectural designs, this very impression of an actual encounter remains the most challenging to address. »As we enter the space, the space enters us, and the experience is essentially an exchange and fusion of the object and the subject«; Pallasmaa describes the all-encompassing effect that architectural encounters have on their perceivers (Pallasmaa 2014: 232). Vice-versa, »as the space enters us, we enter the space« as anticipation in the design process. This mutual condition illustrates the involvement of lived experience and corporeal encounter in actual architectural space, such as in its anticipation in the design process. Moreover, the intersubjectivity of experience in general and the distinct subjective, individual impression finds a nuanced differentiation in Pallasmaa's observation: As the individual object blurs to form the totality of an architectural expression, its perception includes both an individual, subjective attempt and an intersubjective, generic sensual encounter. In this sense, the body appears to be an »archive in motion«, an assemblage of lived experiences, embodied memory and associations (cf. Wehren 2016). Integrating the methodologies from contemporary dance and the work of Sasha Waltz into architectural research reveals the resemblance between the two disciplines. Procedural analogies become evident as commonalities; Waltz's in-situ *Dialogue* series exploits architecture's potential as the impulse to generate the movement figures inscribed into the space, whereas her productions rather highlight the reciprocal interrelation between the spatiality of the body and the corporeality of architecture. The adaptation of different locations in Berlin as venues and working spaces, has an influence on the development of the work. Each of the interim uses provides valuable impulses for the development of Sasha Waltz's work. By working in the respective spaces and elaborating site-specific performances for each venue, these places are closely linked to the development of the work.

Analogies between the figures of movement conducted in a particular space and the configurations and gestures initiated by the space itself are essential for the consideration of architecture as a realm of corporeal experience: One's own body is drawn upon as a medium of architectural experience. Aiming for corporeal access to the experience of architecture, we are eager to develop architectural designs that elicit the nuanced sensations of an actual experience already during the development process. Experiences of architecture indispensably depend upon an attentive body. As the transdisciplinary investigation of contemporary dance and architecture grants access to the body as a medium to experience space, it makes the tacit, pre-reflexive, body-based knowledge explicit and adaptable to the design. With the pronounced emphasis on Waltz's handling of architectural spaces, the procedural, multisensory, and sensorimotor dimensions of architectural perception are fostered. It is the aim of this research to exploit the potential held by the human body to experience the sensory aspects of architecture – including its memory, envisioning, and anticipation – in order to include its capacities and genuine knowledge in the repertoire of established cultural techniques of architectural design, such as sketching, drawing, model making, visualization or description.

References

Condia, Bob (2019): »What Architects Do: Construct Culture«, in: Alessandro Gattara/ Sarah Robinson/Davide Ruzzon (eds.), *Intertwining, Baukultur*, 02/2019, Mimesis International.

Mallgrave, Harry Francis (2018): *From Object to Experience: The New Culture of Architectural Design*, London: Bloomsbury Publishing.

Merleau-Ponty, Maurice [1945]: *Phénoménologie de la perception.* – English translation: *Phenomenology of Perception*, transl. by Colin Smith (2003 [1962]), London/New York: Routledge & Kegan Paul.

Pallasmaa, Juhani (2001): »Lived Space. Embodied Experience and Sensory Thought«, in: *The Visible and the Invisible*, OASE (58), Amsterdam: Sun Publishers, 13–34.

Pallasmaa, Juhani (2014): »Space, Place and Atmosphere. Emotion and Peripheral Perception in Architectural Experience«, in: *Lebenswelt: Aesthetics and Philosophy of Experience*, 230–245. doi: 10.13130/2240-9599/4202

Schlagenwerth, Michaela (2008): *Nahaufnahme Sasha Waltz. Gespräche mit Michaela Schlagenwerth*, Berlin: Alexander Verlag.

Weibel, Peter (2014): »Between ›Performative Turn‹ and ›Installative Turn‹«, in: Christiane Riedel/Yoreme Waltz/Peter Weibel (eds.), Sasha Waltz. *Installations, Objects, Performances.* Ostfildern: Hatje Cantz.

Wehren, Julia (2016): *Körper als Archiv in Bewegung. Choreographie als historiographische Praxis*, Bielefeld: transcript Verlag.

Researching Non-Conscious[1] Dimensions of Architectural Experience

Marcus Weisen

Editorial Summary: Entitled »Researching Non-Conscious Dimensions of Architectural Experience«, Marcus Weisen's contribution explores the investigation of pre-reflexive ways of knowing, sensory thought, and the embodied mind. He introduces the micro-phenomenological interview as a successful methodology to exploit immanent, non-conscious aspects of architectural experience. He emphasizes the relevance of investigating the individual, subjective perspective in architectural research, proposing the first-person description of experience as a starting point from which to derive insights into overarching, essential principles of lived experiences of, and encounters with, architectural spaces. Tracing the elusive, embodied dimensions of architectural experience, he aims for an »embodied rationalism« in architectural research. [Uta Graff]

Keywords: Unconscious; Pre-Reflective; Tacit; Lived Experience; Micro-Phenomenology; Experiential; Experimental; Research Methodology; Non-Dualistic Epistemology.

The Realm of Perception

The academic study of perception still focuses predominantly on the sense of sight and reflects the resilience of »ocularcentrism« in Western culture (Levin 1993). When, in 1961, Marshall McLuhan pointed to the need for »re-balancing the senses« (Howes 2004), immersive and installation art had already begun to shift the paradigm of what constitutes perception from sight toward bodily experience, a shift borne out in reflective artist practices and in art

---

1 In this article we use the term »non-conscious« to cover references in theoretical writings on architectural experience to pre-reflective and pre-reflexive experience (phenomenology) and unconscious experience (depth psychology, cognitive psychology). We are interested in particular in the possibilities of passage between e.g. pre-reflective experience and reflective thought.

Corresponding author: Marcus Weisen (École Normale Supérieure, Paris, France); marcus.weisen1@gmail.com
Open Access. © 2021 Marcus Weisen, published by transcript Verlag.
This work is licensed under the Creative Commons Attribution 4.0 (BY) license.

150 Marcus Weisen

»Unconscious and Conscious Interplays Between Experiencers and Architecture«
Steven Holl: Kiasma Museum, Helsinki, 1998.
Photographer: Marcus Weisen, 2016.

criticism. Architectural thinking, on the other hand, has been remarkably slow in engaging with multisensory lived bodily experience. Not until the 1990s did a noted momentum of reclaiming sensory experience in architectural discourse arise (Pérez-Gómez/Holl/Pallasmaa 1994). During the same decade, sensing and feeling (spüren) began to take center stage in emerging studies on urban and architectural atmospheres in Brazil, Germany, and France. »Everything suggests that we are witnessing an in-depth movement which reconfigures our ways of thinking today's ambient world [...] in every case it's about engaging with the question of experience and paying special attention to sensory perception« (Thibaud 2010).

Bodily experience, movement, peripheral vision, feeling and sensing are at the core of architectural experience and of feelings of rootedness and participation in the world (Pallasmaa 1996). A lived understanding of whole-body perception is therefore central to the design of nurturing and life-supporting environments. While architecture is undoubtedly enriched by academic disciplines that focus on the body, such as phenomenology, neurosciences and evolutionary biology, there is no better way to understand it than deliberate bodily engagement with the lived experience of architecture itself.

In architectural experience, sensory perception, memory, imagination, social imprint, emotion, cognitive processes, and incidental factors are intertwined. This highly complex experience resists investigation by the methods of the hard sciences – a view already expressed by Merleau-Ponty (Hahn 2017). Architectural experience is to a large extent unconscious, a point Pallasmaa has been making since 1980 (MacKeith 2005). This makes lived architectural experience very difficult to study. An implicit, widely held and largely unquestioned view discerns the boundaries rather than the possibilities of perception. There is ground for perceptual optimism, however. It is a common experience of artists, meditators, dancers, practitioners of yoga, Qigong, body therapies, and indeed, of any other form of practice, that the threshold of conscious perceiving and experiencing is lowered through a listening attitude.

The Research Project – The Quest for Architectural Encounter

This doctoral research project, to be completed in 2022, seeks to deepen the understanding of elusive and non-conscious dimensions of architectural encounter. In this research, perception is both a gateway and an inseparable part of architectural encounter. The term is sometimes used spontaneously by lovers of art and architecture to denote salient experiences of positive valence. It resists being defined. It refers to singular situated, sensory, emotional, and existential experiences of singular buildings and environments which are very difficult to convey. A description of architectural encounter is being evolved bottom-up from the interview materials. What happens, for example, when I enter a hospitable building? When I am inspired to joyfully run up the ramp at Steven Holl's Kiasma Museum? When a feeling of connection with the city and its people washes over me as I look out of a window at Peter Zumthor's Kolumba Museum? What happens to me, to the building, to the space in between?

This research project applies the micro-phenomenology interview developed by Claire Petitmengin in the late 1990s to architecture for the first time. It allows fleeting architectural experiences to become conscious to an extent that the hitherto little studied cultural, bodily, existential, and professional practice of sensing architecture would not on its own. Interviewees often make the startling observation that they can recall experiences of which they might not otherwise have become aware (Vermersch 2002).

The Significance of Researching Fleeting and Non-Conscious Architectural Encounter

In 1930, Alvar Aalto praised »the value of the fleeting moment« in domestic architecture (Schildt 1997). More recently, Pérez Gómez ascribed »essential architectural meaning« to elusive and largely pre-reflective architectural experiences (Pérez-Gómez 2016). Pallasmaa views the loss of fleeting and »unconscious architectural communication« as a root cause of the much critiqued inhumanity of modern architecture (Pallasmaa 1980, in: MacKeith 2005). In the absence of the affordance of such nurturing interrelationships, human beings »cannot thrive in [the architect's] house, its apparent beauty will be of no avail – without life it becomes a monstrosity« (Rasmussen 1959). A subtle and respectful conscious and unconscious understanding of the invisible textures and dynamics of architectural experience is then a prerequisite for the design of life-supporting environments.

Research Aims

The specific research objectives were to identify:

- How the findings of the empirical micro-phenomenological research supports, extends or varies from the architectural phenomenology of writers such as Juhani Pallasmaa;
- The design intentions and strategies of Peter Zumthor and material qualities of Kolumba Museum, the case-study building, which favours the emergence of encounter;
- The potential of the micro-phenomenology interview as a tool for knowledge creation in architecture.

Methodologies

In this research project, micro-phenomenology interviews are brought into dialogue with key texts from the phenomenology of architecture written by architects with a gift for evoking lived experiences. The materiality, presence, and agency of Kolumba Museum (2007) co-shapes the research.

Twenty-three interviewees gave a total of thirty interviews in three interview phases. Most interviewees were from the cultural professions (artists, arts managers, art historian, opera singer, composer, architect). Prior to the interview, they explored Kolumba at their own pace (40–75 minutes). They were briefed that the researcher was interested in what they sensed, felt, experienced or thought during the visit. In the interview, they first briefly described their experiences (5–10 minutes). A short salient experience was then selected for an in-depth interview (40–50 minutes). At the end of the micro-phenomenology interview, a semi-formal exchange took place, in which interviewees expressed their emerging thoughts and impressions regarding the experience and the building (10 minutes).

The Micro-Phenomenology Interview

»Becoming conscious of the pre-reflective part of our experience requires a break with our habitual attitude« (Petitmengin 2006). The micro-phenomenology interview leads the interviewee away from the natural habit of analyzing and evaluating. Instead, it prompts the verbalization of concrete lived experiences. The interviewee is guided to evoke a past experience, recalling it in its bodily and sensory dimensions. Empirical micro-phenomenology studies a wide range of lived experiences academically, such as meditation, the visual arts, depression, children's play, and the patient-doctor relationship.[2]

Methodological Alignments and Divergences

Micro-phenomenology is a second- and first-person research method. It has affinity with research methods in environmental and architectural phenomenology (Seamon 2000) and with experiential research methods applied to multisensory urban and architectural ambiances (Thibaud 2015).

Inherent to research on encounter is the quest for research methods suitable for epistemologies that bridge the subject-object divide and seek to evolve knowledges of being with, rather than the distant knowledge of. These have existed for millennia in meditative, somatic, craft and design practices, and are being developed within academic fields, not least in the domain of urban and architectural ambiances. Feminist theorist Karen Barad proposes touch as a paradigm for knowledge (Barad 2015).

Rather than treating interviewees as purveyors of »information«, this research project approaches the deep well of their embodied experiences with the same respect with which it seeks to approach the building. And Kolumba Museum, a work of great complexity, is being approached in a way similar to a literary work. At the edge of extreme rigour, the hermeneutics of empathy of literary critic Jean Starobinski acknowledge the knowledge-benefit of surrendering to the work (Starobinksi 1961).

In contrast to neurosciences, which develop knowledge by extreme reduction of parameters in laboratory experiments, this project embraces the multifactorial complexity of situated architectural experience as the life-ground of enquiry.

Emerging Lessons for Architectural Research and Practice
Provisional Findings and the Space Opened by Surprise

To provide an insight into the interpretive work building up from reflection on concrete architectural experiences, we briefly summarize and discuss a few interviewee experiences here:

---

2 Cf. www.microphenomenology.com

a.) a European immigrant to Cologne (Köln) makes the joyful realization that she belongs to Cologne's deep history as she walks past a lone-standing case with Colonia-style Roman glassware toward the large window bay nearby. She is then overcome by a feeling of happiness. She speaks to herself: »I am of Köln. I am here, simply here«.

b.) a stressed opera singer anticipates that nothing much will come of her visit. Then, on the second floor, she feels that the building is there for her personally. As she looks out of a window bay down to the street where people are walking in the rain with and without umbrellas, she feels a strong connection to all people in the world.

c.) an architect enters the museum with a sense of sadness and thoughts of his departed mother. The feeling is amplified in the foyer at the sight of a big flower vase. The sadness starts to dissolve in the vast space of Roman excavations at the sight of the warm glow of a red brick in the medieval wall – rounded by erosion and lit up by the sun through a small fissure in the wall.

d.) an arts manager sometimes visits Kolumba to restore herself. In interview, she describes the healing presence of the *Reading Room*. She evokes the bodily feeling of her back »straightening up« on her previous visit as she mounts her bike outside the museum.

Several interviewees experienced joy, happiness, and gratitude, which are bodily-mental states (e.g. example a.). This surprised the researcher, as these themes are only vaguely treated in critical literature. Descriptions of concrete experiences of improved wellbeing (c. and d.) are a rarity in architectural thinking. The experience of the straightened back invites comparisons with Pallasmaa's 1999 descriptions of the sense of verticality and dignity afforded to humans beings by living architectures (MacKeith 2005). Experiences a. and b. constitute lived evidence of the capacity of resonant architecture to enhance the sense of self and participation in the world (Pallasmaa 1996).

A few of the interviewees described discreet, yet powerful symbolic experiences. Standing on the top of the lofty staircase on her way down, an interviewee saw herself fly. Another one felt the sensation of being in a whale's body. One interviewee felt walking through narrow *Room 20* to high *Room 21* as a journey through a birth canal. Such experiences are rarely documented.

They are flickery events that become more visible in micro-phenomenological interviews. We should assume them to be meaningful.

Experiences a. and b. helped identify Kolumba windows as »attractors of experience«. This prompted the researcher to re-read Pallasmaa's various writings on the power of »primary architectural images« (e.g. Pallasmaa 2002), such as the door, stairs, and window to engage unconscious experiences. This, in turn, re-directed the focus to Zumthor's unusual skill in designing such primary architectural images. This again, turns attention to their rootedness in the pre-reflective embodied memories of the architect's childhood experiences (Zumthor 1998). The meaningful existential experiences made at Kolumba's windows evidence the successful communication of Zumthor's design intention to enhance the visitors' relationship to the city.

Relevance of Micro-Phenomenology for Perception- and Experience-Based Research in Architecture

Micro-phenomenology helps fine-tune descriptions of the complex reality of the interplays between the experiencer and architectural form, materiality, presence, and atmosphere.

The evocation of lived experience renders material texture to existential person-place encounter. It makes it more visible and eliminates the abstraction of philosophical and scientific discourse without denying its value.

Micro-phenomenology in architecture is, of course, still very much at a pioneering stage. As a transversal method, however, it has been applied in academic research and educational practice for more than three decades. As it develops, it can in principle, be applied to widen concrete understanding of every aspect of architectural experience and embodied knowledge, e.g. of:

- The experiential dynamics of healing architectures and of inhospitable architectures;
- The barely communicable felt experiences of »ordinary« architecture for the everyday;
- The numerous tacit knowledges which underpin the effectiveness of the architect's professions;
- the unconscious and intuitive dimensions of the design process. Alvar Aalto, Juhani Pallasmaa, Alvaro Siza, Peter Zumthor, and Francesca Torzo (Torzo 2018) provide singular fragmentary, yet arresting insights into creative design processes, which deserve respectful study;

- Sensing competences in architectural education and in innovative professional training. Even the simple experience of being interviewed in the micro-phenomenology method heightens awareness of perception and helps expand perceptual skills.

For an Embodied Rationalism in Architectural Research

The present research project is one of a growing number of projects that analyze elusive embodied and infra-verbal architectural experiences. This field is currently experiencing an evolution of methodologies, such as urban walking, urban choreographies, and dance, as well as sensory and bodily experimentation. Such projects rank first-person experience as a central component and seek to overcome the methodological confines inherited by Cartesian subject-object dualism, which has long been philosophically and scientifically defeated.

Thibaud is among the few scholars to develop a meta-discourse on methodologies for researching elusive and largely unconsciously experienced architectural atmospheres. »If ambiances are currently developing into a research domain, they in turn question the scientific paradigms on which we lean to study them« (Thibaud 2015). From this, he draws a logical conclusion: »Setting off on the quest for ambiances means finally accepting to explore new tools of investigation, new forms of knowledge and categories of analysis«. He even recognizes the need for »risking new forms of writing«.

At a time when the lid on tacit knowledge, and on unconscious and intuitive experience, is being lifted in architectural discourse dominated for decades by a narrow »techno-rationalism« (Williams Goldhagen 2008), we may look back for roots of this thinking and practice in the traditions of architectural thought. Aalto's 1935 vision of an »extended rationalism« furtively sketched out in his short article »Rationalism and Man« (Schildt 1997) deserves a reappraisal. Aalto held intuition in high respect. »An analytical, rational approach to the multiplicity of human needs [...] ›can be adopted also in architecture‹. Nevertheless, ›there will always be more of instinct and art‹ in this process – intuition, he asserted elsewhere, ›can be astonishingly rational‹« (Williams Goldhagen 2008, quoting Aalto).

An extended rationalism irrigated by intuition in architectural research, which seeks a more fluid passage between pre-reflective experience and conscious thought, seeks to make the tacit more explicit and values first-person experience as integral to research, is a rationalism transformed. It is an embodied rationalism (Williams Goldhagen 2008) which sensitively tunes into the subtle life-textures of hospitable and health-supporting architectures and the project processes that generate these. It is dedicated to research as a way of getting in touch.

References

Barad, Karen (2015): »The Inhuman That Therefore I Am«, in: *Difference: A Journal of Feminist Cultural Studies* 3(23).

Hahn, Achim (2017): *Architektur und Lebenspraxis: Für eine phänomenologisch-hermeneutische Architekturtheorie*, Bielefeld: transcript Verlag.

Howes, David, ed. (2004): *Empire of the Senses: The Sensual Culture Reader*, London: Berg Publishers.

Levin, David Michael, ed. (1993): *Modernity and the Hegemony of Vision*, Berkeley: University of California Press.

MacKeith, Peter/Pallasmaa, Juhani, eds. (2005): *Encounters: Juhani Pallasmaa: Architectural Essays*, Helsinki: Rakennustieto.

Pallasmaa, Juhani (1996): *The Eyes of the Skin: Architecture and the Senses*, Chichester, UK: John Wiley & Sons.

Pallasmaa, Juhani (2002): »Primary Architectural Images«, in: *School of Architecture*, St. Louis: Washington University in St. Louis.

Pérez Gómez, Alberto/Holl, Steven/Pallasmaa, Juhani (1994): *Questions of Perception: Phenomenology of Architecture*, San Francisco: William Stout.

Pérez Gómez, Alberto (2016): *Attunement: Architectural Meaning after the Crisis of Modern Science*, Cambridge, MA: The MIT Press.

Petitmengin, Claire (2006): »Describing One's Subjective Experience in the Second Person: An Interview Method for the Science of Consciousness«, in: *Phenomenology and the Cognitive Sciences*, 5(3–4), 229–269.

Rasmussen, Steen Eiler (1959): *Experiencing Architecture*, Cambridge, MA: MIT Press.

Schildt, Göran (1997): *Alvar Aalto in His Own Words*, Helsinki: Otava.

Seamon, David (2000): »A Way of Seeing People and Place«, in: Seymour Wapner/Jack Demick/Takiji Yamamoto/Hirofumi Minami (eds.), *Theoretical Perspectives in Environment-Behavior Research*, New York: Plenum.

Starobinksi, Jean (1961): *L'oeil vivant*, Paris: Gallimard.

Thibaud, Jean-Paul (2010): »La ville à l'épreuve des sens«, https://halshs.archives-ouvertes.fr/halshs-00502591/document, accessed January 12, 2021.

Thibaud, Jean-Paul (2015): *En quête d'ambiances, éprouver la ville en passant*, Genève: Métis Presses.

Torzo, Francesca (2018): »Paraphrasing Virginia Woolf for Freespace«, Biennale di Architettura 2018, https://youtu.be/--ju_d7CTNM, accessed January 12, 2021.

Williams Goldhagen, Sarah (2008): »Ultraviolet: Alvar Aalto's Embodied Rationalism«, in: *Harvard Design Magazine*, 27.

Zumthor, Peter (1998): *Architektur Denken*, Baden: Verlag Lars Müller. – English translation: *Thinking Architecture*, Baden: Verlag Lars Müller, 1998.

Archival Research
Ferdinand Ludwig

The investigation, categorization and evaluation of historical sources such as bequests, reports, plans or norms forms the basis of archival methods, which are – along with others – part of most research projects in the field of architecture. In fact, even typical design projects often include some basic forms of archival studies. For instance, in-depth research of the history of a site is an essential prerequisite for any context-specific design. According to the architectural theorist Albena Yaneva »buildings are not limited to their static appearance in Cartesian space but dynamic, hybrid entities reaching far beyond built form« (Yaneva 2012).

Ferdinand Ludwig

Digging deep in architectural archives may reveal that systems of regulations, codes, and order play a more important role than we, as designers, might be willing to admit. Our architectural world might be shaped much more by such systems than by the individual »heroes« of modern architecture we admire. This insight is particularly important in the context of »Research Perspective in Architecture« because researching architects may well be talented designers, but they should never classify themselves as genius – because this self-image makes any scientific questioning of their own design work impossible (see chapter »Reflections«). As the contributions to this chapter show, this may lead to relativize the role of well-known architects, but also to discover and honor completely forgotten or unknown designers.

Archival Research   161

Archival research is not understood here in the sense of classical architectural history, in which historical knowledge represents an intrinsic value. Rather, the aim is to explore the potential cross-fertilization between research methods that deal with historical documents and architectural design. Often, archival documents are available only to a limited extent and archival records give information only in context – and therefore require the designer's interpretation. Therewith, archival research can be understood as research by the designer, closely linked to, and synergistically influenced by, design practice.

References

Alasuutari, Pertti (2010): »The Rise and Relevance of Qualitative Research«, in: *International Journal of Social Research Methodology* 13(2), 139–155.

What the Files Reveal:
Making Everyday Architecture Talk

Benedikt Boucsein

Editorial Summary: Typically, design projects leave traces in building archives. Benedikt Boucsein sees great potential in this practice, as it can be used for a research methodology that explores archival material from the designer's perspective, especially for work that is otherwise not archived. In his text Benedikt Boucsein illustrates this through the example from everyday architecture of the reconstruction period after World War II, which he denominated as ›»Grey Architecture«. One major insight of this research was that the building files were more important for the research than the actual buildings, and that working in the archive helped make this particular architecture »speak« for the first time, unveiling how the built environment is produced. He concludes that archival material may, especially for everyday architecture, be more important than the actual building, and that the designer's view is decisive in understanding this material. [Ferdinand Ludwig]

Keywords: Everyday Architecture; Grey Architecture; Building Archive; Reconstruction; Mode; Representation.

Building Files and the Specific View of the Designer

According to the architectural theorist Albena Yaneva, buildings are not limited to their static appearance in Cartesian space. Rather, she describes them as dynamic, hybrid entities reaching far beyond the built form.[1]

---

[1] Yaneva· »A building or any other architectural work – master plan, design proposal, development strategy – is not a coherent and self-contained entity placed in a space, designed in an architectural practice, built on a site; it is rather a dynamic network of real entities. Defined on the basis of numerous situations of coexistence of these entities, it is made of many spatial pluralities as they enfold in time. It is hybrid and ›could be understood as the intersection of a range of forces, from political to the natural, from the real to the metaphorical. A balance, indeed, of colossal forces‹ (Till 2009: 56)« (Yaneva 2012: 107). See also: Latour/Yaneva 2008.

Corresponding author: Benedikt Boucsein (Technical University of Munich, Germany); boucsein@tum.de; http://orcid.org/0000-0001-7894-9513
Open Access. © 2021 Benedikt Boucsein, published by transcript Verlag.
This work is licensed under the Creative Commons Attribution 4.0 (BY) license.

Buildings exist equally in representations such as plans, renderings, and photographs, and a building's physical form cannot be understood separately from these media.

With regard to the archive, Yaneva's hypothesis is highly interesting: It assigns the archival material a role that can be equal to or even more important than that of the actual building. Accordingly, it seems worthwhile to put Yaneva's hypothesis at the beginning of a reflection that analyzes the archive for architectural research.

In doing so, this text will focus particularly on the role and potential of building file archives.[2] Building files on a parcel's development are stored with the local building authorities and are an independent source of information that represent the building itself in a different way. Depending on the complexity of a project's history, these archives can contain numerous plans, as each building application is contained within them. They can also contain correspondence between the architect and the authorities, between the authorities themselves, or copies of relevant official decrees.

In particular, the text will focus on how the building file archive can be made fruitful for research on everyday architecture. Here, building files are especially valuable, as the design of the actual built structures is not explained through its formal appearance: They are predominantly shaped by external influences and not by formal criteria. Further, the protagonists of such buildings usually leave few written traces, and private archives or interviews are rare. Accordingly, the design decisions of these builders and architects have to be tracked, for example, by tracing modifications in the archival material, or by comparing building files from several houses in the same street. The material can help answer questions such as if all overarching rules were respected, if parts of preceding projects were kept and adapted, if there were choices that seem to have been arbitrary as they were changed in the next instance, et cetera. Read this way, the building files can help reveal valuable information about a specific building. As an example for everyday architecture strongly reflected in building archives, the text will

---

2 This text is based on a notion of »building« in cultures where building file archives play an important role, as opposed to vernacular architecture, for instance. Here, oral tradition takes over the role of the archive: Certain properties of vernacular architecture are only understandable when taking this tradition into account, they are in Yaneva's sense inherently connected to it.

focus on the everyday architecture of the West German reconstruction era after World War II.

Finally, in the context of this volume, a further goal of the text concerns a better understanding the potential of the architect's perspective in such an analysis. When working in the archive, the archival material speaks to the architect as traces of another architect's design efforts – the result of processes that are inherent to the core of the discipline and have been intensively trained during studies and in practice. It can be assumed that this particular viewpoint of the designer enables them to better understand how these components of the built environment were formed, but it has to be better understood how exactly this can take place.

The Case: West Germany's Grey Architecture

Considering its visual omnipresence in West German cities, the everyday architecture of the reconstruction period after World War II (ca. 1945–1965), denoted »Grey Architecture« by the author,³ had been ignored by research for a surprisingly long period. While the general circumstances of post-war reconstruction, which probably represents the greatest collective building effort of the 20th century (Tönnesmann, in: Boucsein 2010: 7), are well known, the character of the everyday architecture of that period has only been more closely regarded during the last decade. Before, it seems to have been generally regarded as a non-architectural side product unworthy of attention. And indeed, it was produced under significantly distinct conceptions compared to those valued and practiced in the »high« architecture of the time that was discussed in magazines and other publications. To the university-educated designer, this architecture is opaque, or mute.

Obtaining an »Architectural Definition«. The Role of the Archive

According to Christian Norberg-Schulz, the main problem of building history and theory is the question: Why does a building from a specific epoch have a certain appearance? (Norberg-Schulz 1965: 20) To answer this question for the particularly difficult case of West Germany's Grey Architecture,

---

3 Two main studies were conducted on the theme: A PhD project from 2005–2008 at the ETH Zurich (Boucsein 2010) and as part of the research project »Städtebau der Normalität« at the TU Dortmund from 2012–2014 (Boucsein 2018).

the chosen research method can best be described as a mixture of historical, urbanistic and architectural approaches. The first study, conducted from 2005 to 2007, included working with primary sources, such as interviews and archival plan material, through formal analysis of selected buildings, secondary literature dealing with the urbanistic developments of the time, as well as grey literature from the post-war era. The study centered on a particular case study, the city center of Essen.

Building on the knowledge gained in the first study, the second, smaller study, conducted from 2012 to 2014, focused on the analysis of building files corresponding to a particular street in the center of Essen and the resulting discovery of a small private archive of a particular architect. This study reinforced and further refined the architectural definition formulated in the previous study.

In the context of both studies, the work in the archive (mainly the administrative building file archive, although some files were retrieved from the city's historical archive) did not follow any predefined methodological procedure. In principle, every plan in the building files of the selected streets was examined from front to back. Short summaries of the respective building histories were produced while going through the files. Important facts, dates, and names were noted for later reference. Plans that seemed important to understand the development of the project were scanned or photographed and then filed electronically. If an open question remained about specific themes later on, the according files were reviewed in the archive.

Once filed electronically, the plans could be interpreted in a number of ways typical to the designer's perspective. For example, the facades of the approved projects in a certain street were combined in a number of different ways, demonstrating how the street elevations emerged during the reconstruction period and explaining their peculiar appearance. It was possible to reconstruct how the window formats followed the fashion of the respective decade quite directly. And formerly unexplainable facades and floor plans were better understood by analyzing the emergence of a project from the remains of the preceding building, thereby layering the relevant documents over each other.

By analyzing the different sources and connecting the knowledge gained in the archive to multiple other sources, an »architectural definition« to answer Norberg-Schulz's question was formulated. Central to this was the description of the Grey Architects' design method: It was analyzed as additive, contextual, and referential. The Grey Architects did indeed follow a design method, though it was fundamentally different from that of »high« architecture.

Hypothesis: Grey Architecture as a Mode

While the importance of Grey Architecture as everyday architecture of the German reconstruction period had been the motivation for the initial study, it had started from a typological viewpoint. In the course of the research, however, it became clear when employing the historical-urbanistic-architectural approach that Grey Architecture is not a type, but rather a mode (from modus operandi). Subsequently, mode became the guiding hypothesis to understand Grey Architecture.

Mode as a concept to describe architecture is still a marginal notion that has only gained more attention since the beginning of the century – surprisingly, as it is fundamentally important for a deeper understanding of architecture. As Yaneva explains: »if we consider architecture as a mode of activity, we cannot divide and subdivide its objects in styles, design principles and architectural languages. We can only follow the differentiation of the activity into different modes as it impinges on different materials and employs different media« (Yaneva 2012: 108). In a first attempt of systematization, Kimmo Lapintie, turning to the philosophical field of modal logic for reference, lists possibility, necessity, knowledge, and belief, as well as the obligatory and permitted as modal notions (Lapintie 2007: 38). Independent from these studies, different modal conditions were carved out in the study on Grey Architecture: Technology (e.g. infrastructure or building technologies), economy (e.g. ownership, labor costs), society (e.g. networks, fashions), planning (e.g. power of authorities, parcellation), and legislation (e.g. building laws and masterplans).

Looking at these conditions, it becomes clear that external circumstances play a dominant role in how architecture is produced: The modal perspective shows that architecture is not primarily the product of the architect's will, but rather strongly depends on external circumstances (Boucsein 2012). As Jeremy Till states, »architecture is [...] shaped more by external conditions than by the internal processes of the architect. Architecture is defined by its very contingency, by its very uncertainty in the face of these outside forces« (Till 2009: 1) – a property of architecture that is often forgotten both in education and research.

It must be noted, though, that the notion of mode has a different significance for »high« architecture than for everyday architecture. In »high« architecture, modal conditions are usually perceived as something that must be overcome through the power of design. Accordingly, these architects often strive to at least partially conceal modal conditions and react to them by appropriate design methods, as Reyner Banham reflected in his essay »A Black Box. The Secret Profession of Architecture« (Banham 1996). This is also possible because »high« architecture is usually not as strongly influenced by external conditions as everyday architecture: Due to specific client-architect relationships, less restrictive budgets, or resources of the architects, external modal conditions can be transformed in the design process in a subtle, complex, and more elaborate way.

Everyday architecture, in contrast, does not work against the strong modal conditions it is subjected to. It does not have the means, resources, and mandate to do so. Rather, it works with the conditions in an affirmative manner, translating them directly into architecture.

In this light, everyday architecture in general and West German Grey Architecture in particular can best be understood and analyzed as a mode – as the product of strong external post-war conditions, which are directly reflected in built form, but also the result of a specific education, as well as client expectations. All of these factors are reflected quite clearly in the building files that were examined in the course of the study.

The Archive: A Piece of the Puzzle

Working in the archive was a decisive component of the research on Grey Architecture: It helped make this particular architecture »speak« for the first time. In hindsight, the files served as the most important anchor in the research. Working in the files also delivered certain unforeseeable results, influencing the direction of research in an unplanned manner.

As it was especially decisive for the research to constantly shift the scales of observation, the building files served as an anchor. By linking the information from conventional secondary sources (as well as Grey Literature from the local context of the city of Essen, gathered from other occasionally obscure municipal archives and libraries) to what could be observed on the block and building scale, it was possible to contextualize the way in which post-war architects worked with (and often also against) the authorities. Interviews with persons that had experienced the reconstruction period were also used to contextualize what was observed in the building files. At the same time, the building files served as the best material to test central hypotheses, as they represented the actual development of these particular buildings at that particular time.

Working in the building files also led to surprising insights that further informed the direction of the research. For instance, in the second research project dealing with the most important shopping street in the city of Essen, reviewing every building file in that street revealed that large parts of it had been built by the same architect, Hans Engels, whose name is today completely forgotten. By locating his daughter, it was possible to retrieve a small, largely photographic documentation of his work. His activity, interrupted by a premature death, proved to be quite extensive, extending throughout Western Germany and incorporating diverse tasks such as social housing, commercial buildings, parking garages, and office parks. Furthermore, internal documents between the authorities regarding their experiences with Hans Engels were found in the building files: They revealed that he worked almost ruthlessly and solely in the interest of his clients, sometimes starting to build before having been granted permission. The example of Hans Engels shows that working with building files can uncover the history of individual architects who influenced the everyday architectural production of that time, helping to understand how such architects worked.

In hindsight, it appears that the building files were more important for research than the actual buildings. This reaffirms Yaneva's hypothesis about buildings as hybrid, dynamic entities: Depending on the research question, other aspects of these entities come into the foreground. The archive additionally helped maintain a certain level of abstraction and distance from the object of study. Surely the research would have taken a different direction if it focused on the material aspects of the respective buildings, such as their details, building materials, and atmospheres.

Making Everyday Architecture Talk

Reviewing the study on West Germany's Grey Architecture from the perspective of the archive reaffirms Yaneva's hypothesis that buildings are dynamic/hybrid entities reaching far beyond their actual built form. In consequence, this also means that there is no clear duality of existence / non-existence for buildings, but that they undergo different stages of existence. This is especially important for everyday architecture, which is often continually modified throughout the years, making the notion of an »original« secondary. It must be noted here that most of the authors of this architecture would agree to this, as they viewed their work as pragmatic and provisional responses to a state of emergency after the war, and as they usually did not attach importance to notions of authorship.

Moreover, it can be concluded that, as the built object decreases in importance as a type, or as a material form, and as its networked and temporal character increases in significance, mode as a category becomes more central in understanding it. The notion of mode relates to the time frame as well as to the multiple thematic connections that everyday architecture has to the economic, legal, technological, and societal influences around it. To gain this modal information, the archival material holds a central significance, as it helps explain influences and decisions. Nevertheless, this can never happen in an isolated way. More information is always necessary to be able to understand mode and modal conditions. The archive can serve as an anchor for gaining knowledge, but it can never be the only source.

Regarding the role of everyday architecture in the city, reflection from the perspective of archival research evidences that this architecture is not to be read as a concrete architectural object, but as a more complex and multifaceted matter. In terms of preservation, for instance, one conclusion may be that it does not necessarily correspond to the nature of everyday architecture to preserve the original buildings. It may be more important to secure typological aspects of the building, in addition to issues such as ownership and production methods. Furthermore, plans and photographs that are stored in public or private archives are valuable, as they can give substantiated information on modal conditions and modal practice. The built form, which has usually been continuously modified throughout the years, becomes less important than the representations that can explain everyday architecture through its modal conditions.

Finally, although archival work is usually not part of an architect's education, students should proactively work in the archive according to their training as designers – and not try to be something else. The designer's view is decisive in understanding mode and modal conditions. It enables them to make the archival material productive for research, to reconstruct design decisions, interventions from the clients and authorities, and the pressure of external circumstances – and to make the everyday architecture, which is often so hard to decipher, talk to us.

References

Handbuch der Essener Statistik, Essen: Stadt Essen.

Banham, Reyner (1996): »A Black Box – The Secret Profession of Architecture«, in: Reyner Banham, edited by Mary Banham, *A Critic Writes: Essays*, Berkeley: University of California Press.

Boucsein, Benedikt (2010): *Graue Architektur – Bauen im Westdeutschland der Nachkriegszeit*, Cologne: Verlag der Buchhandlung Walter König.

Boucsein, Benedikt (2012): »Ohne Modus keine Architektur«, in: *archithese* 6,2012, 2.

Boucsein, Benedikt (2018): »Die nördliche Innenstadt um die Limbecker Straße in Essen. Die Alltagsarchitektur der Einkaufsstadt«, in: Wolfgang Sonne/Regina Wittmann (eds.), *Städtebau der Normalität. Der Wiederaufbau urbaner Stadtquartiere im Ruhrgebiet*, Berlin: DOM Publishers, 156–179.

Lapintie, Kimmo (2007): »Modalities of Urban Space«, in: *Planning Theory* 6(1).

Latour, Bruno/Yaneva, Albena (2008): »Give me a Gun and I will Make All Buildings Move: An ANT's View of Architecture«, in: Urs Staub/Reto Geiser (eds.), *Explorations in Architecture: Teaching, Design, Research*, Basel: Birkhäuser, 80–89.

Norberg-Schulz, Christian (1965): *Logik der Baukunst*, Berlin: Ullstein.

Till, Jeremy (2009): *Architecture Depends*, Cambridge, MA: MIT Press.

Tönnesmann, Andreas (2010): »Vorwort«, in: Benedikt Boucsein, *Graue Architektur – Bauen im Westdeutschland der Nachkriegszeit*, Cologne: Verlag der Buchhandlung Walter König.

Yaneva, Albena (2012): *Mapping Controversies in Architecture*, Farnham, UK: Ashgate.

Architectural Drawings:
Teaching and Understanding a Visual Discipline

Peter Schmid

Editorial Summary: Professional drawing has always played an important role in the training of architects. Plan-drawings have already been sufficiently considered in established architectural research. The research of Peter Schmid presented in this text focuses on so far only scarcely examined architectural sketchbooks as well as various records used for architectural education, such as manuscripts for lectures or notes on perspective theory which belong to the »Munich School« – a tradition of teaching hand-drawing that developed over a period of 150 years through an on-going teacher-student relationship at the Technical University of Munich. He finds that the aim of »Munich School« was not only learning how to illustrate, but also to comprehend architecture through graphic analysis – thereby combining teaching and practice. Against the background that the interest in hand-drawings has significantly increased in recent years, the research helps to refine the role of hand-drawings today as a tool that sets »processes of cognition in motion«. [Ferdinand Ludwig]

Keywords: Sketchbook; Freehand Drawing; Architectural Education; »Münchner Zeichenschule«; Architecture Projection; Perspective Drawing; Analytical Drawing; Friedrich von Thiersch; Hans Döllgast.

The Architectural Drawing as a Profession-Specific »Know-How«

Rem Koolhaas recently put forward the thesis that contemporary architects still work in the same way today as they did during the Renaissance (Michaelsen 2018). A provocative claim, which could immediately be countered by the ease of work and tools provided by the rapidly advancing technical achievements of the digital turn. Koolhaas, however, does not refer to the external circumstances of the working world, but to a certain aspect of designing architecture, which he calls the thinking of »beauty«. Indeed, it seems difficult to imagine that the use of digital tools or the application of Building Information Modeling (BIM) alone is a guarantee of »beauty« in

Corresponding author: Peter Schmid (Technical University of Munich, Germany); peter.schmid@tum.de
Open Access. © 2021 Peter Schmid, published by transcript Verlag.
This work is licensed under the Creative Commons Attribution 4.0 (BY) license.

architectural design. Koolhaas alludes to the theories that have described the thought processes amidst the emergence of architecture since early modern times. In the Renaissance, with the disegno-theories, architects established a body of thought on architectural design in which drawing – or the ability to sketch – was attributed an essential role. The architects of the Renaissance, above all Giorgio Vasari, viewed drawing as a space of possibility which served the creative architect to successively materialize an initially vague idea in a line graphic in order to be able to judge the basic idea – concetto – and to finally transform it into perfect beauty according to the rules of art (Vasari 2012: 98).[1] In fact, the sketch, along with the model, is still a tool that is used today in connection with serious architectural design. Regardless of the external form, whether analogue or digital, the ability to sketch spatial situations is a fundamental requirement for creative work in architecture. The processes that take place during the development of spatial ideas in drawings are procedures which, in the case of practicing architects, mature into schematic experiences, or, in other words, into a »procedure know-how« that is difficult for outsiders to understand or comprehend.

Conversely, it is therefore a logical conclusion that this »know-how« on the part of the insiders is also a basic prerequisite for the scientific description and processing of sketches and architectural drawings. In all scientific disciplines, the direct professional affiliation of the researchers is of course relevant. Even interdisciplinary research projects pursue the method of only one specialist science as a common basis and formulate only one research question which is tailored to the needs of the discipline and whose results are important not only from the point of view of the researcher but above all for the practical user.

In the field of architecture, an important part of the research has long been undertaken by art and architectural historians. This highly specialized discipline is devoted exclusively to research. Other than the architects themselves, art historians take an outside perspective and observe the work of practical architects from a distance. Thereby, they aim to make their research as objective as possible in the first place. The perspective of

---

1 In chapter 15 of Vasari's Book *On Painting* the disegno ist described as: »And since from this knowledge a certain idea and judgement emerges, which in the mind forms the thing that is later designed by hand and then called a drawing, one may conclude that disegno is nothing different than a descriptive imagination, which shows the initially vague idea, that was formed by thoughts, and finally appears as a visible idea« (Vasari 2012 [1550]: 98).

the designing and practicing architect is therefore often lacking – especially in historic reseach. In this respect, art history follows a purely theoretical method, which is based on the scientific understanding of the subject. In simple terms, the questions develop from previous theoretical constructs of thought or theses, which are plausibly substantiated or refuted with the help of archival or textual sources. The highest goal to be achieved is therefore not a definitive statement from the outset, but plausibly argued theories. Although the schism of architectural research and architectural practice undisputedly leads to professional specialization and optimization on both sides, it also obviously requires a constant exchange between the two related disciplines.

Research Field of Architectural Education

In the particular thematic area concerning the subject of sketching or architectural drawing, art history has developed into an independent field of research, hitherto it remains largely closed to architects. Normally, the research culminates in classical catalogues raisonnés on an architect or a group. However, the subject of drawing lessons and even the elaboration of processual sequences during the creation of a drawing are also undertaken within these research projects. The increasing interest in strategies for teaching drawing from the side of art history and art studies has led to numerous survey works in recent years, which have been produced at the University of Hamburg and the Central Institute of Art History in Munich. They do not exclusively pursue a study of history, but also use the knowledge of the observed teaching methods to discuss controversial current concepts and pose questions for the future.

What remains unanswered, however, are the questions regarding the significance of the research efforts for contemporary architecture, or of the transfer of the results into current architectural practice.

For the scientific examination of the drawing theory of the so-called »Munich School«, the question concerning the current possibilities of using the research results for current teaching was decisive from the very beginning and prioritized the question of the methodological approach. The research was directed at educational strategies for teaching the arts at the Technical University in Munich over a period of 150 years ending with the present day.

The Munich lessons in architectural drawing are directly related to the name of its most famous representative, Hans Döllgast,[2] whose freehand-drawings have a high recognition value due to his distinct personal handwriting. Döllgast's teaching, in conjunction with his special style, resulted in the drawing method first being known as the »Munich School«, which already received national attention during his lifetime. He also developed a simple and very instructive teaching method for linear drawing in his lessons, which he presented in several publications toward the end of his teaching. The teaching concept was widely accepted in professional circles and still forms the basis of freehand-drawing lessons in many places today. Hans Döllgast's enormous influence on the »Munich drawing school« is also expressed in the unofficial, but common, designation as »Döllgast School«. It is one of the privileges of the »Munich School«, that until today we can still refer to his teaching methods from the drawing textbooks, which are still in use and form a fundamental foundation for freehand-drawing.

Döllgast's work now dates back more than 60 years. Currently, freehand-drawing and sketching play a rather subordinate role in the architects' timetable. Compared to the considered period of the 150 years of existence of the »Munich School«, today's teaching is subject to completely different conditions and has inevitably changed considerably. The digital turn from the 1990s onwards has finally made freehand-drawing in architecture an exception. In many other universities, the unrestricted belief in progress based on digital possibilities even led to the discontinuation of analogue drawing lessons, resulting in an irretrievable loss of knowledge. In Munich, at least one small compulsory subject was left as it was, through which teaching methods and »know-how« were passed on more or less continuously up to the present day. The fact that hand-drawing has been largely detached from the teaching process raises the urgent question among drawing teachers, including the author, as to what role freehand-drawing can currently play in the creative process of architecture. After all, university drawing classes should not be satisfied with the sole aim of enabling students to produce hand-drawings. It should be just as clear for what purpose this ability can

---

2 Hans Döllgast (1891–1974) studied architecture at the Technical University of Munich under Paul Pfann, Joseph Bühlmann, and Friedrich von Thiersch. He worked with Richard Riemerschmid (Munich-Pasing) and Peter Behrens (Vienna), from whose master class he graduated. He taught at the Technical University of Munich between 1929 and 1956, thus influencing an entire generation of architects through his drawing teaching.

be used. At best, the teaching method should initialize exemplary work-processes with the freehand-sketch, and in this way, assign practical uses to the tool. The positioning of teaching hand-drawings in the constantly changing architectural education is a current challenge which is ultimately decisive for the lasting success of analogue drawing.

Now, one could of course ask why it should make sense for a drawing teacher to deal with the history of his or her own subject, its didactics and methods, in a time where there is obviously no lack of problems. In addition, the period under investigation for the »Munich School of Architectural Drawing« covers the enormous period of more than 150 years and was held in epochs long past, which are now difficult to access. However, it was precisely the unbroken continuity of teaching and the oral transfer of knowledge in the »Munich School« that demanded an introduction to the history and especially to the genesis of the teaching method, enabling one to place the knowledge and know-how in a context of origin and thus understand the intended purpose. Furthermore, the innumerable and changing possibilities of the occupation-specific use of drawing and sketching were exploited in this research, which not only sets the archival drawing collections into the context of their use and thus explains them plausibly, but can also contain core concepts that aid current handling. Furthermore, the story could help us gain clarity about controversial methodological concepts in order to finally be able to include them in currently discussed architectural teaching practices.

The basic precondition and starting point for the research concerned the knowledge of the orally transmitted, traditional form of today's teaching of the »Munich School«; its lessons, method, and the special handling of the projection rules. Without this knowledge and without the knowledge of the urgent challenges facing contemporary teaching, the research question could not have pursued this specific intention.

In order to reconstruct the teaching methods, numerous archival documents were drawn upon, which, when put together in an orderly fashion, finally formed a comprehensible overall picture of the »Munich School«. The teachers' estates and other archival materials are in the architectural collection of the Technical University of Munich, the Städtische Galerie im Lenbachhaus, the Munich City Museum and in private collections.

The basic material can be summarized in the following main groups: The manuscripts for lectures and drawing exercises, the documented blackboard drawings, sketchbooks from the classroom (some of which also have private entries), lecture notes, and publications or scripts for training. These five main groups have never been systematically recorded, scientifically evaluated nor put into context. All of the material had to be digitized and catalogued first. The time required to organize the data took about 80 percent of the time. The results of the archival research were presented in an annotated *Catalogue of Sketchbooks and Sheet-Collections*, the *Biographies of Drawing Teachers*, and the *Course Catalogue* in chronological order and initially formed a fundamental basis of data in the context of this work, but can also be used for future research projects. Indeed, the archive holdings are continually growing. In particular, bequests from the middle to the end of the 20th century are increasingly being added to the collection. In a research project that aims to depict a factual situation up to the present day, it is inevitable that extensive additions from the recent past must be factored in, which could not be taken into account when the work was undertaken.

In order to bring the Munich material into a broader context, drawing-pedagogical instructions or drawing-books,[3] which have been developed in Central Europe from around 1500 until today, were recorded according to lesson topics in order to determine whether the »Munich School« used established schemes or behaved autonomously. In addition, a list of architectural office activities was compiled in order to assign entries made by Munich drawing teachers in their sketchbooks to design projects.

With an observation period of more than 150 years, it should be clear that a complete compilation of all available information was difficult to achieve. Above all, only the most essential aspects regarding biographical information, political backgrounds, and architectural theoretical positions were examined and were only incorporated to the extent that they seemed significant for a description of the Munich drawing-lessons.

The compilation of the material suggested a chronological sequence of developmental steps to the structure of the research work. Paradigmatically,

---

3 From about 1500 onwards, the genre of so-called »drawing-books« and »printed drawing-collections« (for copying) came into being, which were aimed at laymen as well as professional users. They were written by practitioners and reflect the level of knowledge and the basic approach of their respective epochs. Extremely influential were: Alberti's *Della Pittura* published 1436, Bergmann's *Schule des Zeichners* published 1855, Buchotte's *Les Régles du Dessein* published 1743, Burg's *Geometrische Zeichenkunst* published 1845, De Vries' *Perspective* published 1604, Dupain de Montesson's *Science des Ombres* published 1786, Lairess's *Grundlegung zur Zeichenkunst* published 1727, Monges's *Géometrie Descriptive* published 1820, and many more.

the structures of the relevant, thoroughly astute, and profound scientific publications on the subject of drawing or even drawing lessons from the field of art history served as models for the methodical compilation of the material. The applied and long-established methods are capable of precisely describing drawing inventories: from the autographic description of style to the analysis of the basic perspective construction.

Similar to the methods used in art history, the development of the Munich drawing school could also be uncovered on the basis of all the evidence in order to finally retell a plausible story.

The Architectural View

There are, however, other levels of observation of drawings that derive from the special architectural view and the traditional use of drawings. It is the ability of design that enables a special reading of drawings and directs the focus to the content presented. No other discipline is able to describe the various facets of a design process with the tool of drawing and able to trace the stages of the draftsman.

This also applies to drawing lessons, which are primarily a part of the architectural curriculum at educational institutions. This raises questions which are still relevant today in the context of drawing/architecture lessons: Why is this particular architecture being drawn? Why is this particular situation interesting? Even in the art-educational documents of the early-modern period, it is stated that drawing triggers processes of cognition. In the archives of the Munich School, there are series of study sheets that deal with the basic principles of architectural design. The architect is familiar with these topics and the difficulties involved: the joining of materials, for example, or the superimposition of different principles of order. The architect can not only name the principles, but can also recognize the importance, peculiarity or humor.

In the written documents of the archives, the drawing teachers finally name, often in a completely different context, their understanding of architectural-spatial situations. For example, a motif is not drawn because it is particularly picturesque, but because it offers complex spatial sequences and zones of transition.

Two areas of investigation therefore play an important role in the compilation of this research work:

On the one hand, the purely graphic training, the subjects and lessons of which have been presented in drawing textbooks, that encompass the aim of achieving a sophisticated and natural approach to drawing. On the other hand, however, drawing is also a means to an end in the teaching of architecture, with all of the aspects that appear in the basic training of architects. With relevant cross-references, this approach generates typical questions in which the knowledge and experience of a designing architect is the prerequisite for the conception of a research project that aims to advance and enrich the current work on architecture.

For me, as a drawing teacher, it was important to extend the research to the point where the fundamental principles in the conception of drawing lessons could be identified and that the findings from the archives could be used as a stimulus and method for future lessons.

References

Michaelsen, Sven (2018): »Fast die ganze Welt hat sich der Diktatur der Marktwirtschaft unterworfen. Interview von Sven Michaelsen mit Rem Koolhaas«, in: *Süddeutsche Zeitung Magazin*, 20/2018, May 18, 2018.

Vasari, Giorgio (2012 [1550]): Alessandro Nova (ed.), *Einführung in die Künste der Architektur, Bildhauerei und Malerei*, 2nd corrected edition, Berlin: Verlag Klaus Wagenbach.

Archives, Bureaucracies, Architecture: Now You See Me, Now You Don't

Anna-Maria Meister

Editorial Summary: In her text, Anna-Maria Meister focuses on the production and dissemination of norms, normed objects, standards, bureaucratic measures, and administrative processes as social desires in German modern architecture. She states that we must treat them as formal and political acts of »Gestaltung« and critically probe their ideological intent and human consequence since the regulations in place, the order imagined, or the systems constructed were as formative to what we now know as Modern Architecture, as aesthetics or so-called Avant-Garde architects. As a result, rules and codes are »aesthetic tools« rather than mere »bureaucratic impediments«. She claims that it is necessary to research beyond the beaten path to include those contents that are usually left by the wayside, thus revealing and constructing alternative archives and histories. [Ferdinand Ludwig]

Keywords: Archives; Regulation; Norms; Standardization; Activist History; Oral History; Networks; Power Structures; Bureaucracy; Visibility.

What do we see when we look at architecture? And what when looking at its history? These are questions often asked of (and by) architecture historians. And yet, I would argue, they already surmise much of what our task is: a definition of »architecture«, a singular understanding of »history«, and the assumption of visibility. After all, for such a question there needs to be an »architecture« and a »history« that one can even presume to be looking at. While these might sound like sophistic musings, I argue that these are the core concerns in our field – or should be. As a historian and architect, I am interested in the construction of history and the historical construction of architectural production. We know that what we call »history« is not a collection of facts or the remnants of old buildings, but the reconstruction of worldviews. This means that not only do we need to investigate the context of the protagonists or systems we look at, but our own as well – both in practice and in scholarship. Looking at a certain building, image, or file,

Corresponding author: Anna-Maria Meister (TU Darmstadt, Germany); meister@atw.tu-darmstadt.de;
Open Access. © 2021 Anna-Maria Meister, published by transcript Verlag.
This work is licensed under the Creative Commons Attribution 4.0 (BY) license.

we have to understand the layers of its construction; but furthermore, we also need to understand how that very building, image, or file came to be one that we consider in the first place. Why are certain buildings built? Who decides which are maintained or reconstructed? More importantly, what keeps others from coming into being? It becomes clear that the work of the historian is as much one of making the unseen visible as that of the architect. Where architects imagine new spaces, historians are tasked not only with contextualizing those imaginaries, but with excavating and reconstructing how they became possible – and how others did not.

As historians, we have an obligation to look for those who are often overlooked, yet who have shaped and formed the world we live in: Housewives, bureaucrats, but also engineers, cooperations, and collaborative endeavors. All those who have long been considered »remote« or »other«, be it geographically, ideologically, societally or all of the above. This applies just as much to the material – the archive – as it does to people or buildings. The inconspicuous (files, processes, institutional regulations), the non-normative format (oral histories, witnessing) or the lost, destroyed or never collected archives are places we need to search for, rather than continue to gloss over. We must focus on the less-read pages, the missing pages, the crumbling paper or the burnt books, and the files and archives that do not yet exist.

In my work, the material for these acts of construction and excavation is often paper. It serves not only as an archival object or as a record of events, but as a design object itself, as material for bureaucratic measures, and as regulations for curricula and teaching, the frictions and negotiations – the very material that constitutes architects and architecture on a large scale. Paper in architecture is the material on which worlds are imagined, altered, and forgotten. In fact, it is a material of worldmaking not just as fabulous paper architecture or beautiful drawing. Every archive constructs a view of the world, and every drawing rests on a pile of paper thoughts and discourses that came before it.

Of Archives Forgotten, Destroyed, or Not Yet

Paper serves as a clue or guide to evaluate *what* makes architecture and *who* makes and made architecture. To do that, we need to look beyond the »heroes« and analyze the innocent-looking paper stacks, the systems, the bureaucracy, the infrastructure – piles and piles of files. From proportions to standards, architects have repeatedly tried to not only prescribe form, but also exert social and political control. As rules were exported into material form, architecture became an accomplice in constructions of governance. But as we know, »Design Rules« are never neutral, and neither is the technological discourse accompanying their emergence. While typically viewed as a bureaucratic impediment, rules and codes are in fact societal expressions and aesthetic tools. Furthermore, attempts to maximize control through systems often produce unpredictable results. We must ask: What are the architectural, spatial, and political implications of design rules, whether prescribed or self-imposed? How have irrational tendencies been complicit in, or even instrumental to, the formation of design ruleshow design rules? And most importantly: what are the values inscribed in supposedly aesthetic or technological principles, whom do they benefit, and what assumptions are they based on? In short, when looking at norms, standards, bureaucratic measures, and administrative processes, I would argue that we must treat them as formal and political acts of Gestaltung – and critically probe their ideological intent and human consequence.

Looking at paper (literally), we can trace these questions, or rather, we can construct the paper trails that would otherwise remain hidden in plain sight. In my research on norms – taking the term's suspension between social modes of conduct and technical regulations as a basis for my questions – I look, amongst other institutions, at the German DIN Institute (German Institute for Norms, founded under a different name in 1917). Emerging as a large-scale operation initially from a group of engineers, architects, and corporate lobbyists who tried (and still try) to define and design technical norms for literally every object in post-war Germany, in 1922 the institute issued (not coincidentally, I believe) the standardization of DIN A paper formats as the most successful norm of modern life. Paper, here, becomes both a subject of design and an object for designing, ruler and ruled, paper and file. Every painting, sketch, bureaucratic form and print has since fallen within its frame – approved and designed by engineers, mathematicians, and architects to make the world more homogeneous. Tolerances were minimized, dimensions fixed, and outlines drawn on page after page of (in turn) normed paper sheets, forming an ever-growing entourage of norms for all objects and aspects of life in post-World War I Germany.

All of this was done in the name of engineered transparency and the efficiency of technology – but not as a piecemeal process. The search for a transparent system of these almost self-proliferating norms was based on the idea of so-called »Ur-Normen« (foundational norms), a main obsession of the DIN from the very beginning. This was not a merely pragmatic attempt at regulating production, but an endeavor to systematize the world into a safe, predictable place after the first of two World Wars in the 20th century. Architects and architecture were at the heart of these efforts, ready to rebuild, and re-imagine an ordered environment built upon the modernist dream of the tabula rasa.

Now, how does that relate to the question in the beginning of this essay: What do we see when we look at (modern) architecture? I would propose rethinking the question in the reverse: What makes the architecture we look at look like it does? Why can we see *that* architecture and not others? Why are we looking at it in the first place? While these sound like rhetorical exercises, I think we should take them quite literally. Who and what shaped the architecture of our canon? How did they get to that position, and what defined the insiders and outsiders of this canon; those who become known and those who get forgotten, those who could build, and those who were made to disappear? There cannot be one answer to such questions. Rather, we might suggest a strategy: look at what we don't see; bring the flickering blur into focus that lingers between the already written pages; record unheard voices, look between stacks, take files seriously. The regulations in place, the order imagined, or the systems constructed formed what we now know as »Modern Architecture« in early 20th-century Germany at least as much as aesthetics, or even economics – and definitely more broadly than individuals still often referred to as »geniuses«.

This question is by no means a purely historic one, but the archival traces of decision making and negotiation processes help trace aesthetic intentions interwoven with bureaucratic desires, showing time and again their interconnected, inevitable entanglement. At a moment when the design and distribution of information has become a dominant driver of world politics and the economy, the aesthetic and material implications of algorithmic thinking remains under-researched – as do concurrent shifts of agency. A history of proto-algorithmic thinking in the discipline of architecture and engineering is not a mere history of computation or the so-called »digital.« Rather, looking at precedents and mechanics of algorithmic thinking in the pre-digital and pre-computational world by analyzing material objects and their design is indispensable in excavating the production of embedded values of – and through – contemporary information design; an urgent endeavor for both makers and (hi-)story-tellers.

Germany's architectural history of the 20th century has produced a vast literature – and yet, the role of the automation of Gestaltung (rather than production) in the construction of modernity in this specific cultural context is still to be assessed. Reviewing when the rhetoric of technological neutrality drove aesthetic and societal debates will reveal the entanglement of technocratic agency with processes of intentional form-giving. Located in the seams between what is conventionally called »architecture history« (monographic accounts or analysis of large-scale buildings) and the history of science and technology, looking for archives or constructing them through history writing becomes a foundational tool. Treating architectural thinking as inseparable from an aestheticized rationalism uncovers the aesthetic and epistemic convergence between seemingly opposed historical movements and actors. With my research, I hope to bring forth the urge to question a ready dichotomy of design and bureaucracy, and of »neutral« technology and morality. Placing a history of norms, of files, of bureaucratic thinking in spatial vicinity to the execution of architectural promises can unveil uncomfortable friction and productive affinities necessary for our histories to bear on the present.

To do that, we might need to construct the archive rather than find it: these are stories not derived from Gropius's letters, or Mies's drawings, but piles and piles of correspondence, ideas, processes, and documentation. As such, these archives can be built or written, recorded or forgotten, visual or sensual. By looking less at buildings and more at discussions, we might ask questions such as: What was the aim of architecture that focuses on technology and process, what happens to the subject? What does an architect like Walter Gropius hope to gain by making design automatic? What do the residents in his houses smell when the spring comes? Where is the hope for change embedded in both technological and aesthetic visions? And how did they negotiate forms and materials to get there?

Architecture Histories: For Whom?

When we, as historians and architects, go to »the archive« to conduct »research«, I put those terms into quotes because (as we know) all archives are constructed, and research takes many forms and formats. Archives are materialized worldviews and we construct our histories from them.

If architecture has canons, archives reveal their becoming. Architectural design that architects are taught is never self-evident, and the absence of an underlying ideology of any canon illusory. They have precedent, they change – and they must keep changing. Design and research (especially in a field so enchanted with the promise of technological prowess or innovation) is never neutral. We need critical historical and theoretical reflection to ask: How are we complicit as architects, historians, and teachers? How do we need to sharpen our tools, our terminology, and our methods to investigate how ideologies, forms, and power are constructed? How can we make critical reflection central to the field? Because what gets configured, normalized, and controlled by the stories from the archives are ultimately the subjects who occupy, use, and inhabit architecture.

So instead of asking »what, when, or where is the archive of architecture history« we need to dig through the very stuff left on the wayside. We need to unearth and construct those archives that we are sorely lacking. We need to critically assess not only what is our history, but how our histories are constructed – by whom and, most of all, for whom.

Interdisciplinary Research
Katharina Voigt

An inter- and transdisciplinary examination of architecture opens up the possibility of bringing together different substantiated interests in related issues. Interest does not only entail intellectual involvement and attention, but also, according to the Latin etymological root of the term, «inter-est», creates a space in between, in which the act of existing in-between promotes intellectual freedom and creative power. This impulse-giving potential of such anarchistic intermediate zones of the disciplines must be exploited to the fullest extent. The in-between of different disciplines creates a space of possibility which is neither inherent in the disciplines themselves, nor to be regarded as independent of them.

On the other hand, the resulting productive interdisciplinarity, often with a particular acceleration toward the acquisition of new knowledge and scientific insights, reveals the artificiality of setting disciplinary boundaries. The stronger the concept of science was oriented toward an ideal of the universal scholar, the less stringent disciplinary boundaries were drawn. Significant parts of the foundations of today's individual disciplines lie in the thematic sharpening of content, and topics with and against each other, in generalist academic discourse. Bridging disciplinary boundaries, working and researching between and across disciplines, as well as exploiting the potential of the areas between disciplines, encompasses both an innovation of the status quo and a recourse to the beginnings of scientificity.

The terminology of interdisciplinarity diverges in different directions between either an in-between or incorporating state of neighboring or foreign disciplines. The work across or alongside disciplinary borders can hitherto be a matter of methodological approaches from one discipline to the other, or relate to constellations of collaboration of researchers from different backgrounds in a team of overarching disciplines. Interdisciplinary research teams bring together individual scholars from different backgrounds, profiting from the alliances and commonalities of interest, methodology or endeavor as well as the respective differences, contradictions, and frictions between them. Trespassing between disciplines and approaches, the methodological framework as well as the findings multiply tremendously in terms of diversity, variety, and richness. The superordinate disciplines as well as their specific working methods and creation processes rely and depend on genuine knowledge – be it tacit, conscious, explicit or abstract. Linking the knowledge from different disciplines bares the potential to access the tacit knowledge of either discipline by making it more explicit through the shaping of the genuine approach, methodology, and process of creation from each field against the other. The following contributions highlight three different tracks of interdisciplinary research attempts: One emphasizes the distant perspective from the background of one discipline on topics particular to another, the other casts light upon the potential and innovation of cross-disciplinary collaboration in research teams of heterogeneous backgrounds, while the third traces the incorporation of genuine theoretical, methodological, and thematic framing from one discipline to another.

Research / Design and Academia

Susanne Hauser

Editorial Summary: In her contribution »Research / Design and Academia« Susanne Hauser discusses institutional developments and changes in academia since the 1990s, alongside which disciplinary frontiers and thematic as well as methodological approaches have been re-examined and reorganized. She highlights systemic differences in funding as well as uneven particularity in methodological attempts as fundamental reasons for the different recognition of e.g. practice-based and traditional types of academic research in architecture. Against the background of her personal academic foundation in cultural studies, she traces the genesis of the architect's education as a generalist, responsible for design and conception, creation and making. Considering the specific potential of design, she argues for the recognition of designing as a specific approach to the generation of knowledge. [Katharina Voigt]

Keywords: Design; Knowledge; Architectural Education; Academic Institutions; Environmental Models; Aesthetics; Concrete Object; Criticism.

One of the most discussed issues of the last 25 years in cultural studies was – and still is – the notion of knowledge. This was not the case because the humanities were in an exceptional state of crisis, but there were several changes able to disturb the on-going business as usual. One of these developments was a change merely due to political decisions based on neoliberal concepts and convictions. They inspired a redefinition of political aims, of public interest, and of public spending. Public institutions, such as universities, were not funded anymore beyond the absolutely necessary means to keep up their sometimes newly – and usually more restrictedly – defined main function, in the case of universities: education, not in the sense of *Bildung (education)* but in the sense of *Berufsbildung (practitioner's training)*. The new policy of less money for more economically defined aims came along with two new practices. One of them was the funding of project-based research that established the necessity of permanent competition even in fields that were not able to compete in an economic sense. The other practice entering universities during the 1980s and implemented till the turn of the millennium the latest was the practice of permanent evaluation. The combination of these three changes – less public funding for the basic needs of universities, the generalization of project-based research and funding, and the implementation of more or less strict and more or less biased evaluation modes – produced impressive changes in many fields of research. Probably only those branches of science able to define future applications of their research were exceptions as they were already accustomed to project-based funding, externally controlled competitive situations, and to commissions. The process of reorganizing academia had, and still has, locally and nationally specific outcomes, some of which are ambivalent. In Germany, for example, the changes triggered productive interdisciplinary cooperation within universities, while individual research, widely characteristic for the humanities, tended to be less appreciated than collective endeavors. Groups, whose members had never dreamed of working together within huge organizational structures, entered the scene to look for project funding and to produce »knowledge«, preferably proven by dissertations, PhDs, and publications.

For me, as a researcher in architecture with a background in cultural studies, it became evident that the topic of knowledge in architecture had to be explored (cf. Hauser 2005: 21–27).[1] I want to stress again though, that it was not only the discipline of architecture in academic settings that had to change some basic convictions and practices; various disciplines were challenged in their academic habits. The first quest for research in architecture, however, – similar to the quest for research in the arts – belonged to a wider restructuring endevor. It redefined the field of accepted academic knowledge and the realm of what was accepted as academic research. Obviously, the production of knowledge meeting such standards was not one of the key features that architects relied on when they described their practice, and it was not what architecture schools usually saw or even still see as the core of their teaching ambitions. The most defining practice for architects and students in architecture was the practice of designing, the production of new concepts and designs. And obviously, the process of designing, the key activity taught in schools of architecture, clearly did not meet academic standards as such. It is evident that there was a challenge in entering the special activity of designing into the realm of accepted approaches to research. Today, I believe that

---

1 See also the doctoral program »Knowledge in the Arts« (2012–2021), University of the Arts Berlin: https://www.udk-berlin.de/forschung/temporaere-forschungseinrichtungen/dfg-graduiertenkolleg-das-wissen-der-kuenste/.

we are on our way to accepting that there are different kinds of knowledge in academia – and that the very special type of knowledge production defining architecture is an important part of it.

This notion has depended, and still depends, on institutional conditions. There exist architecture departments within schools or faculties of art and design with little affinity to social and cultural studies. Furthermore, there are architecture departments in technical colleges – in Germany Fachhochschulen, in Britain polytechnics. Some architecture schools are close to or a part of engineering faculties, whereas others evolved from beginnings in the art history faculty of universities. Architecture departments and schools differ widely in their approaches to the field of relevant academic issues for future architects, in their attitudes toward the arts, technology, and the humanities – and accordingly to research in general. Nevertheless, they all tend to teach expertise and capability in designing.

So I understand designing as the essential practice in architecture., This motivates my plea for the acceptance of this practice as the distinguished and characteristic contribution of architecture to research and to the production of academic knowledge. I came to this conclusion some 20 years ago when I analyzed two landscape designs and became interested in the process of their development (see Hauser 2006, in: Hess-Lüttich (ed.): 95–104). Both designs implied answers to a variety of heterogeneous questions, among them decisions about materials to be used, about structures to be built, but also answers to fundamental questions like how to define and present the relations of »man« and »nature«. I realized how many different aspects had been dealt with during the design processes, while the results, the finished and finally realized designs, were undeniably entities in their own right. I began reflecting the process of designing as an operation dealing with heterogeneous aspects leading to a synthesis, as well as about the practice of designing as a cultural technique (see Hauser 2013, in: Ammon/Froschauer (eds.): 363–381). In a first and tentative approach, I proposed to read the two inspiring landscape designs as »environmental models« (»Umweltmodelle«). The intention was to indicate the wide scope of their topics and their potential impact. I coined the expression in reference to Jacob von Uexküll's semiotic concept of the »Umwelt« (von Uexküll 1956: 103–159). Uexküll's description of sign-processes as bonds of any living being and the – for this being – relevant traits of its surroundings seemed to offer a promising approach to understanding the manifold aspects of our permanent individual, collective, and societal exchange with our environment. The concept of the environment as a sign-based relation implied the idea that designs were readable as complex offers of sensations, communications, and activities: as new proposals of environmental models. I liked the metaphor and the assumption of a multifaceted relatedness of designs in their elaboration and emergence as well as in their built manifestations and assumed that this perspective provided an adequate approach to the further analysis of the manifold aspects of architecture and landscape architecture.

A second helpful reference for the understanding of designs was due to the observation that we tend to talk about designs as single entities emerging in a process. Presumably, this process starts quite often with a first idea, a first sketch pointing to a future result meeting the aims or the initial intentions of the design (cf. Cross 2004: 427–441).[2] In the course of the process, a variety of decisions about future sensations, communications, and exchanges will be molded into one single result, ultimately called »the design«. This observation led me to Ernst Cassirer's suggestive metaphor of the »crystallization foci«. This is how he understands, in his Philosophy of Symbolic Forms, the origins of conceptual formations, the beginnings of the separation and organization of an unorganised field into meaningful structures, and thus the beginning of language (Cassirer 1990: 135). His vision of a slowly stabilized core and its characteristic structure born out of a non-ordered potentiality provided a useful image for the understanding of the emergence of designs in architecture or landscape architecture, even if this image did not reflect the complexity of the knowledge and methods involved.

I came to the conclusion that at the beginning of a design process, architects or designers do not know in detail how to get their final result. Even the number of aspects to be explored and their relations cannot be listed conclusively. An enumeration of tasks and aspects would reduce any analytical approach to the processing of a checklist and neglect the possible relations of different issues. If we understand designing as an exploratory activity with the potential to create new options, it is clear that operating via checklists is not the defining aspect of this activity. Design processes start with incomplete knowledge and, at least in principle, questionable methods. Without the intention of change, of challenging rules and routines, there is no need for a process whose most important quality is its capacity to produce new

---

2 Cross argues that experienced architects and designers tend to solve and analyze the »problems« (of a certain design) at the same time and produce ideas and concepts already at a very early stage of their acquaintance with a certain project.

results. Doing a design may imply revisions of established knowledge, the questioning of trusted rules and regulations, and the necessity to go beyond common or familiar methodological approaches; Research is required and an expected part of the process. The idea of completeness in the acquisition of useful or necessary knowledge for a design, however, is specific and in so far of interest: Any research will be pursued to exactly the extent that allows for the continuation of the design process. Not each and every aspect of a design has to be tackled with the same curiosity or intensity. Completeness in the sense of conducting exhaustive research on decisive issues is not necessary for the completion of a certain design. The only criterion for the successful closure of the necessary research activity is whether the required answers to the open questions are found according to the unfolding aims of the unfolding design process.

The relevant issues in architectural designs are manifold. They include, for example, the necessity of satisfying basic needs such as shelter from weather and climatic conditions; the spatial organization of social processes; mechanic and constructive questions; aesthetic qualities and choices of materials; functional options such as the adaptability to specific social situations; sustainability; ecological consequences and their monitoring or measuring; financial outcomes of investments. And there may be many more issues at stake. The aspects or layers deemed relevant for a design follow different types of logic. They do not belong to or refer to just one societal subsystem systems theory could identify. This means that their expressions in designs cannot be evaluated according to the same rules, although all of these aspects are involved in the definition of one single design. Thus, the key qualification in architectural design may be described as the ability to synthesize heterogeneous issues, different kinds of knowledge including practices, skills, and aptitudes, and to turn them into one single option. This requires a highly qualified and yet non-specialized approach also implying decisions on sensual matters, as designs propose visual, tactile, and auditory sensations.

Here I want to take up and reinforce the subject of the role of architecture within academic institutions: I assume that the generalist and universal approach and the close affinity of design processes to sensual options are responsible for the unclear status of architecture and architectural knowledge in academic institutions such as universities, colleges, art schools, and academies. As I mentioned before, schools of architecture are found within all of these institutions. It is interesting though, to observe that they all seem to be exceptional compared to their neighboring faculties. Architecture is too artistic to be seen as an obviously serious engineering discipline in technical universities; architecture offers too many pragmatic or profitable solutions for pragmatic problems to be fully accepted as an art in art schools; it is too involved with and dependent on engineering concepts and approaches to impress the humanities still surviving in classic universities; and colleges providing merely practice-oriented courses are observed suspiciously by architects from other schools as they may support less ambitious and more opportunistic habits in building processes. This position of architecture schools among, above, and between other disciplines and practices is a challenge and a special condition resisting specialization in methodology as well as in knowledge. This position is due to the non-restricted approach necessarily implied in seriously innovative work.

This brings me to the question as to how far specialization is an important issue in study programs addressing future architects. Still in 2006, Ivar Holm described the pursuit of »holism« as a guiding principle and thus a regulative idea for architectural education. It should be noted that Holm interpreted the relevance of this concept as a widely shared conviction, not as a fact. Used in this context, however, holism tends to imply »an all-inclusive design perspective which is often regarded as somewhat exclusive to the two design professions« (architecture and industrial design) distinguishing them from other professions involved in design projects (Holm 2006: 173). According to Holm, architectural students and students of industrial design are trained to develop »a« design as a single whole, as a project encompassing all possible traits, and to understand these traits as necessarily linked. They also learn to see themselves as the »natural person to be in charge of the design process« (Ibid.: 174), a definition of the architect's position that has been seriously challenged through economic, technological and conceptual developments since the 1980s (e.g. Anstey et al. (eds.) 2007). Holm contrasts this attitude with the usual approach to education in the engineering disciplines. According to his observations, young engineers learn how to solve single problems on a functional basis and are not expected to deal with the general »holistic« perspective (Holm 2006: 173).

»Holism« may also find a different interpretation that stresses the idea of a perfect control of designs. The necessary precondition is, as Holm realizes, the identification of all possible questions, aspects, and relations of a certain design or of designing in general. Holm quotes Harold G. Nelson and Erik Stoltermann who indeed came to this conclusion (Nelson/Stoltermann

2003). This »holistic« approach requires a complete set of tools or at least a complete set of criteria and standards that only a complete and final »system« can provide. Its ideal expression would be a single tool defining the ends and means of the process of designing. This option challenges the idea of the architect's professional role as well as the idea of designing as a cultural technique with the unique potential to question even its own methodology (see »Einleitung« in: Gethmann/Hauser (eds.) 2009, 9–16). It may also be a form of bringing architectural research to an end before any coherent position on architectural research has been developed.

The question of whether and when a certain design is finished is varied and debatable. The answer depends on intellectual and local contexts and leads back to the idea of the specific environmental model as well as to the thesis that research processes – and also their traces in designs too – depend on aims and attitudes: There is no general rule explaining how and when designs are finished, and they tend to be revised again when it comes to building. In any case, it is by decisions that design processes come to their end. The diagnosis that a certain design is finished, at least for the present moment, is usually backed through different arguments. They may be subject to lengthy discussions. As designs include answers to many heterogeneous questions, it is not surprising that the criteria for these decisions are manifold. Some among the many possible criteria refer to norms, to usual practices of crafts and engineering, and to other trusted disciplines such as mathematics or biology. These criteria seem to be the least problematic, especially if they are based on practices usually seen as reliable, such as measuring or calculating. Functional qualities, the conviction that pragmatic aims are met and that usability will be achieved through the design in question, are also important. Then there is the evaluation of designs according to less well-defined aesthetic criteria such as suitability, unity, and coherence, qualities associated with sensual satisfaction.[3] The results of design processes have to be seen as aesthetic accomplishments and have to show an aesthetic necessity, yet these criteria are not easily explained through generally accepted standards. Designers and trained critics, however, seem to be able to agree on the answer to the question of whether a design shows these qualities of suitability, coherence, or fitness and is worth being accepted as completed in this respect too – even if the evaluations may differ in other aspects.

---

3 These criteria may still be summed up in (interpretations of) Vitruvius' definition of the key requirements in building: firmitas, utilitas, and venustas.

There are several criteria for the judgment of finished architectural designs. They differ from judgments of other results of academic activity and of other approaches to research. Among the desired qualities are what we may call »fitness« in the sense of fitting into a certain condition or in the sense of making a certain condition fit the new design and »suitability«, or »coherence« of a design for the buildings, urban structures or open spaces at stake. Nelson Goodman introduced the »fit« or »fitness« as the ultimate criterion for a critique of a work of art (Goodman 1978: 138; Goodman 1981: 264). I mention this notion, as there is an interesting relation between this approach to the judgment of art and the judgment of results in the development of technology. Goodman's state of »fitting« and the »concrete technical object« in the sense of Gilbert Simondon's term are related concepts in so far as both mark the (preliminary) end of a productive process. Simondon's essay on the philosophy of technology was an innovative contribution to the long European history of philosophical thought concerning concepts of wholeness and unity.[4] According to Simondon, the concrete technical object is completed when the manifold aspects it reflects and the different »forces« it contains are brought together in such a way that the involved powers and functions do not disturb each other, but result in a new arrangement merging the synergies of all implied elements and functions in a harmonious way (see the first chapter of Simondon 2016). This seems to be a useful description of designs too.

This is also quite important for the question of the acceptance of designs as relevant results of academic research: It is interesting to note that Gilbert Simondon and Nelson Goodman do not attempt to fully explain what their respective ideal integrations in a work of technology or in a work of art may mean. Nor do they assume that anyone, including the designers themselves, is able to understand the complexity involved. Simondon's »concrete object« is not completely analyzable by its makers, and the same applies for the works of art and architecture discussed by Nelson Goodman and Catherine Z. Elgin (see Goodman/Elgin 1988: 44). In this respect, the philosopher of technology and the philosophers of signs and representations agree – which I consider highly interesting, as both argue using quite a transgressive manner in the definition of their objects.

---

4 The idea of an inseparable whole, a complex unit, and a single integrated object, has of course been a traditional subject in reflections on art and aesthetics since the 18th century; e.g. Dällenbach/Hart Nibbrig (eds.) 1984.

These criteria, however, cannot be supported through any classic methodology of the sciences or through the hermeneutic approaches of the humanities: The basis for these judgments is aesthetic ability, training, and extensive experience. Whether these abilities survive in present academic institutions is one of the very relevant issues at stake. As long as architecture is understood »as an aesthetics-based network of practices of environmental transformation« (Arteaga 2016, in Arteaga (ed.): 8), the idea of a final definition of design will not be the final idea in designing and the creation of models for new and enriching environments – and may, as I hope, contribute as such to the range of academic research and knowledge production.[5]

---

5 This text is partly based on a first version and its discussion in Arteaga 2020: 330–350. My thanks go to the authors of the book, especially to Alex Arteaga, Mika Elo, Lidia Gasperoni, and Jonathan Hale.

References

Anstey, Tim/Grillner, Katja/Hughes, Rolf, eds. (2007): *Architecture and Authorship*, London: Black Dog Publishing.

Arteaga, Alex (2016): »Architecture Without Walls: An Introduction«, in: Alex Arteaga/Boris Hassenstein (eds.), *Architecture Without Walls*, Berlin: Errant Bodies Press, 4–12.

Cassirer, Ernst (1990 [1929]): *Philosophie der symbolischen Formen, Dritter Teil. Phänomenologie der Erkenntnis*, 9th edition, Darmstadt: Wissenschaftliche Buchgesellschaft. – English translation: *The Philosophy of Symbolic Forms: Vol. 3: The Phenomenology of Knowledge*, transl. by Ralph Manheim, New Haven: Yale University Press, 1965.

Cross, Nigel (2004): »Expertise in Design: An Overview«, in: *Design Studies* 25(5), 427–441.

Dällenbach, Lucien/Nibbrig, Christiaan L. Hart, eds. (1984): *Fragment und Totalität*, Frankfurt: Suhrkamp Verlag.

Gethmann, Daniel/Hauser, Susanne eds. (2009): *Kulturtechnik Entwerfen*, Bielefeld: transcript Verlag.

Goodman, Nelson (1978): *Ways of Worldmaking*, Hassocks, Sussex: The Harvester Press.

Goodman, Nelson (1981): *Languages of Art*, Hassocks, Sussex: The Harvester Press.

Goodman, Nelson/Elgin, Catherine Z. (1988): *Reconceptions in Philosophy & Other Arts and Sciences*, Indianapolis/Cambridge: Hackett Publications.

Hauser, Susanne (2005): »The Knowledge of Architecture – an Essay/Das Wissen der Architektur – ein Essay«, in: *Graz Architectural Magazine* 2, 21–27.

Hauser, Susanne (2006): »Modelldenken in den Wissenschaften«, in: *Dialektik* 1997/1, 105–118. – English translation: »Environmental Models – Landscape Planning and New Descriptions of Nature«, in: Ernest W. B. Hess-Lüttich (ed.), *Eco-Semiotics*, Tübingen: Francke, 95–104.

Hauser, Susanne (2013): »Verfahren des Überschreitens. Entwerfen als Kulturtechnik«, in: Sabine Ammon/ Eva Maria Froschauer (eds.), *Wissenschaft Entwerfen. Vom forschenden Entwerfen zur Entwurfsforschung der Architektur*, Munich: Wilhelm Fink Verlag, 363–381.

Hauser, Susanne (2020): »The Ends of Design«, in: Alex Arteaga (ed.), *Architectures of Embodiment. Disclosing New Intelligibilities*, Berlin: Diaphanes, 330–350.

Holm, Ivar (2006): *Ideas and Beliefs in Architecture: How Attitudes, Orientations, and Underlying Assumptions Shape the Built Environment*, Oslo: Oslo School of Architecture and Design.

Nelson, Harold G./Stoltermann, Erik (2003): *The Design Way: Intentional Change in an Unpredictable World: Foundations and Fundamentals of Design Competence*, Englewood Cliffs, NJ: Educational Technology Publications.

Simondon, Gilbert (1958): *Du mode d'existence des objets techniques*, Paris: Aubier. – English translation: *On the Mode of Existence of Technical Objects*, transl. by Cécil Malaspina/John Rogove, Minneapolis, MN: Univocal Publishing, 2016.

von Uexküll, Jakob (1956): »Bedeutungslehre«, in: Jakob von Uexküll/ Georg Kriszat, *Streifzüge durch die Umwelten von Tieren und Menschen. Bedeutungslehre*, Reinbek bei Hamburg: Rowohlt, 103–159.

What is Architectural Psychology?

Alexandra Abel

Editorial Summary: Alexandra Abel explores the general potential of disciplinary fusion and, specifically, the incorporation of psychology into the field of architecture, aiming for an architectural psychology. In her contribution »What is Architectural Psychology?«, she questions the possible intertwining of the two disciplines, highlighting their reciprocal interconnectivity. She draws specific attention to the substantial ways in which the consideration of psychological findings affect the perception and appropriation of architectural spaces and their sensual and attentive impact on human well-being. In regard to the integration of perceptual and sensory principles into the architectural design, the consideration of psychology becomes inevitable when aiming for a human centered design. [Katharina Voigt]

Keywords: Requirements and Benefits of Architectural Psychology as an Interdisciplinary Cooperation Between Architecture, Psychology and others.

Architecture is (applied) art. It is created for people to perceive and use it. Psychology, on the other hand, is the study of human experience and behavior. One of its branches is environmental psychology, which relates the environment to human experience and behavior. Today, the environment is primarily designed or at least influenced by people, and dominated in turn, by architecture. According to Evans and McCoy, we spend 90 percent of our time in architecture (Evans/McCoy 1998: 85), and the remaining ten percent almost entirely in its immediate proximity.

Unlike the subject area of psychology, the subject area of architecture is tied to evaluation. Architecture is considered to be »Baukunst« (Brockhaus 1987: 82), the art of building and construction.[1] But who decides on the

---

1 Brockhaus encyclopedia defines architecture as »Baukunst«, or the art of building, which is the oldest and most appropriated of the fine arts (Brockhaus 1987: 82). Similarly sensitive to the issue of inclusion or exclusion is the definition in the Duden, universal German dictionary, where three meanings are assumed of architecture as the art of building (as a scientific discipline) as a (more or less) elaborated construction and artistic design of buildings, and as the summary of products of the art of building (cf. Dudenredaktion 2003: 163).

Corresponding author: Alexandra Abel (Bauhaus-Universität Weimar, Germany); mail@alexandraabel.de
Open Access. © 2021 Alexandra Abel, published by transcript Verlag.
This work is licensed under the Creative Commons Attribution 4.0 (BY) license.

criteria of inclusion or exclusion in this case? To free the interdisciplinary discourse from the issue of evaluation and to keep the the overlapping area between disciplines as wide as possible, architectural psychology is defined as the science of human experience and behavior in built environments (i.e. Richter 2013: 21).

Where, how, and with what intention can psychology enrich architecture with its knowledge of human nature? In their encounter, psychology is not the key player. It does not create architecture. It must find a different, virtually adjunct or corresponding position to architecture. It can incorporate this position quite confidently, however, for it has something to offer which architects can use in practice, theory, and research: scientific knowledge of human nature. Architecture as a discipline is much older than (scientific) psychology. And knowledge of human nature has always, varying in depth and thematic focus, been considered an expertise crucial to the design of architecture. The added value of architectural psychology in the interdisciplinary discourse is its scientific content, methods, perspectives, and possibly a transsystemic meta position.

The Offer of Architectural Psychology

What does architectural psychology have to offer in terms of theory, research, and practice? Architectural psychology can sensitize the significant influence of the designed environment on human experience and behavior and can contribute to an understanding of the interrelation between humans and the human-designed and influenced environment. Thus, it searches for explanations behind the observed effects, formulates them in the form of hypotheses, theories, explanatory models, and puts them up for discussion.

To support the communication about and the reflection of this interrelation, it is necessary to introduce psychological terms to the discourse in a clearly defined range of content and meaning. Attention must be paid to the pre-existing language culture of psychological content in architecture, which can be different from the specific terminology of psychologists and non-architects. Architecture conveys itself through perception and interaction. But to make this impact communicable, in the sense of the Latin origin »communicare« – to make common, share, bring into common use (Kluge 2002: 514), and reflexible, in the sense of the Latin origin »(animum) reflectere«, – to turn the mind or the thoughts back or away (Georges 1995: 2267), a language and sign system is required; a system that is preferably equally shared by all participants of communication and reflection, and that at best offers terms for all communicable and reflexive contents.

Thus, (architectural) psychology can act as spokesperson, voice, representative, and mediator for the recipients of architecture, the ones addressing and creating it – the people. This must be the intention of architectural psychology and the intention of an interdisciplinary cooperation between architecture and psychology, which is optional per se and always has to prove and justify its added value. In this sense, from its position as a human science, architectural psychology can generate discourse, preceded by the question: Which kind of architecture do we need? Should architecture increase comfort? Raise life expectancy? Support certain actions, functions? Please our perception? Stabilize or destabilize systems and institutions, power dynamics, and states? And is it even justifiable, in terms of overall ecological interest, to focus so much on humankind, which threatens the survival of the Earth's ecosystem by merely existing?

Against the backdrop of an open discourse, this question should nevertheless find, at least, a preliminary, hypothetical answer: Architectural psychology is the science of human experience and behavior, especially in the context of the space designed or influenced by humankind. Through the examination of the mutual relation between human experience and behavior, and the dimension of space, created or influenced by man, its intention is to support human well-being on one hand, and the continued existence and conservation of the entire ecosystem on the other.

Following the hypothesis that the aim of architectural design is the simultaneous optimal well-being of humans and the entire ecosystem, research must try to operationalize both in order to derive observable and appraisable criteria from it. The well-being of the ecosystem can be operationalized, whether in the form of soil sealing, carbon footprints et cetera, and can then be introduced into the context of design processes. Human attitudes toward the natural environment – such as the assumption of responsibility in the form of ecologically conscious action and the relevance of the natural environment for human well-being – fall into the domain of environmental psychology and thus into the domain of architectural psychology as well.

The World Health Organization (WHO), in its role as publisher of the *ICD* and associated publisher of the *World Happiness Report* as well as of numerous charters in this field, provides a widespread and universally accepted basis for an operationalization of human well-being. The terminology utilized primarily consists of the terms: Happiness, health, (subjective) well-being and life evaluation. Yet, these terms are so similar in their definition that they are sometimes used synonymously. As such, happiness is defined as subjective well-being in the *World Happiness Report 2017* (Helliwell/Layard/Sachs 2017: 13). In contrast, life evaluation is considered to be more related to the concrete living conditions of the individual. Therefore, the *World Happiness Report* does not focus on the evaluation of individually felt happiness, but on the evaluation of life satisfaction, as the purpose of the report is to capture and compare the external living conditions in each country and not the internal attitude of the individual.[2] Health, on the other hand, is »not merely the absence of disease or infirmity« in this context, but »a state of complete physical, mental and social well-being«, according to the pioneering definition of the WHO.[3] Consequently, the WHO's definition of health can be the starting point for an operationalization of factors, which then, as categories, can be respectively examined in relation to the built environment.

Regarding social well-being, for example, architectural psychology has the ability to create awareness of not only the human need for positively perceived social encounters, but also of the opposite need for withdrawal, and can illustrate how both are connected to the affordance of space (term definition »affordance«, cf. Gibson 1966), through proxemics (term definition »proxemics«, cf. Hall 1966), posture, viewing direction, movement et cetera. It can offer methodology as well as pre-existing instruments, such as test and questionnaire diagnostics, interviews, and criteria for content-analytical evaluation of interviews, to gather further insights, and thus put architects, architecture students or representatives of similar disciplines

---

2 »These twin facts – that life evaluations vary much more than do emotions across countries, and that these life evaluations are much more fully explained by life circumstances than are emotional reports – provide for us a sufficient reason for using life evaluation as our central measure for making international comparisons.« (Helliwell/Layard/Sachs 2017: 12).

3 From the Constitution of the World Health Organization (WHO): »Health is a state of complete physical, mental and social well-being and not merely the absence of disease or infirmity.« »The Constitution was adopted by the International Health Conference held in New York from 19 June to 22 July 1946, signed on 22 July 1946 by the representatives of 61 states (Off. Rec. Wld Hlth Org., 2, 100), and entered into force on April 7, 1948.« (World Health Organization: *About WHO, Constitution of WHO: Principles*, https://www.who.int/about/mission/en/, accessed February 20, 2019.

in a position to examine their own issues, whether during their studies, in research or in practice.

Architectural Psychology in the Design Process

To have an impact on the design of architecture beyond the reflection of existing environments, architectural psychology must first and foremost deal with the creation of architecture, and therewith primarily with the design process. In the understanding of its dynamic nature lies the quintessence necessary for a potentially enriching collaboration of architecture and psychology. The more closely the procedures of creation and design in architecture are explored and examined by the means of psychology, the greater the potential for architectural psychology can be revealed.

Indispensable for the understanding is a meta-analysis of the design process, a process that should be entirely unknown to most psychologists. While architects may experience it regularly, they probably rarely reflect it on a verbal or graphic level. This process has to pay attention to many criteria – user requirements, structural engineering calculations, monetary guidelines, building codes, and formalities –, but it also contains a de surplus, the assumption of a creative Aha-moment (Csíkszentmihályi 1997: 119). How much meta-consideration and meta-analysis does the design process need? How much can it tolerate? How can architectural psychology assimilate into this process? And where? How close may the input of architectural psychology come to the creative Aha-moment? How much influence may architectural psychology have on the result of the design process? How visible may this influence be?

The design process at the university level occupies a special position. Usually, it is freed from the restrictions of realization, and focuses on an education in the design process through content and methodology. Based on six years of architectural psychology teaching at the Bauhaus-University Weimar at the Chair of Building Morphology, held by Professor Bernd Rudolf, I am able to make the following meta-analytic observations: At the beginning of the design process, which due to university circumstances is usually restricted to one semester, there is the task, usually freely selected by the students based on interest and inclination. Different motivations, like collaboration with fellow students or a preference for particular lecturers, presumably contribute to the choice as well.

In the initial phase, a diverse input oriented toward the task ensues. This input consists of:

- The assumption of a certain user group.
- Research, field trips to prototypes, constructed or hypothetical reference examples.
- Guided preliminary tasks that aim to activate previously unconscious biographical contents, like, for example, the subject of water in relation to architecture, the examination of their own bathing experiences.
- Field trips to particular places or places where their own draft is to be positioned in the dimension of space.
- Additional knowledge about certain aspects that are important for the task, e.g. knowledge about dementia.

This input consists of the reactivation of personal memory contents as well as new information. Whereas some contents are concretely thought or perceived, others reach the preconscious[4] through associative networks (for the concept of associative networks, see: Collins/Loftus 1975: 407–428). These fluctuating conscious and preconscious contents create an input-cloud, whose composition and consistency changes constantly and which accompanies the students over a certain amount of time (similar to a creative incubation process) until they solidify it and select a concrete design idea. This process is promoted and regulated by presentation deadlines, limitations through guidelines et cetera, and conglomerates in an initial design idea.

As the course proceeds, this first and central design idea develops into an elaborated draft, into which additional parts of the cloud can certainly be incorporated again. Where and how can architectural psychology accompany the design process in the structures of the university?

---

4 The terms conscious, preconscious, and unconscious are not used conforming to Freud's theories, for whom the unconscious for instance is associated with displacement. Here, they denote the distance of the potentially available information in our memory to our conscious mind (see: Zimbardo/Gerrig, in: Hoppe-Graff/Engel 2003 [1996]: 165–166).

It can:

- Observe, analyze, reflect, and support the whole process, influence it if necessary, lead, and accompany a meta-analysis.
- Add concrete scientific content to the diverse input in the first phase, thus feeding into the cloud.
- Support the activation of conscious and preconscious individual contents and accompany their reflection e.g. through processes of introspection and projective procedures.
- Support the compaction and selection with the specification of psychological criteria.
- Offer methodology to include architectural psychology contents after the compaction to a concrete idea – during the elaboration, e.g. in the form of analyses of motion, social density, privacy et cetera.
- Prepare a verbal mediation and explanation of the design that is not only based on drawings and models, but that also reflexively explains the process of the development and incorporates (scientific) psychological elements into the argumentation.

Perspectives

The interdisciplinary cooperation between architecture and psychology appears almost inevitable. Architecture has to consider human factors, while psychology is the science of human experience and behavior. This cooperation, however, presumes the acceptance and the constructive handling of a number of subject-specific particularities: Architecture has always been created for people and therefore has its own culture and tradition of knowledge about human nature. Architectural psychology has to develop a positive and conscious attitude toward this tradition and culture.

Although, or maybe even because it is a young science, (scientific) psychology is very heterogeneous regarding its schools, orientations, and approaches. Its research area concerns a complex reality and metaphysical questions, which explains why, for certain phenomena and questions, there exist parallel theories, models or hypotheses. This might complicate the access to psychology for architects in a cross-disciplinary discourse but must nevertheless be made transparent. One vision for the future would entail a closer link between architecture and psychology, for instance in a shared postgraduate program, as productive cross-disciplinary research can only arise from proximity. The promotion of process- and project-oriented cooperation, in which new approaches are developed together and traditional paradigms are left behind, appears equally useful. Our current reality has produced a number of extremely urgent issues, such as economic and ecological fairness, which obligate both psychology and architecture. Solutions only arise from a cross-disciplinary, open discourse, which should naturally include many other related sciences as well.

References

Brockhaus (1987): *Brockhaus-Enzyklopädie*, in 24 volumes. 19th, completely revised edition. B 2. Mannheim: Brockhaus-Verlag.

Collins, Allan M./Loftus, E. F. (1975): »A Spreading-Activation Theory of Semantic Processing«, in: *Psychological Review* 82(6), 407–428.

Csíkszentmihályi, Mihály (1996): *Creativity, Flow and The Psychology of Discovery and Invention*, New York: Harper Perennial. – German translation: *Kreativität. Wie Sie das Unmögliche schaffen und Ihre Grenzen überwinden*, transl. by Maren Klostermann, Stuttgart: Klett-Cotta, 1997.

Dudenredaktion (2003): *Duden – Deutsches Universalwörterbuch*, 5th, revised edition. Mannheim.

Evans, Gary W./McCoy, Janetta Mitchell (1998): »When Buildings Don't Work: The Role of Architecture in Human Health«, in: *Journal of Environmental Psychology* (1)18, 85–94.

Gibson, James Jerome (1966): *The Senses Considered as Perceptual Systems*, Boston: Houghton Mifflin.

Georges, Karl-Ernst (1995): Tobias Dänzer (ed.), revised by Thomas Baier, *Der neue Georges. Ausführliches Lateinisch-Deutsches Handwörterbuch, Volume 1 A–H, Volume 2 I–Z*. Darmstadt: wbg Academic.

Hall, Edward T. (1966): *The Hidden Dimension*, New York: Doubleday.

Helliwell, John/Layard, Richard/Sachs, Jeffrey, eds. (2017): »World Happiness Report 2017«, in: *Sustainable Development Solutions Network*, New York.

Kluge, Friedrich (2002 [1883]): Elmar Seebold (ed.), *Etymologisches Wörterbuch der deutschen Sprache*, 24th revised and extended edition, Berlin: DeGruyter.

Richter, Peter G., ed. (2013): *Architekturpsychologie. Eine Einführung*, Lengerich: Pabst Science Publishers.

World Health Organization: »About WHO, Constitution of WHO: Principles«, https://www.who.int/about/mission/en/, accessed February 20, 2019.

Zimbardo, Philip G./Gerrig, Richard J. (1977): Psychology and Life, Reading, MA: Addison Wesley. – German edition published and edited by Siegfried Hoppe-Graff and Irma Engel, Psychologie, Berlin/Heidelberg: Springer, 2003.

On the Entanglement between Sociology and Architecture in Spatial Research

Séverine Marguin

Editorial Summary: Coming from a background of sociology, but taking part in the interdisciplinary research network »Re-figuration of Space«, Séverine Marguin describes the »design turn« as a driving force for new directions in the humanities and natural sciences as well as a starting point for new formats and procedures in scientific investigation. She emphasizes the potential of cross-disciplinary research for either discipline involved, as it fosters new insights beyond disciplinary framings. »On the entanglement between sociology and architecture in the field of spatial research« highlights the »design turn« in social sciences as a catalyst for the incorporation of design-based procedures into the humanities, opening new possibilities to reconfigure the thematic field, its methodologies, and its forms of research. [Katharina Voigt]

Keywords: Design Turn; Interdisciplinarity; Transdisciplinarity; Sociology.

A Broad Interdisciplinarity between Sociology and Architecture

Interdisciplinarity is experienced in various forms. Following Julie Thompson Klein's typologies, different patterns of consensus and debate can be identified – stemming from the first major classification scheme in 1970 to recent taxonomies. Klein »compares similarities and differences in a framework of multidisciplinary juxtaposition and alignment of disciplines, interdisciplinary integration and collaboration, and transdisciplinary synthesis and trans-sector problem solving« (Klein 2017: 23). This research project addresses a specific form of interdisciplinarity between design and sociology and, in particular, between architects, planners, and sociologists. It is a broad interdisciplinarity, in which the disciplinary integration proves to be complex, inasmuch as it concerns »disciplines with little or no compatibility such as sciences and humanities [which] have different epistemological paradigms and methodologies« (Klein 2017: 34). Is such an integration even possible? What form (whether multidisciplinary, interdisciplinary or

Corresponding author: Séverine Marguin (Technische Universität Berlin, Germany); severine.marguin@tu-berlin.de; https://orcid.org/0000-0001-6775-2678
Open Access. © 2021 Séverine Marguin, published by transcript Verlag.
This work is licensed under the Creative Commons Attribution 4.0 (BY) license.

transdisciplinary) is needed in everyday research practice? And what consequences can such interdisciplinary encounters have for the respective disciplinary understandings and epistemic cultures (Knorr-Cetina 2001; Keller/Pofferl 2018)?

In order to open the debate, I would like to begin with a small narration about a personal interdisciplinary experience between sociology and architecture, in order to show the complexity it involves. In 2019 I worked as a scientific ethnographer and developed a design-based, experimental research design in collaboration with an architect and an interaction designer to analyze the effect of space on the research practices of our colleagues in a so-called Cluster of Excellence (Marguin/Rabe/Schmidgall 2019). Originally, the project was conceived by the designers together with a spokesperson from the cultural studies department with the aim of finding spatial solutions to increase the productivity of the researchers in the excellence cluster. We were to design spatial settings, test them with quantitative tracking measurements and finally evaluate them. The project functioned as a »showcase«-project of the cluster and received a lot of visitors (e.g. from the field of university and research politics). After forming our team, we decided as project staff to reorient the project and to push it more in the direction of a qualitative experimental basic research project, for which we interfered with irritations as well as optimizations across the 18 different settings. This »problematization« was welcomed by the supervisors – but only up until the time of the new proposal for the next Cluster of Excellence, when they urgently asked us for concrete and proved solutions. In contrast, our methodological as well as theoretical and empirical contribution to spatial research did not appear to count or be of value. One year later and outside of the already completed cluster, we published our project publication as a team and devised five concrete statements at the end of our detailed book, which were specifically addressed to the designers of research spaces (Marguin/Rabe/Schmidgall 2019: 186–188).

This anecdote exemplifies how the recipient and the purpose of interdisciplinary research, which oscillate between different logics, can remain ambivalent right up to the end for both the participants and more generally for such a design-focused research project within the framework of a Cluster of Excellence, funded by the German Research Foundation (DFG). This anecdote – in its complexity – allows me to develop a space to reflect on polycontextural knowledge production at the interface between design and sociology (Marguin 2021).

Scientification of Architecture and Creativization of Sociology

The integration of design disciplines (such as art, design, architecture) into the classical (so far mainly natural and humanities) sciences has become an increasingly important topic in the literature on the history of science and cultural studies. Schäffner (2010) and Mareis (2010) welcome this as a desirable development and assign design an »integrative strength (Kraft) for the different scientific disciplines« (Schäffner 2010: 33). Although increasingly occurring, such a development has not yet been investigated – not for the social sciences nor for architecture.

Based on historical analysis, I claim that the design turn leads to new forms of interdisciplinary collaborations and, in my case especially, the referencing between the disciplines of architecture and sociology. In a first step of the research, I outlined the different forms of historical referencing and collaborations between architects and sociologists since their respective disciplinary foundations. In doing so, I addressed the respective positions held by architectural research in sociology and by sociology in architectural research, both at the level of the disciplinary object itself (»architecture« and »society«) and at that of the disciplines themselves (do architectural researchers work with sociological knowledge or even sociologists and vice-versa?). The result of this literature research conveys that despite repeated attempts at rapprochement, collaborations did not become sustainable until the early 2000s, when, in the course of the so-called »design turn«, fundamental new aspects could be observed, pointing to an integrative quality of both disciplines (Marguin 2021).

This new integration as a bold collaboration massively challenges our respective understanding of knowledge and its relationship to society and even more fundamentally to reality. How do we want to generate knowledge? For whom? For what purpose? There is a disciplinary divide of viewpoints. It is what makes current integrative collaboration so difficult but also so exciting and relevant. These are precisely the normative questions of scientific theory that I am now empirically exploring and whose complex entanglement I would like to address in the sense of an empirical theory of science (Knoblauch 2018). For this multiscale investigation, I pursue a mixed-method approach, consisting of a micro-sociological ethnographical part at the *CRC 1265 »Re-Figuration of Spaces«* (TU Berlin) and a macro-sociological component at the field level. Within the ethnographic investigation at the CRC, I observe the everyday interdisciplinary collaboration between sociologists, planners, and architects and analyze the challenges they face, whether as obstacles or productive frictions (Marguin/Knoblauch 2021). These challenges unfold on practical, methodological, scientific and institutional levels. On a macro-sociological level, the research project aims to illustrate the structure of the relational field of architectural research and identify potential linkages to social-science approaches as well as to other actors (i.e. to practitioners). To this end, I conduct interviews with experts on one hand and create different databases on architectural researchers, and on research projects in the field of architectural research in the German-speaking academic field on the other.

The first observation that emerges from my research, both at the Cluster of Excellence and at the CRC 1265, is that there are two parallel converging tendencies: the scientification of architecture and the creativization of sociology. These two tendencies are both somehow explanations and facilitators of such interdisciplinary cooperation.

The debate about the scientification of architecture is by no means a new phenomenon. Rather, it has marked the academicization of the discipline since the 16th century and especially since architecture was integrated into the technical universities from the second half of the 19th century onwards. It has been recurrent throughout the 20th century – whether in the design methods movements in Ulm, or in the 1970s' student movements, or in the digitalization of design in the 1990s. The ambivalence between a free, artistic, and subjective design practice and the longing for systematization is an important component of the epistemic culture of architects and architectural researchers. Following Kurath (2015), two modes of researching in the academic field of architecture can be observed: The first mode is aligned with the validity criteria and scientific understanding established in other disciplines – whether philosophical, sociological, historical or from the field of engineering sciences. Within our CRC, this mode is quite visible in the great interest of the architects in developing a methodological discourse that follows more sociological rules. This also has an institutional background; architects have to defend their position, especially within the faculty, thereby needing doctoral theses, acquisition of third-party funds, and peer-reviewed articles to remain competitive. An opposite tendency is the legitimization of design research as a concept encompassing design practice as a research practice. However, in German-speaking countries – unlike in English-speaking countries, for example – it is extremely controversial and characterized by a heterogeneity of positions.

At the same time, I would like to put forward the thesis of a creativization of sociology, following Reckwitz's social diagnosis of the »dispositif of creativity« (2012, 2016). In our CRC 1265, sociologists hope to develop new, innovative methods of spatial research from the interdisciplinary work by integrating visual-mapping methods from architecture and planning into sociology among other things (Baxter et al. 2021). Beyond the boundaries of the CRC, there are an increasing number of initiatives in the German-speaking field that are interested in integrating artistic and design methods into social research – whether in the field of sociology or anthropology (Wildner 2015; Fariàs/Criado 2019; Estalella/Criado 2019). This shift of sociology toward design can be interpreted as an »expansion of its innovation zone« (Rammert et al. 2016). In fact, this notion of creativity is thought of as a means of innovation for social research: The hope is that something new will emerge from the collectively and strategically provoked dissonances. It seems important, here, following Rammert, to critically question whether the creativization process in sociology can be regarded as »an imperial expansion of economic innovation criteria or [rather] a liberal extension to social innovations« (Rammert et al. 2016: 4). Or more simply formulated: why should sociology become more creative? At this stage of my investigation it remains unclear whether this imperative of the renewal of sociology around the »practice and semantics of creativity« (Hutter et al. 2016: 28) is rather, in the Bourdieusian sense, field-internally driven, or if it responds to field-external factors.

I present both tendencies equally here, despite the unbalanced tendency, which favors sociology over the design. The scientification of architecture is a common tendency, while the creativization of sociology only exists in its initial stages and at the periphery.

A Design Turn for the Social Sciences

In terms of contemporary diagnosis, such converging developments largely tie in with the need for a »transformative science« (Schneidwind/Singer-Brodowski 2014), understood as the function of science to restructure social areas of life, including changing people's behavior. For this challenge of science's transformative performativity, the design disciplines are relatively highly valued because they include the competency to consider potential changes and reflect on the performativity of their own knowledge production into society. But what does it mean and imply for sociology and its potential to become more creative? And for architecture to become more scientific? In other words, what kind of challenges do such mutual integrative adjustments bring? The pitfalls of such cooperation between design and social science become visible in the interdisciplinary everyday collaboration. The empirical investigation shows that the attempt to appropriate the structural logics of the other field leads to a seemingly inevitable conflict, insofar as the respective logics of the academic fields contradict each other.

In the ethnographical investigation, scholars address their feeling of alienation from their field-specific practice. Designers clearly convey that their participation in a basic research project is not sufficient or remains irrelevant to their peers, if it is not followed by an operative and projective translation into society. The inconsequence, or rather the absence of the project's finality, acts as an insurmountable disadvantage for recognition in their community. For the sociologists, however, it creates the opposite unease: The need for action is perceived as an external compulsion that implies a loss of autonomy. Embedded in its structural logic, the sociologists link it directly to the current debates on the new relationship or »contract between social sciences and society« (Weingart 2008), which should no longer be characterized by disinterest and independence but rather be guided by socially relevant political or economic mandates. This highlights the heteronormatization tendencies at work and points to the controversial debate on the so-called »Mode 2« or triple helix of knowledge production (Gibbons et al. 1994), which suggests an intertwining of scientific epistemology, entrepreneurial application orientation, and efficiency-based strategies of problem solving – and clearly endangers the basic scientific orientation of the social sciences (Gingras/Heilbron 2015). Conflicting polarities are identified during the investigation: practice vs. theory; action or application research vs. basic research; synthetic vs. analytical science. Terms such as action, application, practice, and mission will be almost equated. The amalgam gives the (deceptive) impression of a clear duality as well as an irreconcilable discrepancy between the disciplines.

However, this schematic, polarizing duality is not satisfactory. As the aforementioned anecdote demonstrated in an exemplary way, the positions of the researchers, whether sociologists or designers, are much more complex. Therefore, I suggest breaking the polarity shown above and complexifying it. From the analysis of the disciplinary structural logics, the following two axes become clear: in the sociological field, it is primarily a question of the autonomy/heteronomy of the social sciences, while in the field of architectural research, it is more a question of the compatibility of research and design. The relation of these different elements enables the expansion from the one-dimensional restricted polarity to a two-dimensional space of interdisciplinary spatial research (see fig. on following page).

This gives rise to four different understandings of interdisciplinary research: autonomous with design; autonomous without design; heteronomous with design; heteronomous without design. This spatial modeling is not intended to show ideal types but rather a continuum of research understandings that are relatively more autonomous or heteronomous, or contain relatively or no design aspects. This notion enables thinking about a research practice with design aspects that, despite its dimensions of application, practice or action, would nevertheless take on autonomous traits in its orientation and execution (see the red square on the diagram). A preliminary placement of representatives from the interdisciplinary field of urban and spatial research was realized on the diagram to illustrate the differentiated positioning. It should not be overlooked, however, that a strong imbalance of power is at work here, insofar as the field of sociology has considerably more power in a scientific or academic context than the field of architectural research, which is still in its infancy. In fact, the Design Turn is still at its very beginning and, although very promising, has to contend with greater disadvantage in the classical sciences, especially in the social sciences.

Conclusion

In this paper, I present the initial results of an empirical investigation that I am currently conducting on the relationship between design and the social sciences on the basis of an ethnographic inquiry of the cooperation between architects, planners, and sociologists. I first discuss the current favorable tendencies of approximation between these disciplines, namely a scientification of architecture and a certain creativization of sociology before tackling the main challenges of such cooperation concerning the divergent understanding of knowledge and science.

In order to go beyond the common but deceptive duality between design vs. science; practice vs. theory; action or application research vs. basic research; synthetic vs. analytical science, I have proposed to break down the polarity and complexify it, thereby relating the structural logics to both fields. Such a spatial-visual modeling, which creates the possibility of autonomous creative-social-scientific research, however, raises many questions.

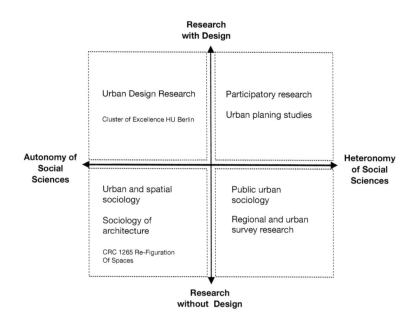

»Modelling a Two-Dimensional Space of Interdisciplinary Spatial Research«
CRC 1265 Re-Figuration of Spaces.
Graphics: Séverine Marguin, 2020.

The first is the question of autonomy. If I have so far dealt exclusively with the autonomy of the (social) sciences (Bourdieu 1975, 1997, 2001; Bernhard/ Schmidt-Wellenburg 2012a, b), the autonomy of architecture must also be considered. Based on the work of Biau (1998) and Aigner (2007), field theory does indeed lend itself well to the analysis of architecture, insofar as it can be understood as a cultural asset. Can one therefore speak of a parallelism between the understandings of autonomy in the social sciences and in architecture? The second question concerns the career possibilities of such hybrid knowledge producers and the risk of their marginalization: in fact, the investigation provides many indications that disciplinary logics continue to be of a strange importance in career formation. A deviation from the disciplinary rules of the game may lead to a dead end, also because what has been learned from interdisciplinary cooperation can no longer be sealed off. The only solution for hybrid knowledge producers is therefore to influence the rules of the game in their own field in order to increase the acceptance of alternative approaches.

References

Aigner, Anita (2007): »Architektur als Feld«, presented at the conference »Profession, Habitus und Wandel«, Humboldt Universität Berlin.

Baxter, Jamie Scott/Marguin, Séverine/ Méllx, Sophie/ Schinagl, Martin/ Sommer, Vivien/Singh, Ajit (2021): »Hybrid Mapping: Visual Methods at the Intersection of Sociospatial Research and Design«, in: *SFB 1265 Working Paper No. 5 Berlin.*

Bernhard, Stefan/Schmidt-Wellenburg, Christian, eds. (2012a): *Feldanalyse Als Forschungsprogramm 1. Der Programmatische Kern,* Wiesbaden: Springer VS.

Bernhard, Stefan/Schmidt-Wellenburg, Christian, eds. (2012b): *Feldanalyse Als Forschungsprogramm 2. Gegenstandsbezogene Theoriebildung,* Wiesbaden: Springer VS.

Biau, Véronique (1998): »Stratégies de positionnement et trajectoires d'architectes«, in: *Sociétés contemporaines* 29(1), 7–25.

Bourdieu, Pierre (1975): »The Specificity of the Scientific Field and the Social Conditions of the Progress of Reason«, in: *Social Science Information* 14(6), 19–47.

Bourdieu, Pierre (1997):*Les usages sociaux de la science: Pour une sociologie clinique du champ scientifique*, Paris, INRA Editions. – German translaton: *Vom Gebrauch der Wissenschaft. Für eine klinische Soziologie des Wissenschaftlichen Feldes*, transl. by Stephan Egger, Konstanz: UVK Verlagsgesellschaft, 1998.

Bourdieu, Pierre/Wacquant, Loïc [2001]: *Science de la science et réflexivité*, Paris: Éditions Raisons d'agir. – English translation: *Science of Science and Reflexivity*, Cambridge: Polity Press, 2004.

Estalella, Adolfo/Criado, Tomás Sánchez (2019): »DIY Anthropology. Disciplinary Knowledge in Crisis«, in: *ANUAC Journal of the Italian Society of Cultural Anthropology* 8(2), 143–65.

Fariàs, Ignacio/Criado, Tomás Sánchez (2019): »Erfahren. Experimente mit technischer Demokratie in Entwurfskursen«, in: Séverine Marguin/Henrike Rabe/Wolfgang Schäffner/Friedrich Schmidgall (eds.) *Experimentieren. Einblicke in Praktiken und Versuchsaufbauten zwischen Wissenschaft und Gestaltung*, Bielefeld: transcript Verlag, 67–81.

Gibbons, Michael/Limoges, Camille/ Nowotny, Helga/ Schwartzman, Simon/ Scott, Peter/Trow, Martin (1994): *The New Production of Knowledge: The Dynamics of Science and Research in Contemporary Societies*, London: Sage Publishers.

Gingras, Yves/Heilbron, Johan (2015): »La résilience des disciplines«, in: *Actes de la Recherche en Sciences Sociales* 210(5), 4–9.

Hutter, Michael/Knoblauch, Hubert/ Rammert, Werner/Windeler, Arnold (2016): »Innovationsgesellschaft heute«, in: Werner Rammert/Arnold Windeler/ Hubert Knoblauch/Michael Hutter (eds.), *Innovationsgesellschaft heute*, Wiesbaden: Springer Fachmedien Wiesbaden, 15–35.

Keller, Reiner/Poferl, Angelika eds. (2018): *Wissenskulturen der Soziologie*, Weinheim; Basel: Beltz Juventa.

Klein, Julie Thompson (2017): »Typologies of Interdisciplinarity: The Boundary Work of Definition«, in: *The Oxford Handbook of Interdisciplinarity*, Oxford: Oxford University Press.

Knoblauch, Hubert (2018): »Von Der Reflexiven Methodologie Zur Empirischen Wissenschaftstheorie«, in: Leila Akremi/ Nina Baur/Hubert Knoblauch/Boris Traue (eds.), *Handbuch Interpretativ Forschen*, Weinheim: Beltz Juventa, 226–244.

Knorr-Cetina, Karin (1995): »Laboratory Studies. The Cultural Approach to the Study of Science«, In: Sheila Jasanoff/ Gerald Markle/James Peterson/Trevor Pinch (eds.), *Handbook of Science and Technology*, Thousand Oaks, CA: Sage Publishers.

Kurath, Monika (2015): »Architecture as a Science: Boundary Work and the Demarcation of Design Knowledge from Research«, in: *Science & Technology Studies* 28(3), 81–100, doi: 10.23987/sts.55343

Mareis, Claudia (2010): »Entwerfen – Wissen – Produzieren. Designforschung im Anwendungskontext«, in: Claudia Mareis/Gesche Joost/Kora Kimpel (eds.), *Entwerfen – Wissen – Produzieren. Designforschung im Anwendungskontext*, Bielefeld: transcript Verlag, 9–32.

Marguin, Séverine, Henrike Rabe, and Friedrich Schmidgall (2019): *The Experimental Zone. An Interdisciplinary Investigation on the Spaces and Practices of Collaborative Research*, Zurich: Park Books.

Marguin, Séverine (2021): »Architecture and Sociology: A Sociogenesis of Interdisciplinary Referencing«, in: *Forum: Qualitative Social Research, special issue The Re-Figuration of Spaces and Cross-Cultural Comparison*.

Marguin, Séverine (2021): »Interdisziplinarität als polykontexturale Wissensproduktion. Über die Kollaboration zwischen SoziologInnen, ArchitektInnen und PlanerInnen«, in: Martina Löw/Volkan Sayman/Jona Schwerer/Hannah Wolf (eds.), *Am Ende der Globalisierung. Über die Re-Figuration von Räumen*, Bielefeld: transcript Verlag.

Marguin, Séverine/Knoblauch, Hubert (2021): »Empirische Wissenschaftstheorie. Wissenschaftsethnografie, experimentelle Methodenentwicklung und Sensitizing Visits im SFB 1265 Re-Figuration von Räumen«, in: Martina Löw/Volkan Sayman/Jona Schwerer/Hannah Wolf (eds.), *Am Ende der Globalisierung. Über die Re-Figuration von Räumen*, Bielefeld: transcript Verlag.

Rammert, Werner/ Windeler, Arnold/ Knoblauch, Hubert/Hutter, Michael (2016): »Die Ausweitung der Innovationszone«, in: Werner Rammert/Arnold Windeler/Hubert Knoblauch/Michael Hutter, *Innovationsgesellschaft heute*, Wiesbaden: Springer Fachmedien, 3–13.

Reckwitz, Andreas (2012): *Die Erfindung der Kreativität. Zum Prozess gesellschaftlicher Ästhetisierung*, Frankfurt am Main: Suhrkamp.

Reckwitz, Andreas (2016): »Das Kreativitätsdispositiv und die sozialen Regime des Neuen«, in: Werner Rammert/Arnold Windeler/Hubert Knoblauch/Michael Hutter, *Innovationsgesellschaft heute*, Wiesbaden: Springer Fachmedien, 133–153.

Schäffner, Wolfgang (2010): »The Design Turn. Eine Wissenschaftliche Revolution Im Geiste Der Gestaltung«, in: Claudia Mareis/Gesche Joost/Kora Kimpel, *Entwerfen – Wissen – Produzieren Designforschung im Anwendungskontext*, Bielefeld: transcript Verlag, 33–46.

Schneidewind, Uwe/Singer-Brodowski, Mandy (2014): *Transformative Wissenschaft. Klimawandel Im Deutschen Wissenschafts- Und Hochschulsystem*, Marburg: Metropolis.

Weingart, Peter (2008): »Ökonomisierung der Wissenschaft«, in: *NTM Zeitschrift für Geschichte der Wissenschaften, Technik und Medizin* 16(4), 477–484, doi: 10.1007/s00048-008-0311-4

Wildner, Kathrin (2015): »Inventive Methods. Künstlerische Ansätze in Der Ethnographischen Stadtforschung«, in: *Ethnoscripts* 17(1), 168–185.

Resumee

Reflection

Ferdinand Ludwig and Katharina Voigt

Keywords: Research Perspectives; Research Reflection; Research Methodologies; Knowledge Creation; Architectural Knowledge; Design Research; Research Funding.

Context

A reflection on the contributions in this issue requires a recollection of the 2019 summer conference »Research Perspectives in Architecture«, as well as a consideration of the themes discussed there. It is important to examine and explore which approaches, ways of thinking, and potentials will unfold on this basis for future research in the discipline of architecture. The initial questions mentioned in the editorial introduction to this volume – Where do we come from? Where are we now? Where are we going? – address the dimensions of past, present, and future, inquiring into the history, current state, and future of the research of architecture. In this regard, we need to reflect on recent developments and changes in architectural research. Bold terms, such as the »research turn« (cf. Archis 2016) – implying the academicization of the architecture discipline, the scientific character of research or the integrity of genuine methodologies of architecture – seek further framing and definition. Although the aim of this reflection is not to fathom these overarching terminologies, they have been consolidated more specifically through a discussion of the contributions in this reflection.

The opening lecture of the conference by Monika Kurath revealed numerous challenges in, and potentials of, research in architecture. Although this overarching approach has not been included in this volume as a contribution (cf. Flach/Kurath 2016), some of its core statements are of such profound relevance that they are worth addressing again in this reflection. Kurath's investigation of different research cultures in architecture – using the case studies of the Bartlett and Columbia Schools of Architecture, along with Cambridge University – reveals interesting insights into the different research cultures practiced at the respective institutions. Her analysis highlights their successes and their potential, thereby distinguishing them from each other. She concludes that one key obstacle to reaching a self-evident nature of research in architecture is based on an often-occurring separation of the research division from the design division in architecture schools. Instead, she proposes envisioning architecture departments as comprehensive entities, which include both design and research, equally. Therewith, she highlights that despite their variety of interests and their plurality of methodological approaches, all fields of the discipline contribute equally to knowledge creation in architecture. Nevertheless, she underlines that »design« and »design research« need to be carefully distinguished from each other and accurately defined.

Architecture as a Research Discipline

The very question regarding the interrelation of scientific research and applied forms of knowledge creation in architecture is explored throughout all contributions included in the conference and in this volume. While the latest shifts toward a further academicization of the discipline have resulted in heated debates, weighing the one against the other, the contributions in this volume are based on a common ground of highlighting the fruitfulness of reciprocal interconnections and contingencies of both. The contributions to this issue exemplify the manifold approaches to research in architecture. The fact that architecture is more than just a design practice, but also a research discipline, is therefore without question. In this respect, the original methodologies and ways of working become crucial, as they are the key to addressing research in architecture through architectural means. As Jan Silberberger underlines with his study on methodologies of teaching and knowledge transfer in architecture schools, the design process is more rigorous and more clearly structured than often supposed. On the contrary, well-established scientific approaches – as for instance those of the Natural Sciences – appear to be more liberal and more creative than we believe on first sight. While it has been a long road to approve design as part of the methodological spectrum in architecture – and partially still is – the notion of »design« has long since been adapted to the natural scientific discourse, as researchers in this field speak of »designing a setup«, and »designing a research proposal«; thus, integrating the design process in the conception of a research project most naturally contributes to its methodological framework. This is where a debate about the understanding of research and science in architecture begins, which is also reflected in this issue's different contributions.

The closer architectural research is to other established sciences and the more methods it borrows from these sciences, the more it is acknowledged as «scientific«. There is nothing at all wrong with this transfer and adaptation of research approaches from other disciplines; it is good scientific practice in all interdisciplinary fields. But this approach cannot answer the question of how research is to be recognized in what we can call the »core of architecture«: Architectural design. As Uta Graff explores in the opening chapter »Research Perspectives in Architecture«, the structured, consecutive, organized, and methodological ways of knowledge creation in architecture are numerous and abundant. Furthermore, the distinction often made between theoretical research and practice-based research is therewith put to the question. Dag Boutsen clearly articulates this redundancy:

> »I detest this tendency of some to push architectural research in the direction of applied research. Nothing seems less appropriate. It exists, to a certain extent, but it's the wrong direction. We shouldn't see theory and practice as oppositional. Fifty percent of the curriculum of design education consists of studios and subjects around mixed media. So, when you want to expand research in the service of an educational program, it's necessary to situate that research in a practical realm.« (Boutsen 2016: 24–25)

Understanding architecture as a research discipline, as Kurath promotes it, underlines that research has the potential to contribute fruitfully to the central fields of the discipline, i.e. the design. With regard to the possible research goals for the achievement and application of research results, Boutsen asserts that »research *by* design« and »research *through* design« signify »research *on* design« (cf. Boutsen 2016). Ultimately, research in architecture should always be directed toward and contributing to the design. Methodologically speaking, any approach to gain design knowledge – systematic, testing, creational, analytic or evaluative – should be considered as a serious basis for research. The more specifically we know how we design, the more eager we are to integrate genuine architectural methods into research.

Architect as Researcher

In her text »Reflexions on the Plurality of Methods in Architecture«, Oya Atalay Franck argues that architects are not trained (and maybe not even able) to conduct research, and therefore should avoid trying to do it. Instead, she frames their role as generalists who are responsible for the »organization of the interdisciplinary analytical and synthetical process and the translation of the knowledge gained from this interdisciplinary work into spatial manifestation«. She argues that »the domain of the architect as ›maker of spaces‹ extends to all areas of human presence and all levels of scale« and that this approach causes manifold requirements that »differ obviously from place to place, from scale to scale, and from use to use.« In her eyes, this context-specific approach eludes a systematic, generalizable approach, which is indispensable for research. Franck certainly acknowledges that architecture requires structured processes for problem solving. However, she adds that the reduction of architecture to »mere *problem solving* is robbing it of its key element, the magical quality that architectural spaces and structures have, when they become art«. She subsequently asks: »how can methodological rigor and academic transparency be applied to a discipline which relies so heavily on intuition and on artistic creativity, on that which has to be felt but cannot really be explained?« In this context, she refers to the field of architectural research as »dirty«, because it is not in a laboratory, where agents and factors can be limited, but in the real world. This perspective is nevertheless contrasted by many of the other contributions in the issue, as they highlight the methodological structure, systematics, and clarity of the design process, fostering the potential that identification and investigation of these working methods can provide when applied to research.

According to Franck, architecture is by no means alone in this contextualization of research in the real world, but rather shares its fate e.g. with sociology, anthropology, or medicine. She continues that a holistic medical approach, which regards the patient in all dimensions of »health«, has the same difficulties in finding scientific acknowledgment (and thus ultimately also research funding) as design-related research in architecture – in contrast to laboratory-based medical research, »where huge amounts of money are poured in«.

Research in architecture suffers from the stigma that it would rob the architect of his or her identity, degrade intuition and creative talent, and rationalize the design process, inevitably leading to feeble, uninspired results. This is a problem that cannot be taken seriously enough. In essence, it is diametrically opposed to the expectations that one should have in research – which underpin all well-established, successful fields of research. In fact, the starting point for research is always curiosity – and is ultimately driven by an open question that cannot be answered easily; a question that requires certain procedures – research methods – to be answered. From this, one could conclude the following: As soon as an architect is of the opinion that a (design) question can be answered without such a systematic, transparent procedure or that this procedure would lead to a less convincing answer, then one should consequently decide against pursuing this research. But this is only partly true: Individual architectural questions – as the generally accepted design practice shows – can of course be answered without a systematic research approach. Yet there is often more than one specific solution behind each design question; there is often a core, an essence, that might be generalizable. It should be noted that the notion of generalizability is often misunderstood by architects. The aim of generalization in architectural research is not primarily a matter of finding a standard solution (e.g. in terms of the built result) with the aim of universal application. Rather, it concerns enabling others to learn from the process of finding a solution in a specific case in order to be able to transfer and further develop this approach to other similar, but not identical, questions. This way of thinking and acting is not very common among designing architects – even in an academic context.

Methodological Adaptions

If a holistic approach to medicine – which is undoubtedly of high societal relevance – is struggling with very similar problems as architectural research, then one should at least consider questioning the criteria of the established sciences and not only the research competences of designing architects. What might help here, are the attempts of e.g. Schöbel et. al assembled in this issue, who, unlike Franck, see high potential for systematic research approaches in the practices of designing architects.[1] For example, in the approach of qualitative abductive reasoning, they see the possibility of systematically collecting, interpreting, and clustering phenomena such as design solutions or built forms – in order to make them available

---

1 »Architects« here is considered as an umbrella term. Landscape architects and urban planners/designers are meant equally.

as »scientific data«. Between this clustering and the typologization common in architecture, they see a great methodological affinity and thus conclude that »the similarity between qualitative research and architectural typologization can be used in the design-specific approaches, if we do the same – accept, adopt, and adjust quality criteria of systematic research in what we call »Research through Design«. In doing so, they point out that »we must embed design […] into a method that enables general, i.e. transferable and verifiable knowledge«. In so far as they identify ways to »operate research through design not only systematically, but also with regard to general knowledge.

The prerequisite for this form of generalization is to shed as much light as possible on the »black box« of design. Yet there is another point to be addressed here: Findings need to be made accessible to others, they need to be communicated and contribute to the overarching discourse. Simply put: One has to publish them and others will have to read them, have to build on them, and also have to indicate what they are building on in their work.

Research Efficacy

The initial questions to plunge into investigation and research are very basic: »what do I want to know and why?«, »what do I have to know to pursue my research?«, »what do I know through my practice and experience?«, »what is already known about my topic?«, »what would the effects of my research be?«[2] and most importantly: which discourse do I contextualize my work in?«, »which track of argumentation and knowledge do I want to contribute to?«, and especially, »who are the recipients of my work?«. Given the broad variety of subareas in the discipline of architecture, it is most reasonable that it would result in a plurality of research interests addressed and methods applied. The different methodological approaches shed light on the varying roles of researchers themselves. The section on experience-based research should be emphasized in this regard, as it empowers the researcher to become part of the research work, contextualizing it in the background of personal knowledge and experience. Researchers are never uninvolved

---

2 These five questions have been investigated particularly in the context of the international PhD event on »Research Practice in Architecture«, initiated by Meike Schalk (KTH Stockholm), Frank van der Hoeven (TU Delft), Torsten Lange, and Andreas Putz (Technical University of Munich), hosted at the Technical University of Munich in October 2020.

in their research. Against the background of the differentiation between architectural design processes and the corresponding perpetual self-reflection and self-examination, the discipline of architecture holds the potential to emphasize the individuality of the individual researchers and to conceive of them as part of the research process. Being a researcher does not only describe an activity, but it also highlights a personal involvement, contributing one's individual background, experience, and position to the discourse and knowledge creation of the discipline.

Among the many different aspects of architecture, there are some that ought to be considered of extraordinary importance, forming the core of the discipline. It would be most natural if research in architecture would address the most common aspects – instead of intensive research in liminal subareas of very specific content. Therefore, it is necessary to outline the entire spectrum of the »core« of architectural research. It would be misleading to relate this exclusively to the built object. In this sense, the contributions in this volume reveal not only methodological diversity but thematic variety as well, ranging from the design of ecological systems (Sungoruglu-Hensel) to performative approaches (Ferreira). At the same time, however, it is also important to avoid the arbitrariness associated with the multiple interpretations of »design« in the sense of »design thinking«. For the purposes of precision, the German terms »Entwerfen« and, above all, »Gestaltung« should be referred to in this volume, which can hardly be translated into English. What is meant with »Gestaltung« is a process of creation in which a material object, a structure, a process or a situation is changed or developed in its – in the broadest sense – aesthetic appearance.[3] Furthermore, it should be noted that all research activities contribute to a broader realm of discourse beyond their individual specific findings. It is crucial to specify the potentials of a research work regarding this superordinate context. The contributions assembled in this volume – as well as those to follow in future issues – convey the diversity of dimensions of architectural knowledge, the plurality of directions unfolding in research or standpoints and perspectives claimed. It becomes apparent that research always includes the position of the researchers, their self-understanding, their background, experience and choices, and their individual involvement in seeking further knowledge and insights.

---

3 Own definition, partly based on: https://de.wikipedia.org/wiki/Gestaltung, accessed November 11, 2020.

After all, we have to admit that it will not be easy to establish design research in architecture as a widely accepted field of research. Ultimately, it will also be a matter of offering researching architects a platform and a base for their work that enables them to concentrate on their research questions – in other words, rewarding and honoring research in architecture. Therefore, it will not be possible without third-party funding, and, as Franck correctly points out, so far architecture often falls out of the picture here. First, because research questions and procedures are not formulated precisely enough and second, because key prerequisites such as the existence of well-cited peer-reviewed articles are not in place.

The first point can be addressed by establishing a research culture as described above. This must be achieved through a good balance between self-confidence and self-criticism. Self-confidence in the sense that architects have to realize that their inherent methods of analyzing design frameworks (see Boucsein's contribution in this issue), systematizing (typologization) and, of course, designing itself, are quite suitable to develop into research methods. Self-critique insofar as that there is a deficit in making a research approach explicit, as well as in defining criteria of how to distinguish between architectural research and design practice – especially if it is practice-based research.

The second point can only be solved strategically: On the one hand, by urging universities and research-funding institutions to recognize the special approaches of architects. And on the other hand, by establishing or expanding publication formats that are specifically tailored to the particular needs of researching architects. In alliance with other recently started journals from the BauHow5 partner universities, *Dimensions. Journal of Architectural Knowledge* aims to bridge this gap. However, it is not a question of establishing a peer-reviewed journal for purely strategic reasons, to simply follow up with the generally accepted index scores for successful research (number of peer-reviewed publications, h-index, cite-score, etc.) with the aim of increasing the success rate of third-party funding. The established sciences show all too well that publishing for the sake of achieving formal, quantitative rather than qualitative criteria ultimately runs the risk of counteracting itself. Rather, the driving force behind *Dimensions. Journal of Architectural Knowledge* is an interest in the content, while the concrete implementation strategically aims to open up new possibilities for architectural research in the future.

References

Boutsen, Dag (2016): »Upgrading the Architect«, in: *Archis* 2(48), 24–27.

Flach, Anna/Kurath, Monika (2016): »Architektur als Forschungsdisziplin: Ausbildung zwischen Akademisierung und Praxisorientierung. Bildungslandschaften«, in: *archithese* (2)2016, 73–80, doi: 978-3-03862-231-4

Gibaldi, Joseph (2008): *MLA Style Manual and Guide to Scholarly Publishing*, New York: Modern Language Association of America.

Oosterman, Arjen et al. (2016): Volume. The Research Turn, *Archis* 2 (48).

Winick, Raphael (1991): »Copyright Protection for Architecture after the Architectural Works Copyright Protection Act of 1990«, in: *Duke Law Journal* 41, 1598.

Contributors

Katharina Voigt

This publication, issued as the first volume of *Dimensions. Journal of Architectural Knowledge*, assembles a selection of contributions from those presented at the international conference »Research Perspectives in Architecture« in July 2019, which was the point of initiation for the editors to further investigate the question how knowledge is constituted, passed on, and invented in the discipline of architecture. The matter of methodologies and structured, coordinated ways of knowledge creation has therefore become crucial as the core of the investigation. The conference was initiated and hosted at the Technical University of Munich by the editors of this issue, funded by the German Research Foundation (DFG), project number 428316702. It was part of the context of the BauHow5 European Alliance of five leading research-intensive universities in Architecture and the Built Environment – as is the journal *Dimensions* itself. The authors are part of the institutions who form the BauHow5 Alliance or the associated networks of the respective universities.

All contributors to this issue work and research in the field of architecture and relate to the discipline of architecture; be it as trained and practicing architects or as practitioners and researchers from different disciplinary backgrounds with specific interest in the matters of the architectural discipline and discourse.

The perspectives on architecture are therefore manifold, as all authors access their investigation starting from their individual standpoint, integrating their personal context of knowledge into their research. As we have been opening this issue, raising the questions »where do we come from?«, »where are we now?« and »where are we going?« in regard to the superordinate tendencies of change and development in the state of the arts for research, we consider it evenly important to raise these questions for each individual contributor. We all have come our individual ways, which have brought us to the perspective we now take, which have shaped and reshaped our view on the world on the large scale, as they have shaped our position to regard the subjects of our research. The individual background can be formative for certain views, approaches to certain questions, or intentions for methodological choices. Therefore, it is inevitable to take into account the background, genesis and intentions of an author in order to better understand the position they take.

The texts collected in this issue stem from authors at very different stages of their academic paths. Contributions from researchers at early or later periods of their doctorate are published alongside those of post-doctoral researchers and habilitated professors. All chapters equally contribute to the overarching aim to constitute an assemblage of positions on methodologies and ways of working to approach research practice in the discipline of architecture. Their biographies are provided in this chapter, to allow the reader to trace where they come from, where they are now, and where they might be aiming to develop their works in the future.

Biographies

Alexandra Abel (Dr.)
studied German studies, philosophy, and psychology primarily in Heidelberg and currently works as an architectural psychologist at the Bauhaus-University in Weimar. Her research focuses on architectural perception, architecture, and communication as well as architecture and health. Her latest publications include: *Klassisch modern – Lebensstile in Weimar*, 2015 and with Bernd Rudolf *Architektur wahrnehmen*, 2018, 2nd edition in 2020.

Oya Atalay Franck (Prof. Dr.)
is an architect, architectural historian and educator. She is the dean of the School of Architecture, Design, and Civil Engineering in Winterthur, at ZHAW Zurich University of Applied Sciences of Switzerland. She acts as an expert in various scientific organizations, such as the Swiss National Foundation of Research (SNF), the Fundação para a Ciência e a Tecnologia (FCT), the Research Foundation Flanders (FWO), as well as in peer-review committees and in quality audits. She is the president of EAAE, European Association for Architectural Education and a founding member of ARENA, Architectural Research European Network Association. Her areas of expertise in research are a. o. design research methods (research by design), design doctorates, artistic research, the profession and education of architects and civil engineers.

Steffen Bösenberg
studied architecture at Leibniz Universität Hannover from 2008 to 2014. He worked as a student employee at the Institutes for History and Theory, Design and Building, and Urban Design. He interned at Cityförster Architecture + Urbanism and worked for architecture offices in Düsseldorf, Hamburg, and Berlin from 2010 to 2014. He wrote his master's degree on the adaptive reuse of the Wapping Printing Plant, London in Summer 2014 and from 2015 onwards wrote his dissertation project titled *Plasticity. Architectural Concept of Urban Industrial Adaptive Reuse*, while working as an architect

at spine architects, Hamburg. From 2018 to 2019 he worked as scientific assistant to the chair »Architecture and Arts of 20th/21st Century« of Prof. Dr. Margitta Buchert at the faculty for Architecture and Landscape Sciences at Leibniz University Hannover. He has been an associate partner at spine architects in Hamburg since spring 2019.

Benedikt Boucsein (Prof. Dr.)

studied architecture at RWTH Aachen University and ETH Zurich from 1999 to 2005. In 2008, he completed his PhD at the Institute for the History and Theory of Architecture, (gta) ETH Zurich, under the supervision of Prof.Dr. Andreas Tönnesmann (*Graue Architektur*, 2010). From 2007 to 2017, he worked as a lecturer and researcher at ETH Zurich, where his final position was at the Institute for Urban Design under Professor Kees Christiaanse. Here, one of the most important themes he focused on was the surroundings of large airports (*The Noise Landscape*, 2017). Since 2007 he has also been a partner at the architectural and urbanistic practice BHSF Architekten, and from 2005 to 2018 he was founder and co-editor of the journal Camenzind. In 2018, Benedikt Boucsein was appointed as Professor of Urban Design at the Technical University of Munich. In 2020, he co-founded the Office for Deep Transformation in Munich.

Margitta Buchert (Prof. Dr. ir. habil.)

is Professor and heads the Chair of Architecture and Arts of 20th/21st Century, Faculty of Architecture and Landscape Sciences at Leibniz University Hannover, Germany. The chair's contents focus on architectural theory, design theory, and design principles as well as wingspans of modernity. Her primary fields of research are »reflexive design«, and »urban architecture«, as well as the aesthetics and contextuality of architecture, art, cities, and nature. She has been invited lecturer and expert in diverse national and international institutions and is academic partner in the innovative, international EU-funded research network: *Communities of Tacit Knowledge, TACK*, initiated by ten leading academic institutions in Europe. The aim of this project is to reveal tacit knowledge forms and to train young scientists to analyze, understand and apply the specific knowledge of architects.

Maria da Piedade Ferreira (Dr.)

is an architect, performance artist, researcher, and curator. Her doctoral thesis, *Embodied Emotions: Observations and Experiments in Architecture and Corporeality* (2016) coins her concept of »corporeal architecture«. Her work explores the connections between architecture, neuroscience, and performance art. Works of hers have been published and presented in international journals and venues, including the ANFA – Academy for Neuroscience and Architecture and the University IUAV di Venezia. She currently teaches neuroarchitecture and performance art at the Technical University of Munich (TUM) and ergonomics, architecture history, design history and art history at the Hochschule für Technik Stuttgart (HFT). In 2020, as a response to COVID-19, she founded the YouTube channel *Corporeal Architecture*, a curatorial project that works as an open-access education and exhibition room which archives and preserves lectures, performances, and artist research outcomes. The photo archive of *Corporeal Architecture* is found at: www.corporeal.persona.co

Uta Graff (Prof.)

holds the Chair of Architectural Design and Conception at the Technical University of Munich. As a practicing architect, she has worked with Peter Zumthor in Switzerland and with architects von Gerkan Mark und Partner in Berlin. She has been a research associate in the architecture program at the Berlin University of the Arts (UdK) and has worked as a visiting professor in the Chinese-German master's program at the China Academy of Art in Hangzhou, China and at UNI.K, the Studio for Sound Art and Sound Research at the UdK Berlin. In research and teaching she emphasizes the processes of architectural design as systematic approaches to knowledge creation, stressing methodological approaches original to the discipline of architecture to be incorporated equally in research and in practice. She is a founder and part of the advisory board for *Dimension. Journal of Architectural Knowledge*.

Susanne Hauser (Prof. Dr. habil.)

completed studies in history, art history, linguistics, philosophy and literature. She received her doctorate in 1989 and habilitated in 1999. Since 2005 she has been Professor of History of Art and Cultural Studies at the University of the Arts Berlin (UdK), Faculty of Design (Gestaltung/Architektur). From 2003–2005 she was Professor and Head of the Institute for Art and Cultural

Studies at the Graz University of Technology, Faculty of Architecture. From 2000–2003 she was Visiting Professor of Landscape Aesthetics at the University of Kassel. She spent the academic year 1995/1996 as Fellow at the Institute for Advanced Studies Berlin. Since 2010, she has been a member of the Deutsche Akademie für Städtebau und Landesplanung (German Academy for Urban Design and Regional Planning; DASL); since 2017 she serves as a board member of the Deutsche Gesellschaft für Semiotik (DGS). She is a founding member of two graduate colleges, funded by the Deutsche Forschungsgemeinschaft (DFG), »Das Wissen der Künste« (»Knowledge in the Arts«, UdK, 2012–2021) and »Identität und Erbe« (»Identity and Heritage«, Technical University Berlin/Bauhaus University Weimar, 2016–2025). Her research focusses on urban studies, landscape architecture, and the history and theory of architecture and design.

Georg Hausladen

studied biology, architecture, and philosophy of science and technology at the Technical University of Munich (TUM). After his graduation he worked as a research assistant on several interdisciplinary projects and in research groups at the TUM on topics such as ecological design, urban climate adaptation, green infrastructure, and landscape planning. Since his graduation he gives lectures on ecology in landscape design, as well as landscape ecology at the TUM. At the moment he is working as a scientific scholar at the Chair of Technoscience Studies at the Brandenburg University of Technology (BTU) in Cottbus where he focuses on the relations between ecology and technology. In addition, he works as a freelance biologist in the fields of landscape planning and habitat design.

Hannah Knoop

is a research assistant for architectural theory at Karlsruhe Institute of Technology (KIT) and an architect in Munich. She studied architecture at the Technical University of Munich (TUM), ETSA Madrid, and architecture theory at the Institute for the History and Theory of Architecture (gta) of the ETH Zurich. She has worked in German and Swiss architectural offices; in 2017 she joined studioeuropa (Munich/Vienna) as an architect. As a research assistant she has worked and researched at the gta of ETH Zurich and at the TU Kaiserslautern. Based on her MAS thesis at the gta ETH, *Architecture in the Vita Activa* (2016), and an in-depth examination of the work of Hannah

Arendt, her current doctoral project focuses on supranational Architecture and how the idea of supranationality expresses itself in architecture.

Ferdinand Ludwig (Prof. Dr.)
is Professor for Green Technologies in Landscape Architecture at the Technical University of Munich since 2017. At the cutting edge of design, natural sciences, and engineering his work centers on architectural concepts in which plants play a central role, thereby broadening architectural knowledge by confronting aspects of growth and decay, and probability and chance in architectural and landscape design. He studied architecture and completed his doctorate studies at the University of Stuttgart where he founded the research group »Baubotanik« in 2007. He is a partner in the office »ludwig.schönle: Baubotanik – Architecture – Urbanism« and has designed and created numerous projects, such as »Plane-Tree-Cube« in 2012, »Baubotanik Tower« in 2009, and »Baubotanik Footbridge« in 2005. He is a founder and part of the advisory board for *Dimension. Journal of Architectural Knowledge*.

Séverine Marguin (Dr.)
is a sociologist and holds a position as the head of the Method-lab in the Collaborative Research Center 1265 Re-Figuration of Spaces at the Technische Universität Berlin. After her doctorate on artist collectives in Paris and Berlin, she was a researcher in the project ArchitekturenExperimente (ArchitecturesExperiments) at the Cluster of Excellence Image Knowledge Gestaltung of the Humboldt-Universität in Berlin. In her research, she focuses on science studies, collectivity, interdisciplinarity, visual research methods, and experimentalization.

Anna Maria Meister (Prof. Dr.)
is an architect, historian, and writer, and Professor of Architecture Theory and Science at TU Darmstadt. She works at the intersection of architecture's histories and the histories of science and technology, focusing on the production and dissemination of norms and normed objects as social desires in German modern architecture. Meister received a joint PhD degree in the History and Theory of Architecture and the Council of the Humanities from Princeton University and holds degrees in architecture from Columbia University, New York, and the Technical University of Munich. She was a fellow at the Max-Planck Institute for the History of Science, Berlin and

her work has been supported by grants and fellowships from the Graham Foundation, the Berlin Program for Advanced German and European Studies, and the DAAD among others. Her writing has been published in *The British Journal of the History of Science, Harvard Design Magazine, Volume, Baumeister, Arch+* and as a book chapter in *Architecture and the Paradox of Dissidence* (Routledge, 2013), *Dust and Data* (2019) or *The Architecture Machine* (2020). She is co-curator and co-editor of the international collaborative project *Radical Pedagogies*; the eponymous book is forthcoming with MIT Press in 2021.

Nandini Oehlmann
was born in Berlin in 1985 and graduated with a degree in architecture in 2013 after studying at the Berlin University of the Arts and the Technical University of Istanbul. She has been an academic assistant to the Chair of Architectural Design and Building in Context at the Brandenburg University of Technology Cottbus and has been working in architectural practice with Oda Pälmke since 2014. She is a doctoral candidate at Berlin Universtity of Arts, researching embodied knowledge in architectural design and has worked as an academic assistant to the Chair for Construction and Design at the Technical University of Berlin since 2018.

Julian Schäfer
is a landscape architect and urban planner, and holds a master's degree in Landscape Architecture. Since 2015 he has worked as a research fellow and has been teaching and researching with Prof. Dr. Sören Schöbel at the TUM on research through design, mapping, and the conceptual, formative design of the city, open space and landscape on a regional and urban scale. His current research project is titled *Public Space in Cultural Landscape*.

Peter Schmid
studied architecture at the Technical University of Munich and at the Czech Technical University in Prague. In 2008 he graduated in Munich with the diploma. Since 2014 he has worked as a practicing architect in Munich. From 2008 on he has researched and taught at the Chair of Architectural Design and Conception at the Technical University of Munich. Since 2014 he has been working on his doctorate on architectural drawing in the education of the »Munich School«, which he completed in 2020. The research project includes the compilation and preparation of the available inventory of sketchbooks

and lecture manuscripts from 150 years of drawing lessons. Architectural drawing in the tradition of the »Munich School« is also integrated in his teaching, with the mandatory subjects of architectural drawing and watercolor painting. Furthermore, in spring 2018 he contributed the findings from his research to the exhibition »Skizzenbuchgeschichten« (Sketchbook Stories) at Pinakothek der Moderne, Munich, in cooperation with the Staatliche Graphische Sammlung München (State Graphic Collection Munich).

Sören Schöbel (Prof. Dr.)
studied landscape architecture at the Technical University in Berlin (TUB), and has worked freelance since 1995 and as a research fellow at the TUB from 1998–2003, when he completed his doctorate. Since 2005, he has held the professorship of Landscape Architecture and Regional Open Space at the Technical University of Munich. His research focuses on the possibilities of, and design methods for, urban landscape architecture on a regional scale in the area of urban open space structures, cultural landscape and rural development, and renewable energies.

Jan Silberberger (Dr.)
is a senior researcher at the Institute for the History and Theory of Architecture (gta) at the Department of Architecture, ETH Zürich, Switzerland. He studied Visual Communication and Fine Arts at the University of Fine Arts Hamburg (HFBK), Germany. In his PhD studies in the Human Geography Unit at the University of Fribourg, Switzerland (which he completed in 2011), Silberberger analyzed decision-making and knowledge creation within jury boards of architectural competitions. Dr Silberberger's current research focuses on methodologies in architectural design and its teaching.

Defne Sunguroglu Hensel (Dr.)
is a trained architect and interior architect, a partner in the practice OCEAN Architecture / Environment, and coordinating manager and a member of the steering committee of the LamoLab Research Centre. She has extensive experience studying at the intersection of architecture, design, and green construction. Her research has focused on advanced design computing, especially in areas of high complexity, data-driven design, design decision support systems, information modeling (computational ontology), and computer-aided design and fabrication. She has taught at the Architectural Association School of Architecture in London, University of Technology

Sydney, Oslo School of Architecture and Design, and the Technical University of Munich. Currently, she is a university lecturer and senior researcher at Vienna University of Technology in the special research area, advanced computational design in the context of the Centre for Geometry and Computational Design.

Francesca Torzo (Prof.)

studied Architecture at Delft University of Technology, Barcelona School of Architecture (ETSAB), Academy of Architecture in Mendrisio (AAM) and University of Venice (IUAV). She completed her diploma at AAM and graduated with honours at IUAV with architect Peter Zumthor, Professor Umberto Tubini, architect Muguel Kreisler, engineer Jürg Conzett. From 2001–2002 she worked as a project architect with Peter Zumthor Architekturbüro and in 2003 with Bosshard Vaquer Architekten in Zurich. In 2008 she started her own office in Genoa. Since 2017 she has been a professor at Bergen School of Architecture, Norway and has lectured at a number of schools and cultural institutions. In 2018 she participated at the 16th Venice Architecture Biennale *FREESPACE* and was appointed fourth chairman of MVSC in Ghent. In 2020 she participated in the Triennale di Milano with her contribution entitled »Chaosmos«. In 2020 she is awarded the WA Moira Gemmill Prize. Her project for the extension of the Z33 in Hasselt has been awarded with the International Piranesi award in 2018, as well as with the Italian Architecture Prize in 2020. The project has also been nominated for the Mies van der Rohe award of 2022.

Katharina Voigt

studied architecture in Hamburg, Munich, and Stockholm. She worked for Stölken Schmidt Architekten BDA in Hamburg and Heim Kuntscher Architekten und Stadtplaner BDA in Munich. She researches and teaches at the Chair of Architectural Design and Conception, Technical University of Munich. Her research focuses on transdisciplinary investigations of architecture, highlighting the lived experience as significant for the anticipation of architectural design, and investigating the integration of sensuality and bodily knowledge in architectural research. She explored the sensual intertwinement of body and space in the terminal phase of life in *Sterbeorte. Über eine neue Sichtbarkeit des Sterbens in der Architektur* (Places for the Dying. On a New Presence of Death in Architecture), 2020. She is a founder and part of the advisory board for *Dimension. Journal of Architectural Knowledge*.

Sarah Wehmeyer

studied architecture at Leibniz University Hannover and worked in architectural practices in Münster, Hannover, and Winterthur (CH). She completed her master's degree in 2015. Since then working in cooperation with Römeth BDA . Wagener Architects in Hannover, as well as a research and teaching assistant at the department a_ku (Architecture + Art 20th/21st century), IGTA, Faculty of Architecture and Landscape Sciences, Leibniz University Hannover. Doctorate in progress titled *The Collage as Practice of Research-Orientated Design* supervised by Prof. Dr. Margitta Buchert. Publications: »Collage«, in: Margitta Buchert ed. (2020), *Entwerfen gestalten. Shaping design. Medien der Architekturkonzeption. Media of architectural conception*, Berlin: Jovis, 202-218; »Produktive Negationen entdecken. Ästhetik des Hässlichen von Karl Rosenkranz«, in: Margitta Buchert (2019), *Das besondere Buch. Architektur Theorie Praxis*, Hannover: LUH, 43–52; »Collages Interactions. A specific form of design and research processes«, in: Margitta Buchert (2018): *Processes of Reflexive Design*. Berlin: Jovis. 124-140.

Marcus Weisen

studied French and German literature and philosophy at the University of Geneva (graduated 1983). He was Arts Officer for the Royal National Institute of Blind People (1987–2002), Health and Disability Adviser to the Council for Museums, Libraries, and Archives England (2002–2007) and is an inclusive museum consultant (from 2007). He is trained in craniosacral therapy (which enhances awareness of internal bodily sensations). His interest in sensory and atmospheric qualities of places arose from shared aesthetic experiences with visually impaired friends. He trained in the micro-phenomenology interview method with Claire Petitmengin and Pierre Vermersch. His latest publications are: »Introduction à Juhani Pallasmaa« (Introduction to Juhani Pallasmaa), in: Mildred Galland-Szymkowiak, (ed.): *Architecture, Espace, Aisthesis* (Architecture, Space, Aisthesis), 2017, and »The Meaning of the Archaic in Architecture Today, Juhani Pallasmaa in conversation with Marcus Weisen« in: Chris Younès, (ed.), *L'Archaïque et ses Possibles en Architecture* (The Archaic and its Possibilities for Architecture), 2019.